AF323721

BEYOND FINTECH

Technology Applications for the Islamic Economy

BEYOND FINTECH

Technology Applications for the Islamic Economy

Hazik Mohamed

Stellar Consulting Group, Singapore

NEW JERSEY · LONDON · SINGAPORE · BEIJING · SHANGHAI · HONG KONG · TAIPEI · CHENNAI · TOKYO

Published by

World Scientific Publishing Co. Pte. Ltd.
5 Toh Tuck Link, Singapore 596224
USA office: 27 Warren Street, Suite 401-402, Hackensack, NJ 07601
UK office: 57 Shelton Street, Covent Garden, London WC2H 9HE

British Library Cataloguing-in-Publication Data
A catalogue record for this book is available from the British Library.

BEYOND FINTECH
Technology Applications for the Islamic Economy

ISBN 978-981-122-230-6 (hardcover)
ISBN 978-981-122-231-3 (ebook for institutions)
ISBN 978-981-122-232-0 (ebook for individuals)

For any available supplementary material, please visit
https://www.worldscientific.com/worldscibooks/10.1142/11885#t=suppl

Desk Editor: Karimah Samsudin

Typeset by Diacritech Technologies Pvt. Ltd.
Chennai - 600106, India

CONTENTS

ADVANCED PRAISES

The author is commended for opening new frontiers offering innovative ideas to realize the potential of Islamic economics and finance. Tech disruption offers a golden opportunity for the advocates of Islamic economics and finance to demonstrate the merits of a risk-sharing based system in action. This valuable volume provides the foundation and lays the blueprint on how to capitalize on this opportunity.

Dr. Zamir Iqbal
Chief Financial Officer of Islamic Development Bank (IsDB),
Jeddah, former Head of World Bank Islamic Finance Center,
Istanbul

Hazik has successfully constructed the idea of Islamic economics practice and its implications when enabled by digital technology, which can give greater beneficial impact towards society in many aspects of life such as poverty alleviation, wealth distribution, MSME empowerment, shared prosperity, as well as sustainable economic development. This book has extensive elaboration in multiple applications from technological instruments in various sectors in Islamic finance and the halal industry, to Islamic social finance and legal modernization and enhancement. This work will be an excellent reference to practitioners and other stakeholders to develop the Islamic digital economy in improving the welfare of society. I believe this book will contribute to the knowledge development of Islamic economy and finance as well since the related topic lacks literature resources in the very first place.

Hazik shows us there are niches that can be filled with technological advancement and innovation in the Islamic economy. In my opinion, he has created a masterpiece. Well done!

Mr. Ventje Rahardjo
Executive Director, National Islamic Economics and Finance
Committee (KNEKS) Indonesia.

As a pioneering effort, the author makes a significant contribution to the Islamic fintech literature by exploring the applications of financial technologies in a wide spectrum of economic and financial topics ranging from smart manufacturing to digital sukuk. I would recommend this book especially for policy-makers and regulators in the financial services industry since it is critical for policy-making and regulation in fintech to understand concrete applications of fintech and to imagine where these applications may evolve.

Prof. Dr. Göksel Aşan
President, Finance Office of the Presidency of the
Republic of Turkey.

As economies has become more dependent on technologies, it is clear that businesses and societies need for integrated and innovative solutions in this era of digital economy. The author synthesizes the applications of AI, Big Data, Blockchain, and IoT for Islamic Finance in specific industries, as well as the importance of cybersecurity and new regulatory measures to deal with new tech in Islamic economy. This book is insightful and well-structured, a good reference for anyone who look to enhance values, break boundaries, promote inclusivity and sustainability.

Mr. Imri Dolhadi Abdul Wahab
Deputy Director, Fiscal and Economics Division, Ministry of
Finance of Malaysia.

Technological disruption in the economy has also affected the science and arts of doing business. Many of the things that were relevant yesterday are becoming obsolete today. To bridge the knowledge gap and market practice, we need important contributions to lay out the concept of technological changes and to shed light on the market potential and its challenges. *Beyond Fintech* fills this gap. It is a mandatory read for both researchers and practitioners within these fields.

Dr. Ashraful Mobin
Managing Director, iFINTELL Business Intelligence Asia.

As economies emerge from the pandemic and humanity rethinks the world after COVID-19, this book offers actionable and timely insights to technologies and applications that can help us build economies back better. *Beyond Fintech* is a must-read for stakeholders who are determined to grasp the opportunity and capitalize on the accelerated digital transformation and subdued legacy resistance. The author's emphasis on the principles of accountability, duty, justice, and transparency cannot be more resonant against the backdrop of pervasive inequalities and deteriorating trust in authorities and systems amplified by the pandemic.

Dr. Alaa Alaabed
Chief Research Officer, Wethaq Capital Markets, Bahrain.

This intellectual piece of contribution is timely and helpful as it nudges the mind to 'deep learning and thinking' at a time where human attention span is getting shorter and technological advancement is overtaking human capabilities. The author's quest to rediscover the soul of the Islamic economy for a better future for everyone through ethically robust and intelligent technologies is commendable. I am sure readers will find the immersion fascinating and insightful.

Dr. Adam Ng Boon Ka
Sustainability Expert, World Wildlife Fund (WWF).

As the global finance landscape is being continually reshaped by innovation, particularly in the areas of fintech, technology has become a major tool in enhancing financial and social inclusion. The book by Dr. Hazik is a step forward in the use of blockchain and digital technology in almost all areas of economic, financial, and social sectors in an Islamic economy. The use of technology has been elegantly discussed in the areas like digital currencies, asset management, supply chain management, manufacturing, social finance, SupTech and RegTech. As such, the present book fulfils a timely requirement for transformation of the systems, and intensively crucial for any economies, particularly that of Islamic countries.

Professor Muhammad Ayub
Director of Research and Training, Riphah Center of Islamic Business, Riphah International University, Islamabad, Pakistan.

FOREWORD

Coming at the heels of the successful publication of an earlier pioneering and groundbreaking book,[1] the present valuable follow up is timely and highly useful for the intended audience it aims to inform. The subject matter it treats is critically important for Muslim countries in particular, and for emerging and developing countries in general. Provided that these countries adopt and implement its guidance, they can potentially experience a grand leap in socio-political-economic development. It is worth recalling the revolution created by cellphone technology which allowed developing countries to leap to the 21st-century in communication in general and in finance and banking in particular, without having to make huge investment in land-base communication technology or in the break and mortar financial institutions. Analogously, new technologies (e.g., AI, blockchain, and IoT) have the potential to create a revolution in reforming and restructuring socio-political-economic institutions without the inefficiencies and distortions that have resulted from the operations of the presently dominant order that have imposed substantial costs to humanity and nature.

A compelling case can be made that informational problems, including moral hazard and information asymmetry, lie at the root of many of the problems that plague human societies. Take as an example the costs of a debt-based financial system that dominates economies at the present. Aside from creating a class of permanent "debt slaves", the system is a source of huge inefficiencies, the cause of lost resources, and a continuous source of financial and economic instability. Even before the coronavirus pandemic, total global debt to GDP was estimated at more than

---

1   Mohamed, H. and Ali, H. 2018. *Blockchain, Fintech, and Islamic Finance: Building the Future in the New Islamic Digital Economy.* Berlin: De Gruyter

300% of GDP at the end of 2019. In the wake of the pandemic, the level of global debt is increasing by leaps and bounds while global GDP is estimated to decline by a minimum of 1%. The frightening debt dynamic — summarized in simple movement of debt upward while the means of validating the debt is moving in the opposite direction — is giving rise to expectation of a pandemic of massive business insolvencies and bankruptcies, as well as to widespread sovereign debt default, thus threatening any post-pandemic recovery.

How did we get to this point? From what is known about human history, it appears that for nearly 3,000 years, humans shared their resources and risks in producing what they needed. Surplus resources were invested in sharing arrangements where returns to productive ventures were shared for using surpluses employed in production processes. At some point in history — roughly during the time of Babylonians — financial surplus holders chose to loan their surplus rather than invest it. In return, they asked for payments of fixed rate specified at the beginning of the transaction. There appears to be two reasons for this change. First, as the economy grew, a rich class emerged with relatively large surplus wealth. This class was no longer interested in exerting effort at direct participation in productive ventures nor in direct supervision of projects where their resources were being employed. Hence, they resorted to a predetermined and fixed rate to the amount of loan, regardless of the outcome of the venture. The same phenomenon seems to have been at work in the 16th-century European economies, where huge surplus wealth accruing to countries from their colonies became a massive source of funds searching for low risk, low return but assured rate of return that would be guaranteed before the funds were committed. As is well known, the Church had, up until that time, prohibited the loaning on interest at the risk of excommunication. The second reason appears to be the erosion in moral/ethical standards in business and finance transactions as societies became economically more prosperous. The result was the growth of information asymmetry and moral hazard. Charging a fixed interest rate on money loaned was therefore preferred to direct investment in ventures where the honesty and integrity of the entrepreneur could not be taken for granted.

There is, however, a critical issue at work with fixed rate debt arrangements. By themselves, agreements on loaning and borrowing money on interest are not risk-free. These arrangements are examples of class of "impossible contracts". According to contract theory, this class of contracts are impossible because they are not incentive-compatible, meaning that the borrower has no incentive to repay the loan and/or its interest. To make these contracts incentive-compatible not only do collaterals become necessary but a huge edifice of laws, administrative, and enforcement institutions such as debt-recovery legislations, courts, and police, are needed to ensure that the borrower has the incentive to repay the loan and its interest. The costs of operation of these institutions, which are ultimately born by taxpayers, are hidden and are not revealed by economies while claims are made that debt is cheaper relative to equity. Additionally, a whole industry emerged, and is ever growing, that produces and manufactures no real product but lives off what it charges for ostensibly managing the risks stemming from informational problems. This is the reason for existence of financial industry as an "intermediary" which represents another source of inefficiency, lost resources, and an additional cost of transactions.

This example can be replicated in analyzing the causes of other political, social, and economic problems. Why do people vote for representatives who end up hurting their interest? The answer is to be found in informational problems. How do political, business, and financial actors get away with corruption? The answer again is informational problems. Similarly, the causes of other costly phenomena such as moral/ethical erosion in business and financial transactions, lack of transparency and accountability in social and political dealings, erosion in and depletion of social capital, weakening of social solidarity, massive environmental problems, and the obscene income and wealth disparities too can be sought in the existence of informational problems. At long last, however, a way to solve these problems appear to be emerging as AI, Blockchain, and IoT technologies make progress. While all economic, political, and social institutions are reeling under the stress of the pandemic, this progress continues and, as it appears, its pace is accelerating. Dr. Hazik's present book and its 2018 companion are not only timely but intensely crucial for developing countries in general and Muslim countries in particular.

With a gifted ability to simplify complex ideas, Dr. Hazik continues his effort at making all concepts related to AI, Blockchain, and IoT accessible and understandable to a constituency that includes policymakers, students, finance professionals, and academics in developing countries in his second Fintech book.

With an active and creative imagination, he not only simply, easily, and smoothly articulates and explains how this technology can be used to effectively address the challenges these countries face presently but also how they can prepare the institutional scaffolding for a sharing, prosperous, and equitable society and its economic and financial system of the future. This is a book that stimulates thinking and generates hope that AI, Blockchain technologies, and the Big Data analytics may indeed hold the key to structuring just and fair societies of the future. It is an enjoyable and exciting read that no library should be without.

Professor Dr. Abbas Mirakhor is a renowned and accomplished economist. He joined the International Monetary Fund (IMF) in 1984, and rose to become its Dean of the Executive Board and retired as its Executive Director in 2008. During his time at the IMF, he was awarded the "Quaid-e Azam" star for service to Pakistan in 1997 by the President of Pakistan. In 2003, he received the Islamic Development Bank Annual Prize for Research in Islamic Economics, which he shared with Dr. Mohsin Khan. In 2005, he was conferred the "Order of Companion of Volta" for service to Ghana by the President of Ghana.

Professor Mirakhor was also the former Holder of the First Chair of Islamic Finance at INCEIF in Malaysia (2010–2017), and has held past professorships in Alabama A&M and Florida Institute of Technology (1968–1984).

INTRODUCTION

The first chapter provides an overview of our research on connecting the various aspects of technology that now shapes the Sharing as well as the Digital Economies. It underscores the integration of IoT, blockchain, and AI into a decentralized intelligence system that has profound possibilities to employ data in innovative ways. The explosion of data has the potential to transform how we view our current processes and possibilities. How we use and analyze data has become significantly important to our economics, and we discuss its transformative adoption in our industries and policy to enable its development. As we grapple with technology's inherent risks, we describe how it can be used as a moral agent. It also describes the structure of the book, where each chapter elaborates on a specific application in a particular economic sector.

Keywords: *Big data, Data science, Policy, Moral agent.*

Contents

1. The Explosion of Big Data

From the early days of industrialization, data had always been available, except that it was not collected. In the new era of advanced digitization, data has become gigantic in terms of volume, processing speed and storage. For an organization in the third industrial era, datasets in terabytes was considered big, but today, a typical organization's datasets are in the multiples of those — in order of petabytes or exabytes. The trend to larger datasets is due to the collection of data from IoT devices as well as additional data derived from analyses of large singular related data sets, as compared to multiple separate smaller sets. These analyses allow for correlations to be found, such as spotting important trends, predicting future course, forecasting disasters, and managing business processes better by extracting exceptional value in real-time via big data analytics. The IoT factor that contributes towards the data revolution is a fundamental shift in the collection of data, where an exponential growth in the number of wirelessly-connected mobile devices interact with various other devices — data communication and generation between devices — was unprecedented.

With the growth of the cloud, organizations of all sizes and industries are producing more data than ever, even up to terabytes per second. Hidden in this data are insights with potential business value. The challenge lies in organizing and analyzing the data to create new business strategies and make organizational decisions. Big Data, data structure, databases, data mining or warehousing technologies, and those of the Cloud need to sync with each other and move in the same direction. The cloud can be a powerful and cost-effective way to deliver capabilities around Big Data analytics and Big Data management. As more and more types of services move onto the digital platform, every click, tap, and swipe on the screens of these devices become invaluable information for businesses that want to capitalize on better customer insights. Is it any wonder then that digital data has become "big" and increasingly significant for companies who want to remain competitive?

1.1. *Types of Data*

With the explosion of Big Data, more organizations store, process, and extract value from all forms and sizes of data. Systems which support big volumes of structured and unstructured data will help data custodians secure and govern data analytics while empowering the end users to analyze the data. Structured data, most universally found in databases that use Structured Query Language (SQL), is organized in a way that lets users select exact pieces, rows, or columns of that database, for e.g., rows with a certain zip code, or the columns with a specific date. Unstructured data, however, has no such architecture and can often include text or images that are not part of the free-form data (for e.g., emails, blogs).

Big datasets,[1] mostly unstructured, require advanced tools, software, and systems to capture, store, manage, and analyze them, all in a timeframe that preserves the intrinsic value of the data.

1.2. *Architecture and Technologies*

New SQL, MapReduce, and Hadoop are the database platforms that are becoming increasingly popular. The architecture of Government of India's ambitious project, Aadhaar, is based on Hadoop handling 200 trillion biometric matches per day, 2PB

---

1   Datasets such as relational data (tables, transaction, or legacy data), text data (web), semi-structured data (XML), graphical data like social network, semantic web (RDF), streaming data, big volume with simple (SQL) analytics or with complex (non-SQL) analytics, big velocity, big variety, large numbers of diverse data sources.

of raw data stored, 100 million authentication requests per day, terabyte-scale data warehouse of 200 million records, 50 million messages per day, and 100 million database transactions per day. The technology spectrum to handle massive parallel processing, streaming data reads, data locality computing, low latency reads, data integrity, and challenges of dealing with distributed data include the Hadoop stack: HDFS, HBase, Hive, MySQL, SEDA, Search: MongoDB, sharded Solutions, Compute Grid: Spring, GridGain, Monitoring: Custom built, Nagios.

In a vendor-neutral approach, the Big Data Architecture is organized around five major roles and multiple sub-roles aligned along two axes representing the two Big Data value chains: (1) the Information Value (horizontal axis) and (2) the Information Technology (IT; vertical axis). Along the Information Value axis, the value is created through data collection, integration, analysis, and applying the results following the value chain (NIST Big Data Reference Architecture). Along the IT axis, the value is created through providing networking, infrastructure, platforms, application tools, and other IT services for the hosting of and operating the Big Data in support of the required data applications. At the intersection of both axes is the Big Data Application Provider role, indicating that data analytics and its implementation provide the value to Big Data stakeholders in both value chains.

For businesses that cannot afford a big data infrastructure of their own, cloud-based big data solutions, for example, Amazon Web Services (AWS), gives a ready platform for users to utilize their cloud computing services. Once a cloud setup or big data infrastructure is done, companies can begin processing their data and leverage the big data technology to their advantage. Nowadays, for elaborate tasks of parallel-processing unstructured data, quantum computers are used.

1.3. *Big Data Analytics and Cloud Computing*

Big Data analytics could be described as high-speed, high-volume, and high-variety information that demands new kinds of processing to enable improved decision-making, process optimization, and insight discovery. Data analytics proliferation has made it critical to analyze data fast to gain valuable insight for organizations to turn terabytes into classified data that are useable to businesses to develop new insights for innovative, new offerings to gain a competitive edge.

Big Data analytics can be done with the software tools commonly used as part of advanced analytics disciplines, such as predictive analytics and data mining. However, the unstructured data sources used for Big Data analytics may not fit in traditional data warehouses. Traditional relational databases cannot handle semi-structured, unstructured, and highly variable data the way open source and other alternatives can. A new class of Big Data technology has emerged and is being used in many Big Data analytics environments. These technologies associated include databases, Hadoop, and MapReduce. These technologies form the core of an open source software framework that supports the processing of large datasets across clustered systems. The challenge lies in its capturing, curation, storage, search, sharing, transfer, analysis, and visualization.

Early big data adopters and top performers already are driving forward on all the big data fronts. In the next few years, millions of big data-related IT jobs will be created worldwide and yet, according to the McKinsey Global Institute, there is a major shortage of the "analytical and managerial talent necessary to make the most of big data". Businesses that successfully harness the power of big data will outperform and outcompete competitors. The MIT Center for Digital Business note that "companies that adopt data-driven practices, and use big data to guide decision making, will have output and productivity that is 5 to 6 percent higher than what would be expected given their other investments and information technology uses". Big data may hold the key to smarter cities, faster medical breakthroughs, greater academic learning, more efficient use of resources, and more profitable companies.

2. The Economics of Big Data and Data Science

The AI Index 2019 Annual Report (Perrault *et al.*, 2019) by Stanford University notes that the "hiring rate has been increasing across all the sampled countries, especially for many emerging markets, not just advanced economies". Figure 1.1 below presents the AI Hiring Index, which is calculated as the percentage of LinkedIn members who had any AI skills.

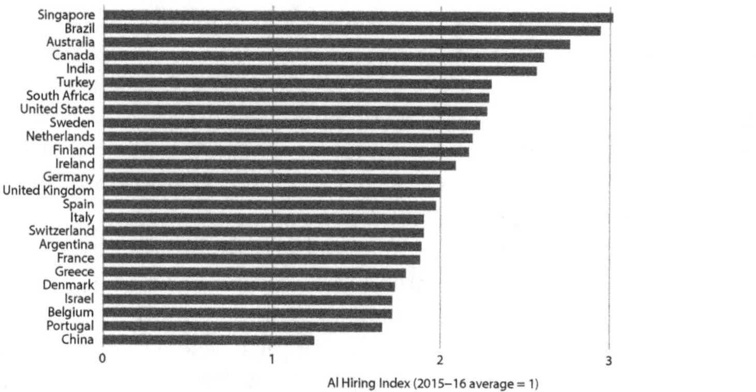

Figure 1.1: AI Hiring Index by Country (2019)
Source: LinkedIn, 2019.

According to the report, the "AI hiring rate is normalized for the different countries by dividing over the total number of LinkedIn members in the country. The growth rate is indexed against the average annual hiring in 2015–16; for example, an index of 3 for Singapore in 2019 indicates that the AI hiring rate is 3 times higher in 2019 than the average in 2015–16". Figure 1.1 shows that the "countries with the highest growth in AI hiring on LinkedIn include Singapore, Brazil, Australia, Canada and India. The rapid growth in AI hiring is also confirmed by job postings data from Burning Glass that shows the share of AI jobs (% of total jobs posted online) grew from 0.1% in 2012 to 1.7% in 2019 for Singapore" (Perrault *et al.*, 2019). Similarly, in the US, the share of AI jobs grew from 0.3% in 2012 to 0.8% of total jobs posted in 2019. Among the sectors, the technology, service sectors, and manufacturing show the greatest rise in demand for AI skills.

In terms of investments, investment in AI startups continues its steady ascent globally. From a total of US$1.3 billion raised in 2010 to over US$40.4 billion in 2018 alone (with US$37.4 billion in 2019 as of November 4, 2018), funding has increased with an average annual growth rate of over 48% between 2010 and 2018 (Figure 1.2a). The report only considered AI companies that received more than US$400,000 in investment. The number of AI companies that received funding was reportedly increasing, with more than 3,000 AI companies having received funding in 2018 (Figure 1.2b). "Between 2014 and 2019 (through November 4), a total of 15,798 investments (over US$400,000) have been made in AI startups globally, with an average investment size of approximately US$8.6 million" (Perrault *et al.*, 2019).

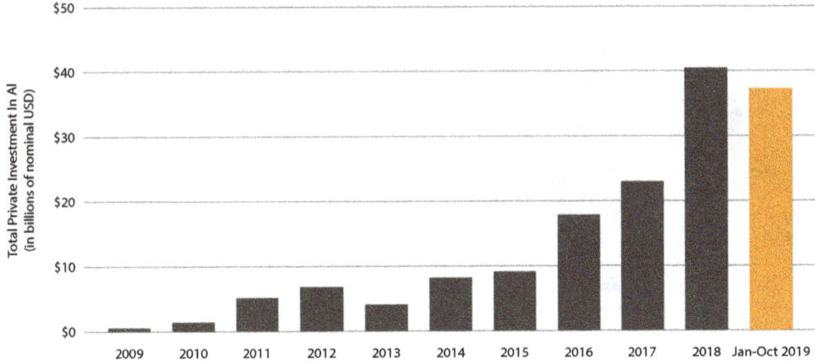

Figure 1.2a: Total Private Investment in AI (US$ billions)
Source: CAPIQ, Crunchbase, Quid, 2019.

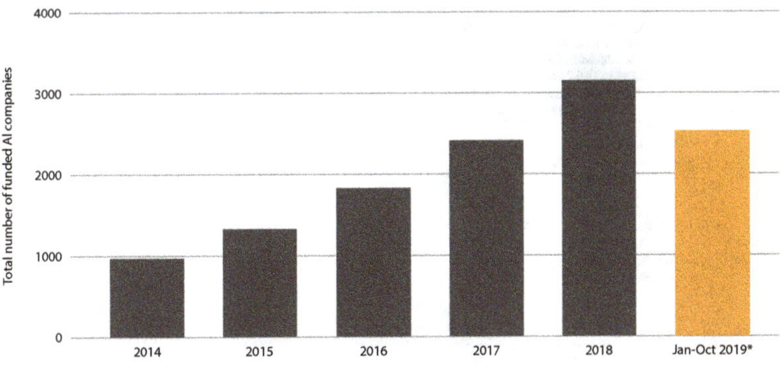

Figure 1.2b: Total Number of Funded AI Companies, World (2014–2019)
Source: CAPIQ, Crunchbase, Quid, 2019.

"The United States remains dominant when it comes to the number of funded startups and, in general, has been a consistent leader in AI funding. However, a select few Chinese firms received exceptionally high levels of investment in 2018, which pushed the country closer to parity with the United States. US, Europe, and China take the lion's share of global AI private investment, while Israel, Singapore, and Iceland invest substantially in per capita terms" (Perrault *et al.*, 2019).

From Figure 1.3a, "Autonomous Vehicles (AVs) received the lion's share of global investment over the last year with US$7.7B (9.9% of the total), followed by Drug, Cancer and Therapy (US$4.7 billion, more than 6.1%), Facial Recognition (US$4.7 billion, 6.0%), Video Content (US$3.6 billion, 4.5%), and Fraud Detection and Finance (US$3.1 billion, 3.9%)" (Perrault *et al.*, 2019).

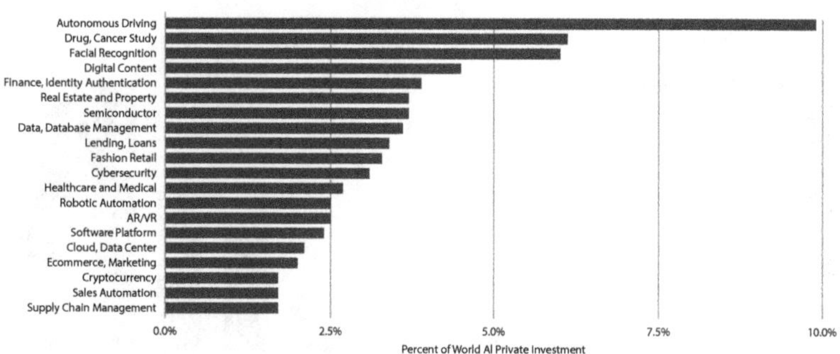

Figure 1.3a: Percent of World AI Private Investment, Startup Cluster (2018–2019)
Source: CAPIQ, Crunchbase, Quid, 2019.

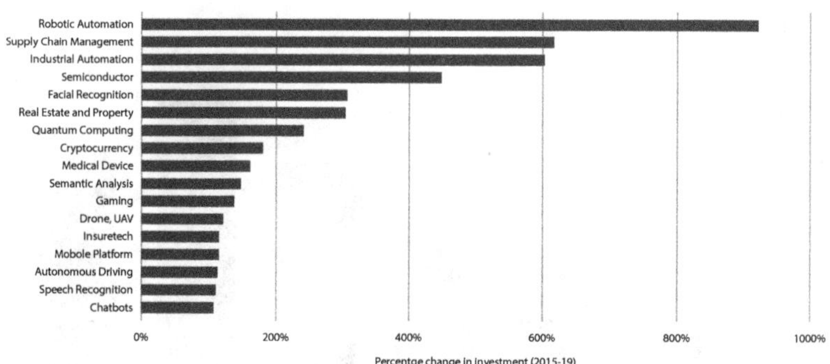

Figure 1.3b: Growth in AI Private Investment, World (2015–2019)
Source: CAPIQ, Crunchbase, Quid, 2019.

Globally, Figure 1.3b shows that "robot process automation grew most rapidly (over US$1 billion in 2018), followed by supply chain management (over US$500 million in 2018), and industrial automation (over US$500 million in 2018). Other sectors like semiconductor chips, facial recognition, real estate, quantum computing, crypto and trading operations have also experienced substantial growth in terms of global private investment" (Perrault *et al.*, 2019).

In terms of industry adoption, companies are most likely to adopt AI in functions that provide core value in their industry (Figure 1.4). For example, respondents in the automotive industry are the most likely to report adoption of AI in manufacturing, and those working in financial services are more likely than others to say their companies have adopted

AI in risk functions. Telecommunications companies are most often adopting AI in service operations, while companies in the pharmaceutical industry tend to apply AI in product development and manufacturing. Respondents in consumer-packaged goods, travel and logistics, and retail are the most likely to report adoption of AI in supply chain management.

	Service operations	Product/ service development	Marketing & sales	Manufacturing	Supply chain mgmt	Risk
All Industries	42	35	27	19	18	17
Automotive	26	43	13	53	18	9
Professional services	36	31	29	10	17	12
CPG	28	12	28	32	29	11
Power & natural gas	49	42	17	21	19	12
Financial services	52	25	43	2	12	42
Healthcare	50	31	19	10	12	10
High tech	49	55	37	12	14	14
Infrastructure	26	43	11	30	13	6
Pharma	19	41	16	41	11	3
Public sector	39	36	6	4	15	12
Retail	47	33	36	14	34	14
Telecom	74	48	28	21	27	30
Travel & logistics	52	20	17	7	31	5

Percent of respondents

Figure 1.4: AI Adoption by Industry and Function (2019)
Source: McKinsey & Company.

McKinsey's study also "surveyed respondents on ten of the most widely recognized risks related to AI, including regulatory compliance, equity and fairness, cybersecurity, and personal and individual privacy. Cybersecurity is the risk most respondents cite their companies are mitigating, about 48 percent of respondents from companies that have adopted AI. Thirty-five percent say their organizations are taking steps to mitigate risks associated with regulatory compliance, and three in ten say the same about personal and individual privacy" (Perrault *et al.*, 2019).

Although concerns on the importance of addressing ethical dilemmas associated with usage of AI are often acknowledged, only 19% of respondents in the McKinsey survey observe their organizations taking serious steps to mitigate such inherent risks associated with the way their algorithms are coded, and only 13% of companies are observed to mitigate risks to equity and fairness, that come from algorithmic bias and discrimination from data assignment.

3. Digital Adoption and Policy Development

Artificial Intelligence (AI) is a highly-evolved area of computer science that strives to create intelligent machines that can replicate certain human behavior without its irrationalities for better predictability and consistency. Advanced AI that utilizes machine learning enables machines to 'learn' from previous data (experience), adjust to new inputs (instructions), and perform tasks through updated algorithms. Through sophisticated algorithms, modern AI systems can be guided to undertake specific tasks by handling huge quantities of data, obtaining insights, and recognizable patterns in the data to act upon. As such, AI has become a hot topic, with much interest on its advantages to the digital economy, especially in the highly regulated financial services industry. McKinsey Global Institute estimates that even with incomplete adoption by 2030, the technology could add US$13 trillion to the world's economy. This would represent a greater relative contribution to prosperity than those brought by such transformative technologies as steam engines in the 1800s and the rapid spread of IT in recent decades (The EIU, 2019).

Similarly, blockchain technology also has the potential to both enrich and improve economic processes and management systems, and progressive corporations have invested and devoted resources to utilize and incorporate blockchain into their businesses. It is clear today that the digital revolution in every sector of the economy is under way, and the world should recognize that these technological advancements are essentially aligned to the principles of the theology that requires and upholds the values of trust, honesty, and transparency. For example, the blockchain poses as one of the main underlying components to enable trust in impersonal economic transactions across highly globalized societies. For one, it will undoubtedly play a crucial role in boosting traceability for fraud prevention. There is a very strong case for decentralized models — for instance, the internet decentralized information and established the Information Age. Blockchain systems along with AI and IoT integration will be the backbone of large-scale implementations of decentralization models, conceived and executed to ascend the intricate multi-dimensional levels of human activity, including those that are still evolving, which could further establish the Moral Economy.

Progressing towards decentralization of economic transactions would make future economic activities less restrictive and increase efficiency. Centralized systems may exist on top of the decentralized system, but they will be few and will act as forms of governance or administrators.

There is a growing realization of AI+blockchain's importance, including its "ability to provide competitive advantage and change work for the better. A majority of global early adopters say that AI technologies are especially important to their business success today" (Deloitte Insights, 2019). Many experts predict that AI+blockchain technology will exert an enormous impact on economic development and the nature of work which will radically reshape the competitive dynamics of many industries. As a result of this, many leaders believe that using these technologies will move them ahead of their competition, and that AI empowers their workforce. It is no wonder that governments are rushing to foster innovation investment, to "establish coursework and education programs, pursue specialization, research and development to support businesses within their borders. Numerous nations have developed AI strategies to advance their capabilities, through investment, incentives, talent development, and risk management" (Deloitte Insights, 2019).

"Organizations often must excel at a wide range of practices to ensure [AI + Blockchain] success, including developing a strategy, pursuing the right use cases, building a data foundation, and cultivating a strong ability to experiment. These capabilities are critical now because, as [AI + Blockchain] becomes even easier to consume, the window for competitive differentiation will likely shrink." (Deloitte Insights, 2019). An MIT Sloan and Boston Consulting Group joint research (Ransbotham *et al.*, 2017) revealed "large gaps between today's leaders — companies that already understand and have adopted AI — and laggards. One sizeable difference, they found, is their approach to data. AI algorithms are not natively 'intelligent'. They learn inductively by analyzing data. While most leaders are investing in AI talent and have built robust information infrastructures, other companies lack analytics expertise and easy access to their data". Their research uncovered "several misunderstandings about the resources needed to train AI. The leaders not only have a much deeper appreciation about what is required to produce AI than laggards, they are also more likely to have senior leadership support and have developed a business case for AI initiatives" (Ransbotham *et al.*, 2017).

Enthusiasm and experience vary among early adopters from different countries — some are pursuing the technology spiritedly, while others are taking a more restrained approach. In some cases, adopters are employing AI+blockchain to improve specific processes and products; others are harnessing this combination of technologies to transform their entire organization.

Regardless of countries' technology maturity level, we learn from their approaches that by examining countries' challenges and how their corporations are addressing them, we can garner some essential best-known practices. For example, leaders in some countries are more concerned about addressing skill gaps, while others are focusing on how AI can improve decision-making or cybersecurity capabilities. There are many paths to technological excellence, and success is not a zero-sum game. Scrutinizing early adopters through a global lens enables a broader perspective for a more balanced approach on their advanced tech-powered journey.

Moving forward, nations and their governments should continue to invest in AI+blockchain and monitor the technology's ongoing impact on their societies. All businesses should continue to improve their AI+blockchain capabilities and install a Big Data Analytics department in their organizations which will be central to their competitiveness. Both will continue to feel a sense of urgency and anxiety as they try to keep up with the rapid pace of tech-driven developments around the world. As such, organizations should contemplate these critical questions when evaluating their own AI and blockchain competitive strategies:

- Should they make small, incremental investments or try to position themselves as AI and blockchain leaders through enterprise-wide initiatives?
- Is it better to develop existing talent or seek talent externally? How do they nurture them?
- How is data viewed, used, and analyzed for competitive advantage?
- When considering the inherent risks associated with AI and blockchain, should organizations face the complexities to be first-to-market or take a more cautious wait-and-see approach?
- Do they have adequate security measures in place?

4. Technology as a Moral Agent

Artificial intelligence, blockchain, and other potentially disruptive technologies form the crucial innovation, structural, and institutional foundation for, not only economic development, but also moral development and practical ethics. The integration of blockchain and AI into a decentralized intelligence system has profound possibilities to employ data in innovative ways. An effective amalgamation of both technologies will enable faster and seamless data management, validation of transactions, and detection of illegal activities, among others.

Good governance is a crucial issue in strengthening the performance of social institutions, viz charities and such foundations, and those pertaining to inheritance and wealth distribution. Although past research has found that good governance in these institutions has been well implemented in some aspects, they, however, have not been implemented comprehensively. As a public organization, the performance of social institutions especially in management and service are the benchmark for the growth of public trust. The principles of accountability, duty, justice, and transparency are the foundation of shaping the framework in achieving good governance in all public institutions (Mohamed *et al.*, 2019). The ability to audit and monitor the movement and transfer of assets to the intended beneficiaries is crucial in dispensing the duty of the authorities, and subsequently establishing trust and improving social capital between citizens and governing authorities. Technologies like the blockchain and AI can operationalize the transparency and accountability that is required of important social institutions that govern the dispensation of inheritance law (pertaining to estates, wills, and trusts), and the management and distribution of endowment and the various forms of charities in order to eradicate poverty, circulate wealth, enhance micro-, small- and large-scale infrastructure for social and economic development, and thus share prosperity for a just social system that enables a more secure and sustainable economy.

In an era of disruption to long-standing economic and governance institutions, digital technologies can reinforce increased use and broader adoption of mobile apps and intelligent systems for traditional social institutions too. The many digital innovations that have helped reshape the financial landscape can help to remove friction, human errors, fraud, and other agency risks from all of the essential steps of charities and other social institutions.

The ability to audit and monitor the movement and transfer of assets to the intended beneficiaries is crucial in dispensing the duty of the authorities, and subsequently establishing trust and improving social capital between citizens, public institutions, and the governing authorities. Providing the public with the appropriate information and the performance of charitable or endowed assets are mechanisms where the entrusted authorities can continually improve on to gain support from the public in obligatory charitable contributions and voluntary endowments. The fall of public trust will result in diminishing pools of endowment assets and reduction in charitable collections, which are critical sources of funds for socioeconomic development of disadvantaged communities. The challenge of theological morality for technology lies in its human creator and not the responsibility of the created; unlike humans, who were created with the choice to uphold moral responsibility by its Creator.

5. Structure of the Book

This book is a follow-up to our first book[2] published in 2018 that provided the linkages between Islamic Finance and disruptive technologies like the blockchain. In the wake of fintech as a new trend in financial markets, the ground-breaking book stressed the relevance of Islamic finance and its implications, when enabled by fintech, towards the development of the Islamic digital economy. While the previous work discussed the crucial innovation, and structural and institutional development for financial technologies in Islamic Finance, this new research explores the multiple applications possible in the various sectors of the economy, within and beyond finance, that can be significantly transformed. These revolutionary applications involve the integration of AI, blockchain, data analytics, and IoT devices for a holistic solution to tackle the bottlenecks and other issues in existing processes of traditional systems.

---

2   *Blockchain, Fintech and Islamic Finance: Building the Future of the Islamic Digital Economy* published by De I G Press (De Gruyter) in 2018 was the first-of-its-kind manuscript on disruptive technologies like the blockchain for Islamic Finance, with respect to theoretical foundation, practical assessment and regulatory implications.

The demand for advance solutions is underscored by the rapid adoption of technology, high-levels of mobile usage, and rising rates of internet penetration, an increasingly urban, literate, and young population, as well as a segment of consumers and micro-, small- and medium-sized enterprises (MSMEs) underserved by traditional institutions. Building the Islamic digital ecosystem is multi-faceted, and it involves various market participants and stakeholders coming together and working towards shared goals of an integrated digital community, increased social inclusion for the disenfranchised, efficient processes, and the seamless cross-border flow of goods and services.

The principles of accountability, duty, justice, and transparency are the foundation of shaping the framework in achieving good governance in all institutions — public or private, Islamic or otherwise. The ability to audit and monitor the movement and transfer of assets to the intended beneficiaries is crucial in dispensing the duty of the authorities, and subsequently, establishing trust and improving social capital between counterparties, even citizens and the governing authorities. Technologies like the AI and blockchain can operationalize the transparency and accountability that is required to eradicate poverty, circulate wealth, enhance micro-, small- and large-scale infrastructure for social and economic development, and thus share prosperity for a just social system that enables a more secure and sustainable economy.

While this chapter lays down the rationale and economics for big data and data science, it also explored the use of technology to meet our own moral standards and emulate such values. Chapter 2 explores the extended use cases of artificial intelligence (AI) together with the blockchain for the sectors within the Islamic Capital Markets (ICM) industry. It proposes a new operational design, where all actors within the capital market sector can work from common ledgers, with collective data-sets in almost real-time, and supporting operations which are more streamlined. The system will also incorporate fraud-detection and compliance enhancements, where applicable.

Chapter 3 recommends putting asset-backed bonds on the blockchain to enable transparency and put forth steps to automate cumbersome processes in asset-backed bond issuances in order to reduce costs and improve efficiency. Significant advantages of using technology to operationalize trust and instil confidence in properly structured and executed financial instruments are discussed on the basis of fulfilling a gap in traditional bond issuances.

Chapter 4 ruminates AI and blockchain applications in asset management, and understand the benefits and the shift in processes that will simplify transaction-tracking and reduce costs, as well as produce novel asset structures that can possibly maximize returns to the investor. Advanced technology has the ability to update and optimize investment strategies by diligently digesting new market data and consequently using them as inputs to project returns and risks for much attuned advisory and customer-centric service.

Chapter 5 provides a strategic discourse on how blockchain can provide additional value to the insurance and takāful industries, understand the change in processes, issues that need to be overcome, along with projected efficiency benefits, anticipated cost-savings, and better overall risk management.

In Chapter 6, we discuss ways as to how technologies like the blockchain can primarily secure personal and confidential patient data, giving permissioned-access approved by the patient herself/himself to related parties like healthcare providers, pharmacies, and health or medical insurers. Patients do not transfer the data to the parties requesting it, but he/she is merely giving them access to view it to enable their work. This protects the privacy of the patients.

Chapter 7 provides a description of artificial intelligence (AI), blockchain, and IoT applications in supply chain management, understand the benefits and the shift in the processes, in digital applications, especially those that impact sustainable practices, such as more agile fleet management, better organization in warehousing and distribution, real-time halal monitoring and tracking, efficient financing and payments of trades, supply traceability, and assurance of halal integrity. By generating digital versions of real-world assets and tracking their pertinent data as a distributed, shared source of information, significant efficiencies and process improvements can be achieved.

Chapter 8 explores the convergence and fusion of various technologies to describe the Factory of the Future. We detail how manufacturing will be transformed in the digital era through technologies that have defined it, such as AI, IoT, and machine learning, to form the Digital Twin and the emergence of Cyber-Physical Systems (CPS). We analyze the shifts in manufacturing practices, and illustrate several key factors that will shape the future manufacturing environment such as manufacturing operations, Lean Production principles, advanced prototype modelling, Industrial Internet of Things (IIoT) and the use of integrated manufacturing analytics, and the transformation of value chains to value network.

Chapter 9 characterizes and examines the benefits, opportunities, costs, and challenges of four key formats, and gives its assessment on the feasibility as well as possibility of practical adoption. It recommends the adoption of a CBDC (non-universal) for the interbank settlement and wholesale payment systems which has a minimal disruption to the economy, stronger monetary policy transmission, and suggests ways forward for adoption of an interest-free monetary system. There is a variety of potential solutions (formats) that can be adopted depending on the attributes and impact of each format on the financial system.

Chapter 10 identifies the use of artificial intelligence (AI) and Distributed Ledger Technology (DLT) to operationalize the specific intents of the Shariah in order to overcome the issues and challenges of traditional fara'id determination waqf administration and zakat collection and disbursement. The utilization of technologies as a mechanism of trust and transparency can improve these institutions, and hence the trust and social capital between authorities and its citizens.

Chapter 11 assesses the key features of the Islamic Digital Economy and its network to foster fair competition, innovation, and the entrepreneurship mindset. We also discuss the regulatory issues that come with technological adoption along with financial stability and consumer protection implications, with suggestions that regulators themselves adopt advanced technologies (SupTech) to embark on the new era of market supervision, regulatory compliance, and monitoring.

This final chapter, Chapter 12, concludes the book by mapping out the ongoing regulatory milestones globally and uses the snapshot between Q3 2019 to Q2 2021 to illustrate the key regulatory priorities by region, and propose how banks can effectively manage regulatory change within their organizations through an AI-driven regulatory management model. We discuss the evolution, challenges, and recommendations for financial institutions (including Shariah compliance) in the change management for regulations using a structured approach that addresses regional priorities.

Bibliography

Aldridge, I., & Krawciw, S. (2017). *Real-time risk : what investors should know about FinTech, high-frequency trading, and flash crashes*. Wiley. Retrieved from http://gen.lib.rus.ec/book/index.php?md5=41c5b796f15ea0e66015278bdac66000

Belliger, A., & Krieger, D. J. (2018). The Digital Transformation of Healthcare. In *Knowledge Management in Digital Change* (pp. 311–326). Springer.

Boland Jr, R. J., Lyytinen, K., & Yoo, Y. (2007). Wakes of innovation in project networks: The case of digital 3-D representations in architecture, engineering, and construction. *Organization Science, 18*(4), pp. 631–647.

Buckley, R. P., & Webster, S. (2016). *Fintech in Developing Countries: Charting New Customer Journeys* (SSRN Scholarly Paper No. ID 2850091). Rochester, NY: Social Science Research Network. Retrieved from https://papers.ssrn.com/abstract=2850091

Deloitte Insights (2019). Future in the Balance? How Countries are Pursuing an AI advantage Insights from Deloitte's State of AI in the Enterprise, 2nd Edition Survey.

Dharmesh, M. (2016). Racing from digital engagement to customer intimacy. Retrieved from https://www.temenos.com/en/market-insight/2016/racing-from-digital-engagement-to-customer-intimacy/

Kenser, K. (2018, March 1). Digital Transformation in Banking and Financial Services. Retrieved June 30, 2018, from https://www.tatacommunications.com/blog/2018/03/digital-transformation-banking-financial-services/

Liere-Netheler, K., Packmohr, S., & Vogelsang, K. (2018). Drivers of Digital Transformation in Manufacturing.

Matzner, M., Büttgen, M., Demirkan, H., Spohrer, J., Alter, S., Fritzsche, A., Möslein, K. M. (2018). Digital Transformation in Service Management. *SMR-Journal of Service Management Research, 2*(2), pp. 3–21.

Mićić, L. (2017). Digital Transformation and Its Influence on GDP. *ECONOMICS, 5*(2), 135–147.

Mohamed, H., Mirakhor, A. & Erbaş, N. (2019). Belief and Rule-compliance: An Experimental Comparison of Economic Behaviors. Academic Press, Elsevier.

Perrault, R., Shoham, Y., Brynjolfsson, E., Clark, J., Etchemendy, J., Grosz, B., Lyons, T., Manyika, J., Mishra, S., & Niebles, J.C. (2019). The AI Index 2019 Annual Report, AI Index Steering Committee, Human-Centered AI Institute, Stanford University, Stanford, CA, December 2019.

PwC. (2017). Digital transformation in financial services. Retrieved June 30, 2018, from https://www.pwc.com/us/en/industries/financial-services/research-institute/top-issues/digital-transformation.html

Ransbotham, S., Kiron, D., Gerbert, P. & Reeves, M. (2017). Reshaping Business with Artificial Intelligence, MIT Sloan Management Review and The Boston Consulting Group, September 2017.

Rüßmann, M., Lorenz, M., Gerbert, P., Waldner, M., Justus, J., Engel, P., & Harnisch, M. (2015). Industry 4.0: The future of productivity and growth in manufacturing industries. *Boston Consulting Group, 9.*

Scardovi, C. (2017). *Digital Transformation in Financial Services.* Springer International Publishing. Retrieved from //www.springer.com/gp/book/9783319669441

Solis, B., Li, C., & Szymanski, J. (2014). The 2014 state of digital transformation. *Altimeter Group.*

The Economist Intelligence Unit, (2019). The AI-enabled Organisation of the Future. Report sponsored by Globality.

AN AI-DRIVEN AND BLOCKCHAIN-BASED ISLAMIC CAPITAL MARKET

New innovative digital and advanced technologies are transforming the way we access and use existing financial products and services. Fintech is becoming disruptive more and more by the leveraging latest and advanced technologies such as blockchain, Cloud computing, Big Data analysis, Internet of Things (IoT), robo-advisors, and artificial intelligence (AI).

This research discusses the crucial innovation, structural, and institutional development for financial technologies (fintech) in Islamic Finance. The blockchain proposes a new operational design, where all actors within the capital market sector can work from common ledgers, with collective data-sets in almost real-time, and supporting operations which are more streamlined. The system will also incorporate fraud-detection and compliance enhancements, where applicable.

This chapter assesses the key features of the AI and blockchain architecture and protocol developments. It identifies areas where AI and blockchain can bring substantial transformational change, while at the same time, identify some of the major barriers to adoption within the capital markets. The AI +

Blockchain model is envisioned execute to scale the complex levels of human activity, possibly even those that have yet to be imagined, which could further establish a truly risk-sharing and just economy.

Keywords: *AI Algorithms, Distributed Ledgers, Marketplace Disruption, Securities Transactions*

JEL Codes: O31, O32, O33

Contents

1. Trends of the Digital Economy

As the Islamic digital economy develops, we utilize technology to operationalize the specific intents of fairness, justice, and accountability so that Islamic economic actors become more efficient ways of doing business and less exposed to unnecessary risks. If regulations are not heeded and rules not enforced, financial systems will collapse. Subsequently, institutions will suffer unnecessary intermediary overhead costs and increased regulatory compliance requirements. Disruptive innovations such as artificial intelligence (AI) algorithms and the smart contracts on the blockchain have the capacity to bring more efficiency and productivity without adding further regulatory burdens to the already heavily regulated industry. In this chapter, we explore the extended use cases of AI together with the blockchain for the sectors within the Islamic Capital Markets (ICM) industry.

Business leaders in the financial industry are trying to prepare for or predict what the financial services sector will look like five to 10 years from now. Will AI replace operations? Will performing financial functions occur in an instantaneous manner in the palm of people's hands? Will there be enough disruption that large banks will no longer exist, since today an asset can be traded electronically in the blink of an eye and then take days to settle. Both the supply-side (investment banks) and the demand-side (their clients) are demanding more — and the market is responding. Some of the main shifts in technology and processes will be discussed later in this chapter.

1.1. *Cloud-based (IoT Infrastructure)*

It appears that public clouds, private clouds, cloud as a disaster recovery (DR), and cloud communications are being used extensively and will increase exponentially as the adoption of cloud-based computing accelerates. All companies, regardless of size, should build with a cloud-based infrastructure in mind, and seriously consider a serverless environment with adequate cybersecurity measures.

Banks are very concerned with security, and the ability to safely store their sensitive information in the Cloud. It should be noted that most of the high-visibility hacks in the past 10 years have affected networks but not one of the cloud providers. It is much easier to protect small amounts of connection points than it is to large amounts of entry points coming into a system. Financial institutions need to find ways to mitigate security fears with the path to future computing, which is all in the cloud.

Cloud computing also serves as an opportunity to consolidate platforms and connectivity. However, it is the role of vendors to provide further efficiencies using cloud computing rather than financial institutions believing that if they simply move everything to the cloud, their processes would be cheaper and easier to maintain.

Going full cloud is like disconnecting from cable; it may not make sense for every player. Some cloud service pricing is flexible in that they charge by the number of minutes used on the platform. This is very encouraging and innovative, as making an upfront commitment no longer necessary. Financial institutions should focus on managing balance sheets, trading, and risk management, while using whatever tools they have at their disposal to provide mobility and competition in their space.

1.2. Clearing Trades and Settlement Transactions

Due to crippling regulatory burdens of keeping larger amounts of capital for over-the-counter (OTC) trades, it is not surprising that the largest clearing houses would support such a migration. However, there are many factors working against the full migration of OTC products to standardized clearable products. Some include the basic fact that there is not *one* model to price these products. Therefore, disagreements on the amount of required collateral prevents the full migration into clearing.

Another obstacle is that banks do not want to create too much transparency in these products, as they provide the bank with huge margins on trading in the current opaque market. Some financial institutions have created direct links to clearing houses and other advancements in the cleared processing of trades. New regulation around trades requires immediate processing activity on these products, and some regulations require full reporting within 10 minutes.

However, what is obviously being missed is that even in the cleared space, 50% or more of the transactions are still voice trades made over the phone. If the industry does not fully automate that part of the cleared trade process, it will not achieve the full compliance needed to create the efficiencies promised by technology. Therefore, the automation of the voice trade is key to the advancement of securities trade processing. By 2022, this concern will be likely addressed and OTC will reach full automation of the trading process.

1.3. *Widespread Use of Artificial Intelligence (AI) and Blockchain*

With the explosion of Big Data, artificial intelligence (AI) technologies are key to understanding and improving the use of this big data. AI is advancing at the fastest pace and will integrate into people's daily lives by 2022 in almost every aspect. For example, the use of AI in multiple platforms tries to achieve two major goals: (1) data quality, and (2) trade breaks reconciliation and remediation. However, the biggest problem is the quality of the data itself. If the quality of the data coming in is poor, then consequently the output will be poor — garbage in, garbage out.

This example shows that the holy grail in terms of digitally-enabled platform's goals is to improve data quality, improve data matching of non-structured data, and help AI algorithms correct data impurities on their own. There is an explosion in the interest around blockchain and the way it could simplify the complexities of the market infrastructure.

Blockchain would drastically reduce costs while improving the ability of financial institutions to synchronize data and transactions. Some experts such as Mohamed and Ali (2019) believe the way to prepare for it is by installing a private node distributed ledger and then preparing to expose it to other players when they are ready. Herein lies the main problem with the implementation of blockchain — it will only work if all the participants implement the technology. To reach this network effect or its true scale potential, one important factor is the ability to define the right use case for the technology.

A main concern today is that institutions are not very selective in the choice of use case when implementing AI or blockchain. This dilutes the importance of the technology and sometimes leads to large investments of solutions being disbanded mid-way. If one is selective in their use cases, and are choosing the right technology partner, they would then have full verification of the success of such technologies by 2022, which will set clear KPIs toward the implementation of these technologies.

1.4. Governance and Regulatory Controls

One area that influences the narrative of the financial institution business model and its future viability is the immense amount of new regulations (Beck *et al.*, 2018) controlling investment capital in the market for the past decade. Complying with the regulations became costly in the global arena. Furthermore, the regulatory attitude toward financial market participants was do or die, leaving no choice or time to think about future strategies.

One of the main criticisms is that most regulators were interested in collecting large fees for non-compliance issues rather than working to reduce systematic risk. New technology was patched on like band-aids put on an open wound. Although some efforts are on the way for deregulation in the US, many new regulations and even tighter frameworks were approved in the EU. It is likely that there will be higher levels of regulations globally, which may distract the strategic views of institutions. Asian regulators are in a more "wait and see" approach, but by 2020, they will catch up. Asian regulators tend to wait for the best methods and then replicate these methods, but if they plan on complying with EU regulations, this will add massive efforts in technology coming into the new decade.

Managing global compliance with these regulations and adjusting the financial institutions systems to be flexible enough to deal with the newest breed of regulation is not the best way to approach this issue strategically (Mohamed and Ali, 2019). Utilities could provide a meaningful stepping stone for further compliance to the ever-changing regulatory environment.

2. Blockchain-based Islamic Capital Markets

A more advanced Islamic securities trading platform on a blockchain protocol, enhanced with sophisticated algorithms, can provide a new way to trade assets without centralized databases or central intermediaries (Mohamed and Ali, 2019). Also, the transparency and anonymous verification protocols inherent in the technology plays a strong function in preventing fraud in all capacities involving banking, and this could correspondingly operate for securities transactions. Moreover, blockchain can help to minimize operational risk and administrative costs from its immutable and transparent nature (Pilkington, 2015; Tapscott *et al.*, 2016; Iansiti and Lakhani, 2017). The information captured on every block along the chain provides trackability for every asset or item of value that was traded ((Nakamoto, 2008; Underwood, 2016; Kosba *et al.*, 2016). Having such historical records provides surety and validity of past transactions and ownership throughout the supply chain.

Practically, digital tokens are issued by a trusted originator or central authority in order to authenticate the product's point of origin (Buterin, 2014; Nærland *et al.*, 2017). From then, every time the product exchange hands (transfer ownership), the tokens move along with the real-world chain of ownership, which is updated and replicated by the historical blockchain of that digital token.

Digital tokens here act as a virtual "certificate of authenticity" that is harder to forge than pieces of paper that represent such authenticity (Morabito, 2017). The end recipient of the product can then verify the chain of transactions from the point of creation, which enables a distributed and demonstrable trust that was not possible before.

Another concern which involves data privacy (Beck *et al.*, 2018; Böhme *et al.*, 2015) among counterparties of trade transactions can be solved by utilizing cryptography in tokenization to protect sensitive data, by only giving permissioned access to information through customized security keys. This would allow for the confidentiality of transactions while provisioning for special access to regulators or governing authorities to carry out their fiduciary duties, where necessary.

2.1. Blockchain as Clearing and Settlement of Securities Transactions

One of the first areas for Islamic capital markets to consider using the blockchain is in payments and settlements. The blockchain can facilitate and enhance payments, without depending on SWIFT or other existing payment methods. Figure 2.1 depicts the technological innovation that can bring about more efficient processing and settlement of transactions. New encryption methods and applications can make highly sensitive data in a shared access environment more secure and private, by only allowing users to reveal selective information to others on a need-to-know basis. Mutual consensus verification through nodes allow the designated parties to verify and accept new updates to the database collectively, without the need for a sole central governing authority. There can be different types of consensus protocols, but the basic idea is that there are ample defenses to prevent manipulation (or cyberattacks) and no weak links (Ross, 2017).

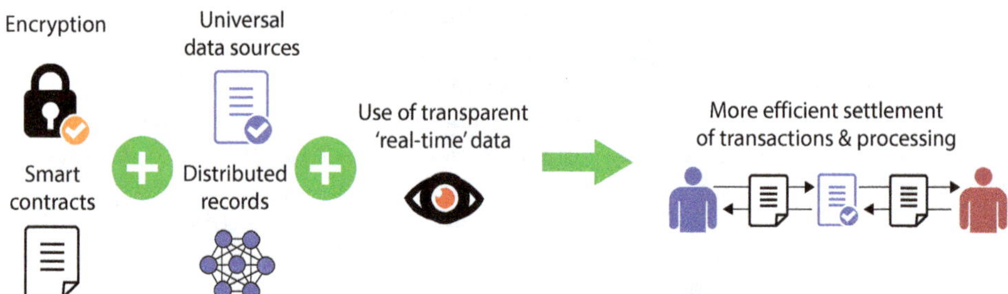

Figure 2.1: Critical Elements in Blockchain Innovation

The smart contracts are coded to deploy commands for subsequent processes (such as payment instructions or transfer assets) when specific terms and conditions are met (Buterin, 2014). Like passive data, they become immutable once accepted onto the blockchain.

Such innovations make it possible for any independent party to work with worldwide data sources, automatically resolving data between all participants (Kosba *et al.*, 2016). Any stored data record can be written onto a block, from asset ownership to contractual terms and payment schedules.

A multitude of data types can be 'hashed', encrypted, and entered into the ledger to create richer datasets than today. Distributed records are stored locally by participants as their golden source of information to replace legacy systems that constantly require alignment of data sets.

One of the best use case for a blockchain is in the clearing and settlement of securities transactions. Currently, the clearing and settlement of securities transactions involve multiple parties, including brokers, custodian banks, stock transfer agents, regulators, and depositories. A single transfer can entail many in-between transactions, which would typically need three days to settle, of which about 20% generate errors, which then has to be corrected manually (Evans *et al.*, 2016). On a smart contract-enabled platform, two trading parties could read and write to a common, trusted, and error-free database. The transaction could be written in legal language and subsequently translated to computer code, which makes the data exchange itself as the settlement. Regulators would not be left out, as this step can be made visible to them on a need-to-know basis. Meanwhile, the brokers for the buyer or seller could trade on a larger blockchain to remove custodians as intermediaries, which would significantly reduce overall transaction costs. Institutions issuing securities, such as corporations and governing agencies, could issue them directly onto the blockchain, effectively replacing stock transfer agents. Figure 2.2 illustrates this shift in settlements.

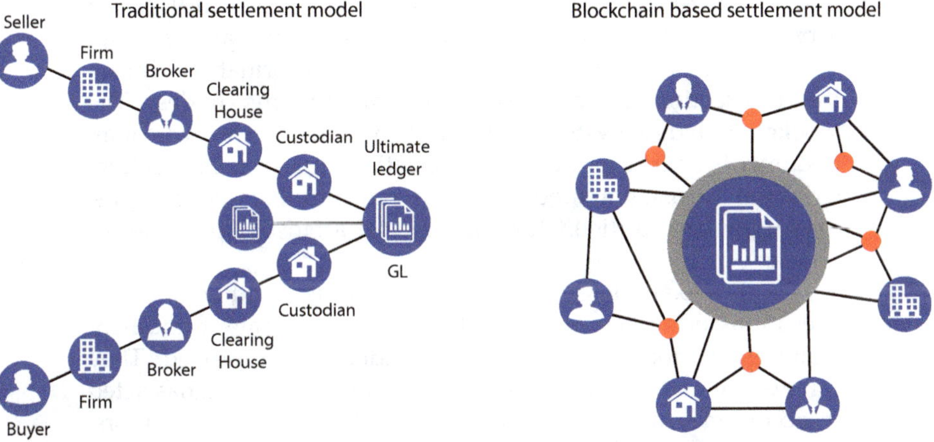

Figure 2.2: Comparative Settlements in Securities Transactions

Blockchain technology would simplify and streamline this entire process, providing an automated trade lifecycle where all parties in the transaction would have access to a single universal source of truth. This would lead to substantial infrastructural cost savings, reduces the scope for data errors, disputes and reconciliation lags, the speeding up of the end-to-end process, and the potential removal of brokers and intermediaries altogether.

2.2. Reduction of Fraud

The growth of fraudulent transactions and cyberattacks has become one of the greatest problems facing the banking industry today. Customarily, bank ledgers have been centralized databases, and being single points-to-entry, are vulnerable to hackers and cyberattacks because all of the sensitive data is located in one main place. Since a single location is easier to find rather than a distributed ledger system, these traditional systems are more susceptible to data breaches and cyberattacks by highly-skilled hackers.

By comparison, the blockchain is distributed (hence not centralized) which makes it less susceptible to this type of malicious intrusion. In addition, the blockchain will enable real-time execution of payments and provide complete transparency, thus enabling real-time fraud monitoring and immediate intervention, where required.

A blockchain is checked before every transaction by independent nodes, before new information is added. Even in a privatized blockchain system, there is real-time analysis and verification of every bit of data and all information during the transaction by pre-determined anonymous nodes. The blockchain ledger system will reflect the previous records of all documents shared and compliance actions for each transaction. Criminal intrusion to modify data become immediately obvious, making it very difficult for hackers and almost impossible for attacks.

For example, such immutable records could be of actual use in ascertaining persons attempting to create fraudulent histories or modify data already recorded and approved. They can also be used to show that an institution like a bank has acted in accordance with the compliance requirements by regulators. Depending on the data protection regulation, the data can be used to spot inconsistencies or actions that may amount to criminal prosecution.

Such advantages over the current banking systems appear to support the migration to blockchain systems, but this would require collaboration and collective participation on the blockchain. Financial institutions must join with regulators and fintech companies to "develop credible, decentralised ledgers permitting rapid adoption of global real-time payments and settlement."

2.3. *Know Your Customer (KYC)*

Know Your Customer (KYC) processes cause significant delays to current banking operations, typically taking 33 to 60 days to complete sufficiently. Apart from its lengthy process, existing KYC practices involve much replication of validation between banks (and other third-party verification agencies or institutions, including credit bureaus).

A typical bank spends millions on KYC compliance every year, as reported by Thomson Reuters Survey, and some banks even spend up to hundreds of millions annually on KYC compliance, Anti Money Laundering (AML) checks, and Customer Due Diligence (CDD). Money laundering, or the act of funnelling proceeds of illegal activity such as drug trafficking, and other illicit activities via legitimate sources or activities, is a profound predicament in the international financial system. The World Bank estimates that the range of money laundering lies between US$2 trillion and US$3.5 trillion annually (3% to 5% of global GDP) as reported in a Goldman Sachs report.[1]

Fines imposed by regulators have increased significantly since 2009, with record-breaking fines levied during 2015. From the banks' perspective, not having one internationally agreed standard makes it increasingly hard for banks to remain compliant, especially when such compliance requirements change from time to time. As the KYC procedures lengthen, it has inadvertently had a dismal effect on the end-user or customer experience.

If KYC protocols utilized the blockchain, customer information can also be utilized by other entities such as car rental firms, credit providers, and insurers, without annoying the customer to start the KYC process all over again. The permission is given by the customer, who ultimately has ownership over his/her own data.

According to the same Goldman Sachs Report, the banking sector can reduce costs by shrinking 10% of its staff with efficiencies from blockchain in its KYC methods, which is estimated at US$160 million in cost savings annually. More savings are projected from employee training, where it is estimated that a 30% headcount reduction is possible, amounting to US$420 million. In aggregate, the overall operational cost savings are anticipated to be around US$2.5 billion dollars.

---

1   Scheider, J. (2016). *Blockchain: Putting theory into Practice.* Goldman Sachs.

3. Applications of the Blockchain to Capital Markets

The blockchain will create efficiencies and greater transparency for every category of capital market and asset classes such as syndicated loans, private placements, asset-backed securities, OTC derivatives, commodities futures, etc. In order to illustrate this, we focus on capital markets and its associated activities, such as post-trade and securities servicing. See Figure 2.3 for an illustration of the basic blockchain infrastructure.

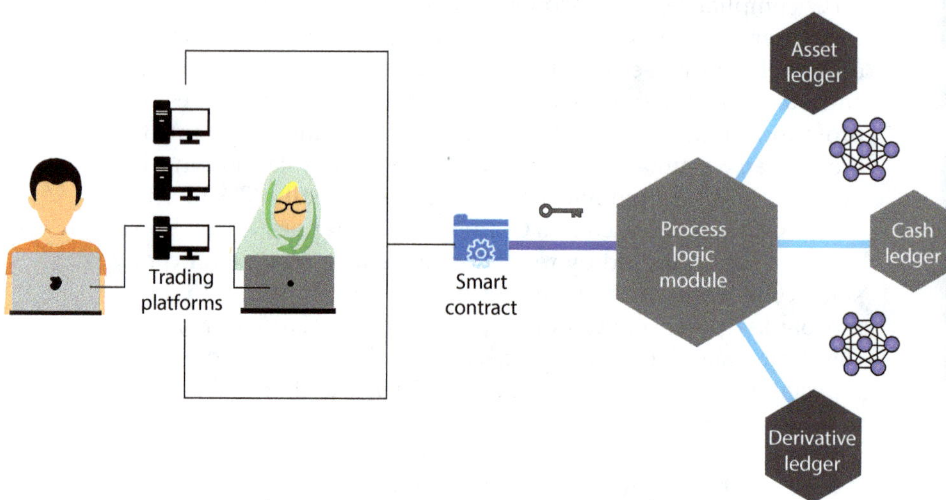

Figure 2.3: Simplified Blockchain Infrastructure for the Islamic Capital Market

3.1. Securities Transaction

Counterparties in a transaction are matched on a smart contract platform, and automatically verify that the other has the means to complete the transaction. For instance, Party 1 has been verified to own a security on an asset ledger, and his/her counterparty has been verified to own cash on a cash ledger. Both parties then jointly 'sign' the smart contract document to unlock their asset or cash, and then transfer ownership to the respective party via execution of the terms. The signed transaction is broadcasted to the distributed ledger to be validated and recorded in a new block, along with a simultaneous update to a cash ledger.

3.2. Asset Servicing and Treasury Operations

Asset servicing refers to a broad scope of financial services like processing payments, cash management, safeguarding assets, and various analytics associated with the assets, etc. Treasury operations are accountable for handling a company's assets and mitigating risks which surface from mismatches between assets and liabilities. AI algorithms can automatically compute exposures by referencing agreed upon external data sources that recalculate variation margin and adjust overall funding needs across parties. Such computational outcomes can be coded onto smart contracts to be deployed to execute required actions. Also, balance sheet providers could immensely benefit from blockchain verification of collateral pledges and secured loans of cash or securities.

Treasury services, particularly payments, could be significantly disrupted by blockchained digital currency (cryptocurrency) or the use of tokens as a medium of exchange. They will eliminate time delays, cut tedious operational processes, and reduce bid/offer spreads in foreign exchange. The need for scheduling, asset movements downstream, and correspondent communication will also be eliminated when settlements are handled on the blockchain protocol.

3.3. Derivative Transaction

Unbundling securities could enable new approaches to financial reconciliation in terms of cashflow and exposures, by enabling specialists to construct bespoke instruments consisting of individual cash flows that meet precise needs in terms of timing and credit risk. These instruments could be financed by issuers selling their own instruments that match the cash flows they expect to achieve, in essence, creating swaps without the need for balance sheet intermediation.

Furthermore, derivative transactions can be created as pre-agreed (and thus pre-coded) smart contracts, securing the agreements of the two contracting parties (such as margin agreements or swap conditions) along with the specified terms and conditions.

In this utopian derivative platform, a central clearing house is still required to novate trades for dealers to net their exposures. It also allows collateral to be posted by escrowing cash on the cash ledger, and allocating assets to the collateral ledger, which is connected to the derivative ledger as well as the asset ledger (depicted as an 'atomic' icon in Figure 2.3).

At maturity, a final net commitment is computed by the smart contracts, and payment instructions will be generated automatically in the cash ledger in order to close out the deal, and complete the contract.

3.4. *Post-trade Processing*

Post-trade processing involves an analysis of a range of middle and back office processes which fall into the post-trade part of an asset's lifecycle, which includes cash, collateral, data management, and inventory, as well as clearing and settlement.

Most delays in clearing and settlement of assets are not due to an asset exchange but due to the way current post-trade settlement processes are set up because of regulatory mandates and proliferation of marketplaces. By streamlining the post-trade processes using blockchain, banks can speed up the movement of assets of value across the capital market and, in turn, save costs, improve liquidity, and reduce collateral needs.

According to a Boston Consulting Group report,[2] the DTCC estimates that moving from T+3 to T+1 would reduce the clearing fund by 25% in a normal environment (saving about US$1 billion worth of collateral) and 37% in a stressed environment (saving US$2.7 billion, as the starting values are higher, with rising collaterals as the stress increases). In doing so, an estimate[3] for the risk reduction to the system can be done too. The Bank of America Merrill Lynch report projects that moving from T+3 to T+2 could possibly save about US$200 million per year, and about US$410 million for T+1 settlement for the US equities market.

3.5. *Finance, Audit, Reporting*

Blockchain enhancements to the capital market infrastructure will impose better enforcement of legal terms due to the escrow-like capabilities in smart contracts for asset servicing. It will be

---

2   https://www.bcg.com/documents/file119009.pdf
3   *How will blockchain change European market structure?* by Bank of America Merrill Lynch

able to reduce friction and accelerate disintermediation across the capital market as the technology itself facilitates trust between counterparties.

Digital identity, AML, CTF, and KYC compliance over a distributed network can help ensure assets and services are accessible to the desired set of investors only, reducing coordination hurdles and regulatory costs. Further, blockchain can improve scalability due to transparent operations and digital interactions with relevant participants across the network via smart contracts. In addition, regulators could be given special access to audit data wherever required, according to its mandate to verify transaction details along with its counterparties, thus improving transparency and transactions oversight.

3.6. Securities Issuance

Securities issuance on the blockchain can help better record the ownership and custody of assets (Conley, 2017). Further, the smart contract can help with automation by carrying out terms of the agreements on the blockchain. Thus, the benefits on the issuance of securities on a blockchain can have many positive ripple effects across the asset lifecycle.

However, mainstream blockchain adoption for issuance will need coordination between market participants and regulators, especially after concerns on ICOs. While the benefits of new infrastructure are enormous, an overhaul of capital market infrastructure in the short term is not likely. Regulatory challenges and acceptance of digitized securities issuance will have to go through significant experimentation and evaluation before any implementation can occur.

The migration of traditional contracts to smart contracts is estimated to save billions of dollars in the several trillion dollar-size of the global Islamic Finance markets. It is indeed significant to consider such progression as our economy evolves, but it will realistically require challenges to be overcome.

4. AI Use Cases for the Islamic Capital Market

Likewise, artificial intelligence (AI) will also play a crucial role to support the digital transformation of the Islamic Capital Market. AI is being used across businesses both to augment existing activities and to automate complex and intensive tasks which would otherwise be cumbersome to execute. Although the use of AI is not new to the capital market (like the blockchain), its use cases today, and moving forward, will be more complex and will be able to tackle more difficult requirements.

The Association of Financial Markets in Europe (AFME) has identified these areas where AI can contribute immensely in their 2018 White Paper (see Table 2.1).

Table 2.1: Artificial Intelligence Applications and Benefits for the Islamic Capital Markets (Compiled from AFME, 2018)

Practical AI Capital Market Applications	**Benefits**
Predictive data analytics to identify 'forecasting events' *e.g., recognizing potential triggers for 'flash crash' events*	• Personalised products and services to meet individual client needs • Automated and predictive resolution of client service issues
Sentiment analysis to determine client needs/ opportunities, *e.g., social media analytics* Algorithms for stock selection, *e.g., development of client trading products*	• Enables existing staff to focus on high value efforts and activities • Improved decision-making based on increased data and simulations • Continuous performance improvements
Natural language document analysis services, *e.g., analyzing and extracting key data from unstructured or semi-structured documents* Natural language generation for document writing, *e.g., performance and financial data commentary reporting*	• Reduced investment costs for market entry of new products • Reduced transaction breaks and exceptions, and increasing data quality • More rapid entry into and development of new markets • Increased standardisation and commoditisation of existing products and services

Practical AI Capital Market Applications	Benefits
Smart matching for trades, *e.g., predicting manual intervention required to complete trades* Internal compliance for identifying patterns and behaviors, *e.g., analysis of trader activities for market abuse surveillance* Market abuse and financial crime surveillance, *e.g., identification of complex trading patterns in large data sets*	• More efficient processing of information • Increased ability for firms to report, and supervisors to evaluate large and complex data sets • Mining of both structured and unstructured data sets • Better use of data to prevent and detect fraud, money-laundering, and market abuse
IT support analysis on system outages and root cause, *e.g., detection of cyber-attacks and point of entry of attack*	• Reduced time required to detect and respond to cyber threats
Rules-based and machine learning exception management, *e.g., processing interest claims on late payment*	• Better assessment of financial and non-financial risks

The proposed use of AI technology should be risk-based and come from a principle-based approach, focusing on addressing the potential risks to clients or to financial stability. However, the application of technology requires rules-based guidelines in order to minimize regulatory and legal uncertainties or oversight. Inherent potential risks associated with technology also need to be addressed. The development of the AI Ethics Guidelines, and accountability and liability mechanisms for decisions made by a self-learning AI also has to be considered from its implementation.

5. Challenges in Market Adoption

AI and blockchain technologies present powerful opportunities to facilitate the coordination of all means of financial transactions, enabling more intricate collaboration in a high-trust environment.

Practically, AI with blockchain technology is a better structural model operationally, and the consensus-based AI + Blockchain model has the potential to provide a market model of straight-through-processing, from execution to post-trade, in a secure, transparent, and efficient manner.

Although the blockchain presents many use case benefits and improvements, it is also crucial to apply the technology relevantly, in areas that it would bring the most benefits, and where existing technology cannot. Not all processes need an economy or a payments system, or peer-to-peer exchange, or decentralization, or robust public record-keeping. The likely outcome is that the different components of digital disruption, like AI and the blockchain, will be integrated within the existing infrastructure or ecosystem to help to streamline many existing cumbersome processes and remove significant inefficiencies correlated to reconciliation. Banks will be looking for ways to become more efficient and improve client services, and regulators will be interested in increasing transparency and optimizing execution and settlement.

5.1. Other Challenges on Moving Ahead

Blockchain functions as a distributed system and thus its value will mostly depend on collaboration with all actors in the value chain like customers, service providers, payment systems, and regulators (Voshmgir, 2017). Given that the nature of blockchain technology implementation is that it requires a network to be achieved before benefits can be truly recognized, it is obvious, as explained, that it can achieve enormous monetary savings for financial institutions; but most importantly, it can be the new architecture of trust for which the possibilities could be truly endless. For the industry as a whole, building trust begins with technology experts and start-ups, regulators, and other market participants to identify the challenges around it, and leverage upon blockchain's open and decentralized nature.

The AI + Blockchain model for capital markets will be centered around creating efficiencies, and capital markets should start with a holistic understanding of technology limitations as well as regulatory (in the absence of an intermediary or in cross-border transactions), and operational requirements regarding, for example, data protection and standardization. As an innovative technology, blockchain presents a range of options to innovate by adopting the way of working of start-ups, partnering with, or acquiring them. The key to shaping the future of the blockchain financial ecosystem is getting involved in partnerships and industry activities early on.

6. Conclusion

The promise of the blockchain enhanced with AI creates the possibility of coordinating our transactional activities through a strong mechanism of trust and transparency within the now global economy. The blockchain is the technology that would operationalize the mechanism of trust as we progress from personal exchange to impersonal exchange due to globalization. It will enable banks to facilitate trade transactions between their clients by offering greater transparency, more automation, and lower risk. As capital markets stakeholders consider where and how to implement blockchain, they must understand that this technology is still frontier in many respects. The general understanding of the full potential of blockchain is also far from complete, which adds to the resistance and sometimes, confusion. Over the course of the research, the authors faced how dramatically misunderstood the elements of blockchain still remain. The cost is also often excessive when measured against the relatively small size of the orders at the beginning. However, over time, technology will improve and there will be thought leaders who will able to leap over current obstacles with transformative ideas to unleash the blockchain's true potential.

No doubt, adoption will be fragmented during the initial trials and implementation. Looking further ahead, the authors will eventually present a map of interconnected (private blockchain) networks, cautiously being integrated with legacy systems. The grander vision is towards a more robust and efficient system that will only take place when we replace and digitize processes, effectively removing bottlenecks and inefficiencies.

Bibliography

Antonopoulos, A.M. (2014). *Mastering Bitcoin: Unlocking Digital Crypto-Currencies*. Sebastopol, CA: O'Reilly Media.

Association for Financial Markets in Europe, AFME (2018). *Artificial Intelligence: Adoption in Wholesale Capital Markets.* White Paper, April.

Bacha, O. I. and Mirakhor, A. (2019). *Islamic Capital Markets: A Comparative Approach (2nd Edition).* INCEIF — The Global University of Islamic Finance, Malaysia. World Scientific Publishing.

Beck, R., Müller-Bloch, C., and King, J. L. (2018). Governance in the Blockchain Economy – A Framework and Research Agenda. *Journal of the Association for Information Systems* 19(3).

Böhme, R., Christin, N., Edelman, B., & Moore, T. (2015). Bitcoin: Economics, technology, and governance. *Journal of Economic Perspectives*, 29(2), pp. 213–238.

Buterin, V. (2014). *Ethereum White Paper – A Next Generation Smart Contract & Decentralized Application Platform.* https://github.com/ethereum/wiki/wiki/ White-Paper. Accessed on 12 March 2018.

CapGemini Consulting (2016). *Smart Contracts in Financial Services: Getting from Hype to Reality.*

Conley, J. (2017). *Blockchain and the Economics of Crypto-tokens and Initial Coin Offerings.* Vanderbilt University Department of Economics Working papers 17-00008.

daCosta, F. (2013). *Rethinking the Internet of Things: A Scalable Approach to Connecting Everything.* New York: Apress, 2013.

Dawson, R. (2014) "The New Layer of the Economy Enabled by M2M Payments in the Internet of Things." Trends in the Living Networks, September 16, 2014. http://rossdawsonblog.com/weblog/archives/2014/09/new-layer-economy-enabled-m2mpayments-internet-things.html.

Evans, P., Aré, L., Forth, P., Harlé, N. and Portincaso, M. (2016). *Thinking Outside the Blocks: A Strategic Perspective on Blockchain and Digital Tokens.* December 1.

Gansky, L. (2010). *The Mesh: Why the Future of Business is Sharing.* New York: Penguin Group.

GitHub. *Blockchain Based Proof of Work.* GitHub. March 2014.

Iansiti, M., and Lakhani, K. R. (2017). The Truth about Blockchain. *Harvard Business Review.* Retrieved from https://hbr.org/2017/01/the-truth-aboutblockchain. Accessed 5 July 2017.

Kosba, A., Miller, A., Shi, E., Wen, Z., and Papamanthou, C. (2016). Hawk: The Blockchain Model of Cryptography and Privacy-preserving Smart Contracts. In M. Locasto & K. Butler (Chairs), *2016 IEEE Symposium on Security and Privacy* (pp. 839–858), The Fairmont, San Jose, California, 23–25 May, IEEE Computer Society, Washington, DC. Retrieved from https://doi.org/10.1109/SP.2016.55. Accessed 4 July 2017.

Lee, T.B. (2013). *Bitcoin Needs to Scale by a Factor of 1000 to Compete with Visa. Here's How to Do It.* The Washington Post, November 12, 2013.

Mohamed, H. and Ali, H. (2019). Blockchain, Fintech and Islamic Finance — Building the Future of the New Islamic Digital Economy. De I G Press, Boston/Berlin.

Morabito, V. (2017). Blockchain Value System. In *Business innovation through Blockchain*. Cham: Springer International Publishing.

Nakamoto, S. (2008). *Bitcoin; A Peer-to-Peer Electronic Cash System* (Self-published paper), pp. 1–9.

Nærland, K., Müller-Bloch, C., Beck, R., and Søren, P. (2017). Blockchain to Rule the Waves – Nascent Design Principles for Reducing Risk and Uncertainty in Decentralized Environments. In *Proceedings of the 38th International Conference on Information Systems*. Seoul.

Nofer, M., Gomber, P., Hinz, O., and Schiereck, D. (2017). Blockchain. *Business and Information Systems Engineering*, 59(3), pp. 183–187.

Omohundro, S. (2014). *Cryptocurrencies, Smart Contracts, and Artificial Intelligence*. Submitted to AI Matters (Association for Computing Machinery), October 22, 2014. http://steveomohundro.com/2014/10/22/cryptocurrencies-smart-contracts-and-artificial- intelligence/

Pilkington, M. (2015). Blockchain Technology: Principles and Applications. *Research Handbook on Digital Transformations* (pp. 225–253). Retrieved from https://doi.org/10.4337/9781784717766.00019. Accessed 5 July 2017.

Ross, E. S. (2017). Nobody Puts Blockchain in a Corner: The Disruptive Role of Blockchain Technology in the Financial Services Industry and Current Regulatory Issues. *Catholic University Journal of Law and Technology*, 25(2), pp. 353–386.

Schenider, J. (2016). *Blockchain: Putting theory into Practice*. Goldman Sachs.

Swan, M. (2015). *Blockchain: Blueprint for a New Economy*. O'Reilly Media, Inc.

Szabo, Nick. (1996). *Smart Contracts: Building Blocks for Digital Markets*. Extropy, No. 16.

Tapscott, D., Tapscott, A., and Kirkland, R. (2016). How Blockchains Could Change the World. McKinsey&Company. Retrieved from http://www.mckinsey.com/industries/high-tech/our-insights/how-blockchains-could-change-the-world. Accessed 5 July 2017.

Underwood, S. (2016). Blockchain beyond Bitcoin. *Communications of the ACM*, 59 (11), pp. 15–17.

Voshmgir, S. (2017). Disrupting Governance with Blockchains and Smart Contracts. *Strategic Change*, 26 (5), pp. 499–509.

DIGITAL SUKUK ISSUANCE FOR BUSINESS FINANCING

Research consistently show that small- and medium-sized enterprises (SMEs) face greater constraints on access to finance than large firms, due to issues of information asymmetry, lack of collateral, and higher cost of servicing loans. In view of the large contribution of SMEs to output and employment in emerging Asian economies, it is critical to enhance the access of SMEs to finance in a way that is consistent with sustainable growth and financial stability. In this chapter, the author recommends putting asset-backed bonds on the blockchain to enable transparency and put forth steps to automate cumbersome processes in asset-backed bond issuances, in order to reduce costs and improve efficiency. Significant advantages of using technology to operationalize trust and instil confidence in properly structured and executed financial instruments will also be discussed. The author will also make these recommendations on the basis of fulfilling a gap in traditional bond issuances, which is currently occupied by the loan markets.

Keywords: *asset-backed financing, decentralized credit rating, risk-sharing instruments, sustainable finance, trust tokens.*

JEL codes: O31, O35, P45

Contents

1. Introduction

Small- and medium-sized enterprises (SMEs) are the backbone of most economies in the world. In Asia alone, they account for more than 97% of all enterprises, and between 32% and 87% of total share of employment outside the agricultural or farm-based workforce in Asia[1] (ADB, 2015). Compared to the larger firms, SMEs have long been significantly under-served financially, with very limited access to the traditional funding from formal banking institutions. Some 85% (or 365 million to 445 million) of SMEs in emerging markets have suffered from credit shortage, estimated in the range of US$2.1 trillion to US$2.5 trillion within the

---

1   Compiled from sources: Office of Small and Medium Enterprise Promotion (OSMEP). 2015. White Paper on Small and Medium Enterprises in Thailand 2015. Government of Thailand; Government of Japan, Ministry of the Economy, Trade and Industry. 2015. 2015 White Paper on Small Enterprises in Japan: Take-Off Time for Micro Businesses. Tokyo; and SME Corporation Malaysia. 2015. Annual Report 2014–2015. www.smecorp.gov.my/index.php/en/resources/2015-12-21-11-07-06/sme-annual-report/book/7/Array

developing world.[2] Of this, 45% (US$900 billion to US$1.1 trillion) is estimated to occur in East and Southeast Asia. Some 85% (or 365 million to 445 million) of SMEs in emerging markets have suffered from credit shortage, estimated in the range of US$2.1 to US$2.5 trillion within the developing world.[3] The European economy is "expected to suffer from the economic slowdown, with 2020 growth forecasted at 1.4% by the European Commission, a 0.2 percentage point downward revision from earlier estimates" (EIF, 2019). These numbers would be readjusted to negative as the world contends with the Covid-19 pandemic. In August 2019, the ECB's composite borrowing cost indicator for Euro area corporate lending reached a "new record low of 1.52%, undercutting the earlier record of May 2018 by 4 basis points".

One of the challenges in SME financing is that their size can be too hefty for microfinance, but are too little to be realistically served by traditional corporate banking models. One other issue that limits SMEs' access to credit is their spread across the nation and around the region. Asia's growth story thus far has been centred in its capital cities and financial centres. While a significant number of SMEs are still concentrated in the capital cities, the remaining are fragmented across other cities in the rest of the country. Most SMEs face poor access to finance in the region's dominant conventional banking-system models. Low bank loans to SMEs can be attributed to several factors, including the trickiness of evaluating SMEs' creditworthiness caused by scant information, especially on repayment behaviors, and hence requiring more collaterals to guarantee loans extended. SMEs also incur a higher cost to serve (as a percentage of loan size) by traditional banks and, in such cases, the lack of government involvement to sponsor credit guarantees does not help the situation. As such, government intervention via policy support should provide long-term financing to growth-oriented SMEs because the nature of the banking sector's short-term credit cycles in the region and rigid banking regulations (UNESCAP, 2017) are not making access any easier. Furthermore, the

---

2   Asian Development Bank (ADB), 2015, Asia SME Finance Monitor 2014, Manila: ADB, available at https://www.adb.org/sites/default/files/publication/173205/asia-sme-finance-monitor2014.pdf.

3   Compiled from OECD (Economic Outlook for Europe, Southeast Asia, China and India, 2018) and World Bank Data.

dominant conventional banking system models make SMEs more vulnerable to financial shocks because these firms do not have a prospect to de-risk by varying their funding sources during financial crises.

Ensuring improved and adequate access to finance for SMEs has long been a concern worldwide, particularly in emerging Asia, hence the directives of various international (i.e., World Bank, IMF, etc.) and regional (i.e., ADB, ASEAN, ECB, MENA, etc.) organisations to encourage greater access to more diversified sources of financing for SMEs. A complementary goal to improve financial inclusion and literacy becomes necessary in order for the SMEs' increased engagement in the financial system. Such inclusion is to be achieved through expanding the number and scope of financial intermediary facilities to benefit a wider circle of underserved communities, especially the SMEs.

Several key factors impede SME lending and results in poor financial inclusion of SMEs:

i. Low SME coverage by credit bureaus/registries increases the cost of SME credit risk assessment;
ii. Inadequate reach limits traditional banks to service SMEs in the physical and digital spheres;
iii. Internal banking regulations dictate higher risk weights to SMEs loans, which in turn raises lending costs; and
iv. Lack of cash flow visibility compels traditional banks to adopt strict collateral-based credit risk models, which hinder lending to SMEs without collateral.

An analysis of individual countries in Asia reveals that the support SMEs receive from financial institutions to help finance their businesses does not reflect their contributions to their country's GDP and employment, despite being the critical drivers for growth. In general, SME loan volumes in the region are less than 40% of their contribution to GDP, and constitute less than 20% of total loans, according to IMF data.[4] This actually presents a sizeable opportunity to alternative financiers in the SME market segment, as well as an untapped resource for the SMEs with regards to their financial needs. In Europe, SME loan volumes in the region are less than 40% of their contribution to GDP, and constitute less than 20% of total loans, according to IMF data. According to the EMN–MFC Survey Report 2016–2017

---

4   Financial Access Survey, IMF, 2017.

(EMN, 2018), the microfinance sector has been steadily growing over recent years. In 2017, the surveyed Microfinance Institutions (MFIs) disbursed almost 700,000 microloans with a total volume of over €2 billion. Overall, in 2017, MFIs reported almost 1 million total active borrowers, with a gross microloan portfolio outstanding of €3.1 billion. When considering a six-year time span (2012–2017), these indicators reach a growth rate upwards of 50%, confirming the dynamism of the microfinance sector in Europe. This actually presents a sizeable opportunity to alternative financiers in the SME market segment as well as an untapped resource for the SMEs with regards to their financial needs.

Currently, there is very limited information tailor-made to SMEs in their search for, and access to, investment finance in Asia. Of the available information, the focus is largely on the traditional sources of finance on the supply side. There is virtually no information on alternative sources of loan and equity funding potentially suitable to the financing needs and requirements of the regional SME. Additionally, no information (such as guidebooks and checklists) exists on how, when, and where SMEs can access alternative sources of finance.

2. Types of Alternative SME Financing Available Globally

While the big traditional banks remain broadly averse or unable to offer credit to SMEs, the alternative financing industry has been growing by leaps and bounds, but all this growth has turned the industry into an evolving mix of non-traditional lenders, accessible platforms, and innovative products.

Today, as increasing numbers of small business owners seek non-traditional funding platforms, the alternative financing industry keeps expanding with new, yet similar-sounding products. The most popular forms of alternative financing available to small business owners can be segmented to:

1. **Non-bank Financial Institutions**, such as credit unions, Community Development Financial Institutions (CDFI), and micro-lenders. Microenterprises and social enterprises are important contributors to employment and social value, especially in countries with high unemployment rates. European microenterprises in 2018 recorded

by far the strongest growth, both in value added and employment, compared to other enterprise size classes.

i. According to the data from the latest EIF SME Access to Finance (ESAF) Index, microenterprises have perceived a slight decrease in the external financing gap indicator. However, the share of enterprises which see access to finance as their most important problem has increased and remained higher among microenterprises than among their larger peers.

ii. Microenterprises, in general, use less bank loans than their larger peers, as they are more likely to be rejected if they decide to apply for a bank loan. Typically, they do not choose to apply for a bank loan due to insufficient collateral, high interest rates, and excessive paperwork without a high chance of approval.

iii. Customers, as they get rejected by or discouraged from banks, often apply for a microcredit from Microfinance institutions (MFI). MFIs do not always charge lower interest rates than banks, but they are less demanding in terms of collateral and guarantee requirements.

2. **Asset-Based Financing**

   i. **SME Guarantees** are credit guarantees which "remain the most wide-spread instrument in use across countries" to ease the SMEs' access to finance (OECD, 2018) and are particularly relevant "in those countries where a network of local or sectoral guarantee institutions is well established" (OECD, 2013).

      a. AECM statistics show that Turkey, Italy, and France are the top three countries in terms of both the volume and the number of outstanding SME guarantees.

      b. Relative to GDP, Turkey, Hungary, Portugal, and Italy have the largest markets.

   ii. **SME Leasing** Programs (also known as a "sale and leaseback") allow the SME owner of a property or other valuable asset, such as equipment or vehicles, to "sell" it to a lender and then rent it back during a set period of time. Under this arrangement, the original SME property owner can quickly free up working capital while retaining possession and use of the property. Some leaseback agreements permit the lessee the option to buy back the property at a future date. During the tenure of the leaseback, however, the buyer obtains tax benefits from the agreement, such as being credited for depreciation of the property.

    a. Leasing is an important additional instrument to facilitate access to short- and medium-term financing for SMEs, ranked second after traditional bank-related products.

    b. During the first semester of 2019, Euro area SMEs state that the availability of leasing or hire-purchase has improved the most compared to other external financing sources, but SMEs still signal an increased need for it.

    c. Leasing is mainly used for investments in property, plant, or equipment.

    d. Estonia, Finland, and Germany are the countries with the highest proportion of SMEs using leasing, contrary to countries in the south of Europe.

    e. Leasing as a financing source is more prevalent among industrial and construction firms.

    f. The use of leasing grows with firm size.

3. **Peer-Based Alternative Financing**

    i. **Peer-to-Peer Lenders**, or P2P lending, is a form of financing that occurs directly between individuals or "peers" without the involvement of a traditional financial institution. Loan amounts are typically small, at a maximum of US$10,000. Loan terms are also quite short ranging from one to five years. Much of the success of P2P lending is a result of the social networking power and infrastructure of the Internet. P2P lending sites offer an online marketplace where borrowers and lenders can come together. Often, there will be several private lenders per borrower who each share in partially funding a given loan amount. These sites usually provide documentation and verification services, as well as an evaluation of the borrowers' creditworthiness and the risk involved in lending to them. Contracts cover the loan's terms and conditions as well as the repayment schedule and tax payments as agreed by both parties.

    ii. **Crowdfunding** allows business owners and entrepreneurs to raise funds by requesting a small amount of money from many different people online. By utilizing the power of the Internet, entrepreneurs can pitch their ideas to a large group of people, who will respond by investing a small portion of the investment required, if they are interested in the campaign or cause. There are several forms of crowdfunding platforms such as donation-based, equity-based, and reward-based, depending on its different structure and objectives. For the purposes of this discussion, the author is only focused on the equity-based crowdfunding where business capital is raised through crowdfunding, and repaid with a certain amount of pre-agreed return on capital for a given tenure.

4. **Private Capital**

    i. **Business Angel Funding** is a method used to raise monetary contributions from a private investor who is an affluent individual who provides capital for a business start-up, usually in exchange for convertible debt or ownership equity. They are also known as angels, informal investors, angel funders, or seed investors.

    ii. **Private Equity and Venture Capital (PEVC)** (often used interchangeably with private equity, although they serve different phases of business growth) is a form of financing that is provided by firms or funds to small, early-stage, emerging firms that are deemed to have high growth potential, or which have demonstrated high growth (in terms of number of employees, annual revenue, or both). Additionally, venture capital is usually only used with high growth industries, where risk is much higher. In these cases, there are little or no assets to back the loan in the event of default, so the likelihood of obtaining a loan is much lower, and the potential pay-outs must be drastically higher to result in a successful investment.

    iii. **Private debt funds** have gained importance as an alternative asset class for investors and a new financing source for SMEs and mid-caps. The most developed and largest private debt market was the US, while Europe was the region with the second largest share in global fundraising in 2018. Europe is frequently stated to be the most important target region of private debt investors. The number of European debt fund managers has grown considerably.

2.1. Recent Trends on Non-Traditional SME Financing in Asia Pacific

In general, it appears that as a country's per capita GDP rises, the alternative finance volume per capita also rises, possibly reflecting the growth of both financing needs and higher disposable income per person for alternative funding and investment activities.

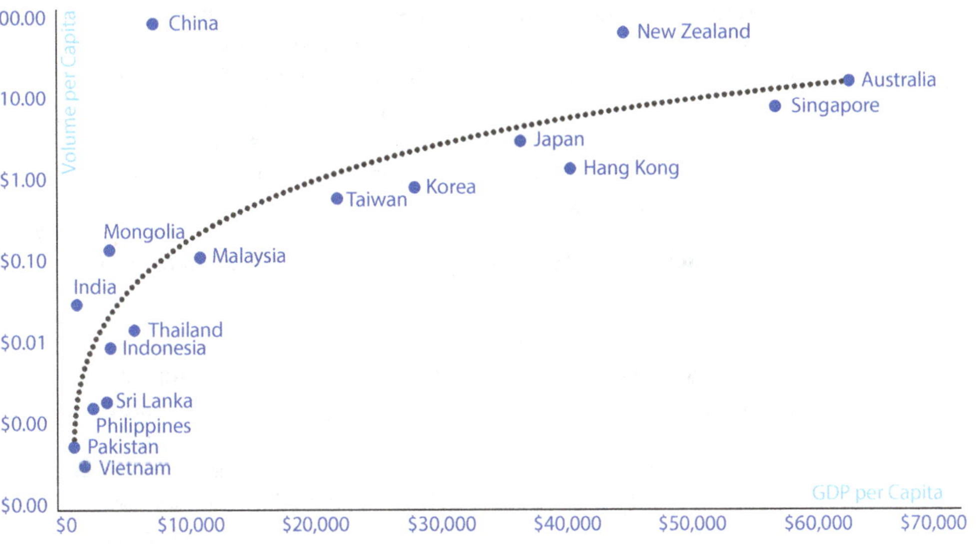

Figure 3.1: Total Alternative Finance Volume per Capita versus GDP per Capita in Asia-Pacific (US$)
Source: Harnessing Potential — The Asia-Pacific Alternative Finance Report. https://assets.kpmg.com/content/dam/kpmg/pdf/2016/03/harnessing-potential-asia-pacific-alternative-finance-benchmarking-report-march-2016.pdf.

Also, there are several trends that will shape the landscape of non-traditional SME financing in Asia. These market forces and key enablers are:

1. **Investment diversification key to growth and resilience**

   Trade prospects and business opportunities are strong within the Asian economies. Meanwhile, the increase in cross-border investments suggest that Asian business leaders are laying the groundwork for regional expansion and long-term growth. They understand the necessity to continue growth in their local markets and grow new markets, or risk losing their market share in the industry.

2. **Accelerating digital connectivity and addressing data security risks**

   Astute digital strategies are imperative for businesses as the proliferation of new technologies such as Internet of Things (IoT) revolutionises the global economy, driving new business models, and forging closer relationships with customers and business partners. Asian CEOs are already investing in connected devices and data collection to not lose out in the competition. With many organisations in the region at the nascent or adolescent stage of the digital curve, Asian business leaders tend to look to regulations as a safeguard and guide to manage data-related risks.

3. **Balancing policy and market factors in cross-border investment decisions**

   The regulatory environment is a strong consideration to business leaders looking at cross-border expansion. No longer are fast-growing markets enough to entice investors to make big bets. Ongoing global economic uncertainty, coupled with increasing paucity of unchartered markets, are calling for more stringent calculations on the projected risks and rewards from investing in a foreign market. Regulatory conditions and past regulations matter as a prerequisite in business leaders' investment decisions.

In Europe, the SME lending market[5,6] "plateaued during the second and third quarter of 2019, hovering around

---

5   Huerga *et al.* (2012) show that "small loans are a good proxy for the SME lending market".

6   To better reflect lending conditions to SMEs specifically, rather than small loans in general, the data excludes interest rates on revolving loans and overdraft, since these instruments are used independently of firm size.

€37.5 billion"[7] (Figure 3.2). The EIF (2019) reported that following the crisis, "SME lending initially contracted, after which it picked up pace early 2014 and has been on the rise ever since. The graph also depicts the share of small loans in total lending, to illustrate how the SME specific segment diverged from the overall lending market". The EIF observed that during the pre-2014 contraction, the "share of small loans in total volumes also dropped. This implies that the credit contraction caused by the financial crisis was felt more severely by SMEs. However, during the recovery thereafter, the share of small loans in total lending increased significantly, stabilizing at about 17% by the end of 2017".

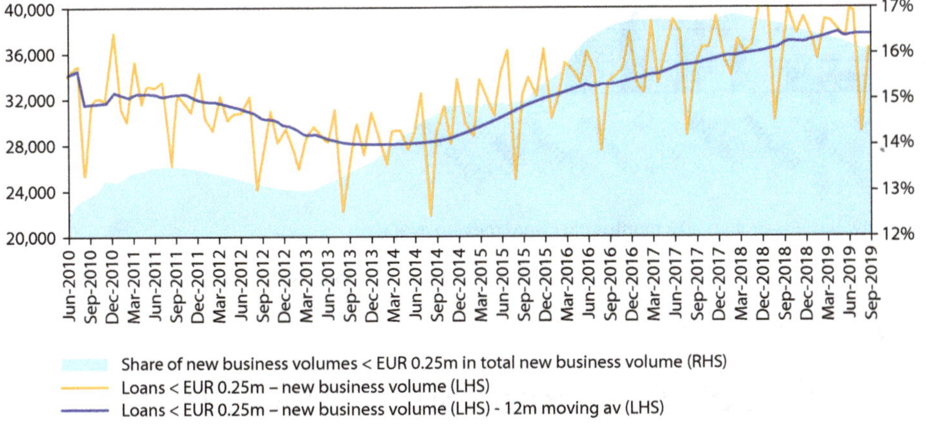

Figure 3.2: Small loans (< €0.25 mil) to NFCs (12 months backward moving averages)
Source: EIF (2019) based on ECB Data Warehouse.

In the report, it is observed that small loans are relatively more important in the credit market of vulnerable countries. From Figure 3.3, in Spain and Portugal, for example, "small loans make up 40% and 35%, respectively, of new loans granted to non-financial corporations (NFCs). For September 2019, both shares stayed roughly constant compared to the same month in 2018. Also, in Italy this share is relatively high at 25%. In Austria, the Netherlands, Slovakia, Belgium and Germany, the proportion of small loans in total new business volume is much smaller and does not exceed

---

7   The EIF report "calculated as a 12 month backwards moving average to abstract from the strong monthly fluctuations typically found in lending new business volumes".

10%". The "relative importance of small lending decreased most in Lithuania, where it fell by another 4 percentage points, a trend that was also observed in the previous edition of the ESBFO" (Kraemer-Eis *et al.*, 2019). For the remaining countries, no significant year-on-year changes for small business lending were noted.

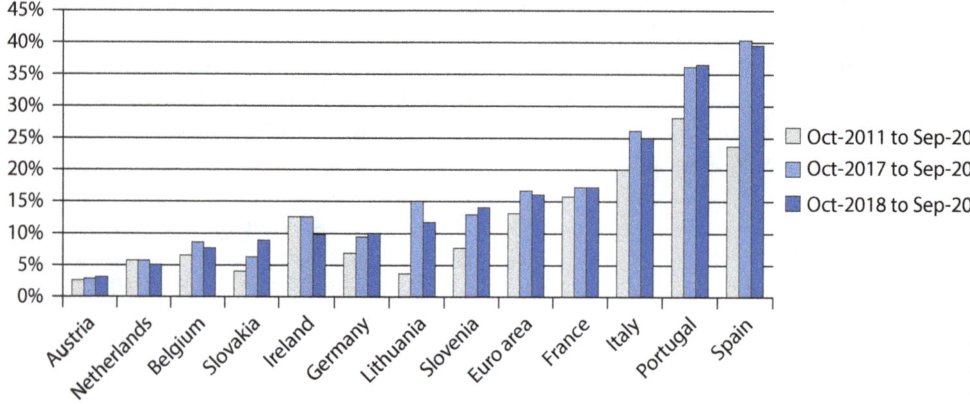

* NBV: New business volume, 12 months backward moving average.

Figure 3.3: Small loans (< €250,000) with respect to total NFC lending (NBV*), by percentage and country
Source: EIF (2019) based on ECB Data Warehouse.

3. Blockchain-based Sukuk (Decentralized Asset-backed Bond)

The model of the sukuk security is derived from the conventional securitization process, in which a special purpose vehicle (SPV) is set up to acquire assets and to issue financial claims on the assets. These financial assets claims represent a proportionate beneficial ownership to the sukuk holders. However, there are several key distinctions between conventional bonds and sukuk. Conventional bonds are debt-based and coupon payments are interest-based and may not be necessarily linked to the performance of the bond. Sukuk,[8] however, are Shariah-compliant

---

8   In the old Islamic era, *sakk* (plural is sukuk), which is related with the European root "cheque", is any legal document that represents a contract of transference of rights, obligations or revenues earned according to the Shariah. Empirical evidence shows that sukuk was a financial certificate broadly used during medieval Islam for the transferring of financial obligations deriving from trade and other commercial activities.

financing structures typically based on a profit-sharing payment and risk-sharing undertaking through ownership of an asset for a given tenor. Islamic Finance prohibits interest payments on loans and the sale of debt, hence issuing trust certificates, like the sukuk, enable entities to raise required capital through securitizing assets without giving up ownership in perpetuity. Sukuk are usually issued for a fixed tenure and ownership rights return to the issuer once the certificate expires. Conversely, sukuk investors own the securitized asset for the tenure of the sukuk and have recourse to the asset in cases of defaults or non-payment of shared profits. Unlike loans,[9] which does not earn the lender anything in Islam, sukuk issuances are a permissible way to raise financing for a profitable project and share the earned profits.

The sukuk market represents an affirmation of Islamic legal principles in the Islamic capital market transactions where the market should be free from any elements or activities that are prohibited in Islam, such as asymmetric advantages and deceptive ambiguity. Sukuk are one of the most popular and commonly used financial instruments in the Islamic capital markets. Sukuk has also been a popular approach for governments seeking to finance infrastructure projects, due to their fixed profile and enhanced credit features. However, the legal complexity and overall cost to issue sukuk has kept it out of reach for most MSMEs, corporations, and cooperatives.

Issuing sukuk on the blockchain is a revolutionary way to ease the complexity and lower the barrier to entry for smaller entities through efficiency and transparency in the issuance. In a blockchain-based sukuk, the trust certificates are issued as tokens underwritten by smart contracts (e.g., Ethereum protocol), which captures the ownership of the underlying asset and payments to the investor. The assets underwritten will be under escrow by a licensed legal entity or under the charge of a custodian bank. This is an important function to ensure performance on the issuer and provides recourse for the investor. In short, the smart contract encodes business rules directly into the underlying payment

---

9   In Islamic financing, loans are only in two forms — *qard* or *qard hassan*. In both types, no earning is permissible as they will be deemed as interest. Lending, specifically bank lending as we know it, is viewed as a risk-transfer exercise rather than a risk-sharing one, and hence should not be rewarded with a profit without taking on any real risk.

currency itself — the blockchain itself enforces the contract rules regarding payments and transfer of ownership.

3.1. AI-enhanced and Blockchain-based Sukuk Structure

Traditionally, the first step to creating a sukuk structure is through defining the obligations between the issuer and the investors against the underlying asset which is verified suitable (Figure 3.4). The appropriate structure is then determined by the issuer, and it must originate from one of the typical Shariah contracts (see Appendix A). Normally, the names or types of sukuk is determined by the Shariah contract in which both the issuer and investor entered into at the first place. Some important factors for considering a sukuk structure include economic objectives of the issuer, availability of assets, the level of debt that the company has, credit rating of the issuer, the jurisdiction's legal framework, and the tax implication of a structure.

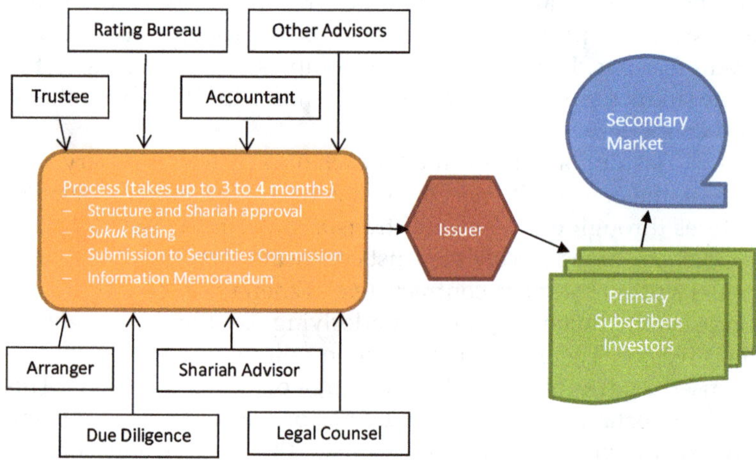

Figure 3.4: Traditional Sukuk Issuance Process and Setup

In the blockchainized version of the sukuk, the papers (trust certificates) issued to the primary subscribers and investors are distributed to them as (crypto) tokens, which represents their portion/ownership of the underlying asset and/or dividend payment (Figure 3.5).

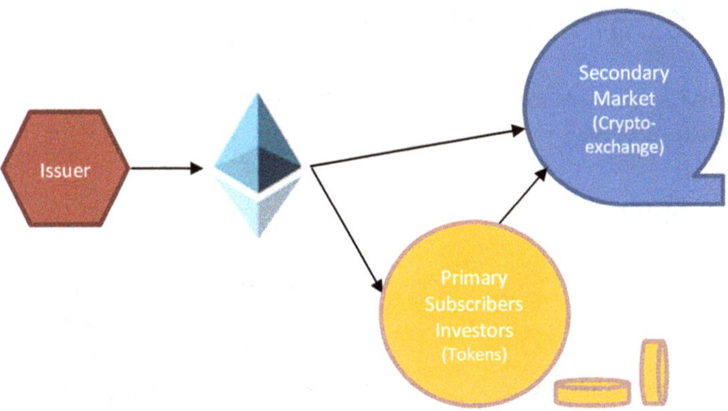

Figure 3.5: BC Sukuk Issuance Process and Setup

The process becomes much leaner and less cumbersome, with the:

- due diligence verification done via blockchainized KYC and identity of issuing shareholders,
- rating of sukuk based on assessment of issuer and asset done via automated market valuation methods,
- Shariah compliance and assessment done by an automated AI-driven review process, and
- legal terms and allocation of dividends/payments done via smart contracts.

Appendix B describes the different modules integrated within the AI-BC Sukuk Platform. For such a platform (or any other platforms really) to work, there has to be trust that the platform is run by credible, trustworthy personnel. The blockchain (on the Ethereum network, in this case) provides that element of confidence as it is the mechanism to enable trust and enforceability within its systems of processes and accountability. In an era that is geared towards decentralization, it is important to note that while decentralization allows us to circumvent a lot of formal time-consuming processes, including tedious regulations, we must not forget that without regulations, self-regulation becomes of utmost important. If the finance industry does not want to be heavily policed then we need to do right even when no one is watching. The blockchain ensures and operationalizes these aspirations through its immutable transparent transaction ledger system.

3.2. Commercial Considerations

In the issuance of any bond or sukuk, there are several commercial considerations:

Size of Issuance

The size of the issuance will be driven by the size and market value of the identified assets to be tied to the sukuk structure and deemed suitable. This is to ensure that there is a right to recourse in cases where there are defaults and non-payments of dividends. In the AI-BC-based sukuk, we wish to occupy a space where most bonds and sukuk issuance do not take place because it is considered too expensive, as the cumulative fees incurred are the same for an issuance of US$500 million or US$1 billion, hence the issuer usually goes for the higher amount. In the proposed blockchainized sukuk structure, the fees are already low and we target issuances which is in the range of US$1 million to US$100 million, which are normally taken out as loans because they are considered too low for an issuance because it would make it expensive. Here, we provide a strong viable alternative to loans and conventional issuances.

The size of the issuance can also be a one-off (standalone) or a series (program), setting the amount of financing the issuer is targeting to raise in the upcoming two to three years or all at once, just like traditional issuances, depending on the issuance strategy. Also, just like traditional issuances, the issuer will have the flexibility to increase the program size at any point, by issuing more tokens (without exceeding market value of the underlying asset), to make adjustments for further capital-raising out of the capital markets upon raising the initial maximum indicated size.

Tenor

According to islamicfinance.com,[10] majority of large-sized Rule 144A/Reg S offerings were issued via dual- or triple-tranches since 2012, combining a 10-year tranche with a five- and/or a 30-year[11]

---

10   https://www.islamicfinance.com/2015/05/*sukuk*-issuance/

11   For corporations and MSMEs, it may be more reasonable to issue five- or 10-year tenors, or dual-tranche of five- & 10-year notes.

offering. They reported that the 10-year note is an existing investor preference for a Rule 144A/Reg S US$ benchmark transaction, as evidenced by both MENA- and CEEMEA-based issues during 2012 to 2013. They also noted that the five-year tranche will allow the issuer to take advantage of strong Middle Eastern and Asian demand, particularly Islamic investors, and accordingly achieve the most aggressive pricing. The proposed platform can also offer drop-down options for commonly-used sukuk contracts according to the asset pledged against and the typical tenor for different contracts used.

Coupon Format

Although the majority of the international US$ issuances (both from the GCC and the broader emerging markets) have initially comprised of fixed rate notes, it is recommended that floating rate notes are used to cater to market uncertainties. However, it is up to the discretion of the issuer with respect to the structure and objective of the capital-raising and use case.

Currency

The issuance platform will be built on the Ethereum protocol so the tokens can be issued (ERC-20). However, these can be pegged to a preferred currency (domestic or international) as the tokens can be opted to be used only as a technological proxy to value or means of exchange for virtually any sovereign fiat currency.

3.2.1. Decentralized Credit Rating

The current credit ratings are usually carried out by credit bureaus. The calculation of the credit score varies between the models used by different agencies and bureaus, but the general scoring system by FICO (US-based) is the standard for other regions too. These factors that are included are typically credit or payment history, income or revenue and debt accumulated. Under this system, businesses (banks, entrepreneurs, etc.) and credit bureaus have to transfer information and personal data between one another, regularly sent back and forth, opening them up to security risks each time and leaving sensitive data potentially vulnerable to cyberattacks and unscrupulous hacks. Also, credit histories are not portable across countries, forcing individuals to re-establish their credit track records whenever they relocate. Borrowers in markets with less developed financial and regulatory infrastructure struggle to access credit as lenders have limited identity and scoring data to base credit decisions. Lastly, the current credit system underserves the ones who need it most. Credit systems rely on historical debt repayment information and therefore cannot easily accommodate users who are new to credit. This is especially prevalent among minorities, the underbanked, and the youth, and in the case of issuing bonds and sukuk, entities with little or no credit histories.

A decentralized credit rating platform could potentially upgrade this archaic system to a more efficient and robust global credit infrastructure that reduces fees, increases accessibility to credit, and makes credit scoring fairer. With KYC and identity on the blockchain, fraud is far less rampant since every credit check no longer requires the exposure of sensitive personal data because the desired information can reach the intended party with dramatically less risk of vulnerability through encryption of the underlying data. Also, with an AI-enhanced and blockchainized digital ID system, the current and historical debt obligations that are tied to a user's ID can be monitored (real-time) and tracked to better reflect a given user's creditworthiness. For entities raising bonds and sukuk, this system will be able to report all identities associated with the issuer, be they board of directors or management teams. This level of transparency enables self-regulatory measures necessary for decentralized systems.

3.3. *Sukuk (Debt Capital Market) versus Loan Market*

Since the global financial crisis, liquidity in the bank loan market has decreased and despite several rounds of quantitative easing, global borrowers have shifted their financing from loans to the availability of asset-backed sukuk and asset-based bonds.

In addition, the sukuk and bonds markets have allowed corporations to extend tenors beyond the traditional five-year sweet spot of the syndicated loan market, to 10-years and 30-years, and with much higher amounts. The aggressive pricing levels have been achieved in the sukuk and bonds markets on the back of large investor demand, providing corporations (and governments) with the opportunity to invest and fund their capital expenditure/acquisitions by raising cheap senior capital without having to dilute their equity beyond the tenor.

3.4. Benefits of BC Sukuk/Trust Certificate Issuance

Some of the benefits of the blockchainized sukuk issuance is its simplicity and speed of execution. All documents (trust deed, terms of agreement, and subscription agreement) are negotiated at the time of the establishment of the issuance program, so negotiation at the time of each issuance is minimized, and issued almost immediately. This reduces execution risk drastically, and provides access to "reverse enquiry" and private placement market.

There are also obvious and significant cost efficiencies. The automation of due diligence processes via blockchainized KYC/ID, market valuation of the asset, and integrated AI compliance systems will not only save costs but save time and unnecessary resources. New issuers can be onboarded much quicker too. Once established, the program helps reduce the costs of subsequent drawdowns, especially when multiple tranches per annum are issued, compared to a standalone issue.

Decentralization of these qualified underlying assets enhances the issuer's profile in the international investor community, and the transparent blockchain ledger system improves transaction visibility, which would allow for cross-border investment and enable international reach more easily. With accessibility and proven structural funding flexibility, the ability to raise attractive funding in the international capital markets can be demonstrated.

4. Conclusion

It is beyond any doubt that the global nature of the 2008 crisis has highlighted the increased interdependence of the world's economies. The challenge is to craft a sustainable system that is grounded in prudent and shared risk approach, on top of being effective and dynamic. Practical risk-sharing cannot take place without it being performance-based. Without accountability on both sides of the contracting counterparties, no discerning person would be willing to partake in any venture that would risk their capital or resources.

BC sukuk, much like social impact bonds, can be designed to promote innovation in addressing capital requirements to solve social problems. Innovation is inherently risky, and some projects may fail to achieve performance targets, leading to losses to the investor and the loss of confidence in the project. Digital innovation, like all innovation, is inherently risky, but a Digital Sukuk model which succeeds in raising the required funds and does so by effectively spreading the risk of the project among the investors and shareholders, instead of transferring the entire risk to the borrower like in the loan markets, may bring benefits such as financial stability that is worth the innovation risk. A more compassionate and just economic system based on risk-sharing provides much-wanted solutions for financing through modifications in financial structures by "removing the debt culture from the private sector, introduction of risk-sharing instruments and real asset price signals that determine the rate of return based on the real sector of the economy" (Mohamed, 2016). Corporations, central banks, and governments can have these types of risk-sharing instruments, which could be used to regulate the supply of credit and even foreign currency debt, and the terms at which it is available. Abolition of interest, absence of interest-bearing securities and, having recourse to an underlying valuable asset, will in turn greatly reduce financial instability in any economic system, conventional or Islamic, resulting in a stronger and more sustainable global system.

Lastly, it is important to highlight that the unrestrained "search for yield" or narrow profit-seeking behaviors can induce a risk of mispricing of some assets, including digital assets, as well as the reversion to risky practices that have resulted in repeated financial crises. "The search for yield movement has led to a reduction in premiums in certain market segments, the magnitude of which can lead to a disconnection between performance and fundamentals of assets" (EC, 2017). In an overactive secondary market, "excess demand thus creates a risk of disconnection between the valuation of securities and their structural, credit and liquidity risks". The parochial pursuit for profit may lead such investors to be less cautious and discerning about highly risky and complex products. This has to be curbed by updating regulatory toolkits for new financial instruments and reviewing existing ones.

Appendix A

Common Types of Sukuk	Nature	Features
Ijarah (Lease-based)	Represents ownership of asset, its usufruct or services (the "Underlying Asset")	The sukuk are akin to trust certificates bearing ownership in the leased asset and the rights to the cash flow stream arising from it as well as proceeds from sale of the assets.
Mudarabah (Partnership; entrepreneur-investor [silent partner])	Represents equity ownership of units of equal value in the issuance and are registered in the names of holders on the basis of ownership of shares in the scheme.	Returns due to the holders as owners of capital are distributed according to the percentage of ownership. Losses are borne in totality by the sukuk holders in accordance to percentages of the shares owned, unless the losses are attributed to the negligence and/or wilful misconduct of the mudarib (entrepreneur), who will be responsible for the same.
Murabahah and Istisna' (Cost-plus and Contracted Venture)	Evidences of indebtedness arising from sale of asset.	The claim is on the obligations arising from the applied contract of exchange. In this case, the sukuk does not represent ownership on the physical asset as the ownership of the asset has been transferred to the obligor, though in certain cases, depending on the credit strength of the obligor, assets are provided as collateral or security to the indebtedness.

Common Types of Sukuk	Nature	Features
Musyarakah (Joint Venture)	Represents ownership of units of equal value in the equity and are registered in the names of holders on the basis of ownership of shares in the scheme.	Returns and losses due to the holders as owners of capital are distributed according to the percentage of ownership.
Wakalah (Agent-based)	To fund various asset, goods, or services acquisition, which are then entrusted to an agent to manage on behalf of the owners.	Capital providers have ownership over the various asset, goods or services acquired by the sukuk issuance according to their contributing percentage.

Appendix B

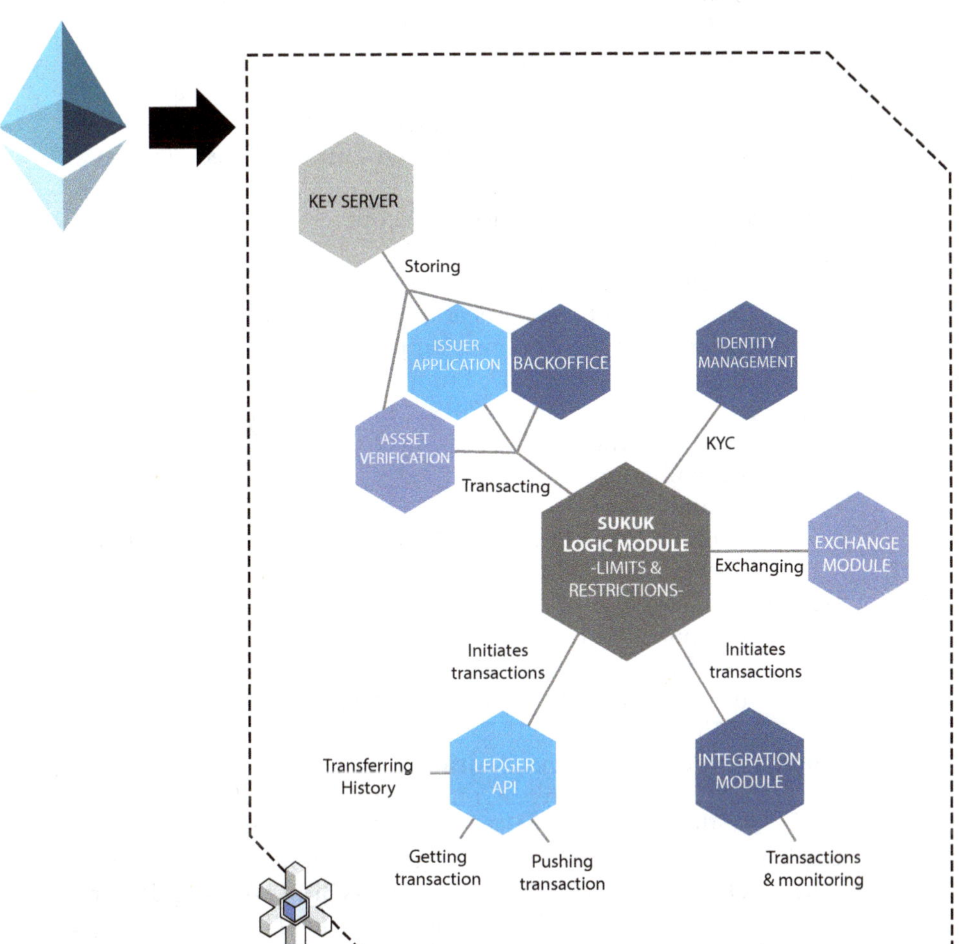

Bibliography

Asian Development Bank, (2013). ADB–OECD Study on Enhancing Financial Accessibility for SMEs: Lessons from Recent Crises. Mandaluyong City, the Philippines.

Asian Development Bank, (2015). Asia SME Finance Monitor, Manila.

Asian Development Bank Institute, (2014). SMEs Financing in Developing Asia: Opportunities and Constraints.

Symposium on Financial Activity of Households and SME Sector and the Regional Economy, Osaka, Japan. 30 October 2014.

Asian Productivity Organization, (2015). Innovation and SME Financing in Selected Asian Economies. Tokyo, Japan.

EMN (2018). Assessing the European Market Potential of Business Microcredit and the Associated Funding Needs of non-bank MFIs. February 2018.

EMN-MFC (2018). Microfinance in Europe: Survey Report 2016–2017. December 2018

European Commission (2017). Analysis of European Corporate Bond Market. Analytical report supporting the main report from the Commission Expert Group on Corporate Bonds November 2017. European Union.

European Investment Fund (2019). European Small Business Finance Outlook, December 2019. Working Paper 2019/61. Luxembourg.

Frost, J., Gambacorta, L., Huang, Y., Shin, H. S., and Zbinden, P. (2019). *BigTech and the Changing Structure of Financial Intermediation*. BIS Working Paper.

Gustafsson-Wright, E., Gardiner, S. and Putcha, V. (2015). The Potential and Limitations of Impact Bonds: Lessons from the First Five Years of Worldwide Experience. Global Economy and Development Program. Brookings, July 2015.

Huerga, J., Puigvert, J. and Rodriguez C., (2012). Enhancements on ECB MFI interest rate statistics. In: OECD — The statistics newsletter. Issue No. 55. March 2012

Kaplan, S.N., and Lerner, J. (2016). Venture Capital Data: Opportunities and Challenges. NBER Working Paper 22500. August 2016. Published in Haltiwanger, J., Hurst, E., Miranda, J., and Schoar, A. (eds.), *Measuring Entrepreneurial Businesses: Current Knowledge and Challenges*. 2017.

Kraemer-Eis, H. and Conforti, A. (2009). *Microfinance in Europe. A Market Overview*. EIF Working Paper 2009/001. http://www.eif.org/news_centre/research/index.htm.

Kraemer-Eis, H., Botsari, A., Brault, J, and Lang, F. (2019). EIF Business Angels Survey 2019 — Market sentiment, public intervention and EIF's value added. EIF Working Paper 2019/60. EIF Research & Market Analysis. 20 November 2019. http://www.eif.org/news_centre/research/index.htm.

Liebman, J. and Sellman, A. (2013). Social Impact Bonds: A Guide for State and Local Governments, Harvard Kennedy School, Social Impact Bond Technical Assistance Lab. June 2013.

Mohamed, H. (2016). "Early Warning Indicators and Macroprudential Policy Tools". In *Macroprudential Regulation and Policy for the Islamic Financial Industry*. Chapter 6, pp. 101–119. Springer International Publishing Switzerland. http://link.springer.com/chapter/10.1007/978-3-319-30445-8_6.

OECD (2013), "SME and Entrepreneurship Financing: The Role of Credit Guarantee Schemes and Mutual Guarantee Societies in supporting finance for small and medium-sized enterprises", OECD Working Party on SMEs and Entrepreneurship, CFE/SME(2012)1/FINAL.

OECD, (2017). Financing SMEs and Entrepreneurs 2017: An OECD Scoreboard.

OECD (2018), Financing SMEs and Entrepreneurs 2018: An OECD Scoreboard, OECD Publishing, Paris.

Shonozaki, S. (2017). Traditional & Alternative Business Models for SME Financing in Asia. ESCAP Workshop on SME Access to Finance and the Role of Development Banks in Asia and the Pacific and Latin America Session 3, 27 September 2017, Bangkok, Thailand.

Shonozaki, S. (2015). Financing SMEs in Asia and the Pacific: Trends and Challenges. Workshop on International Trade Finance, Logistics and Business Development Session 7 (1), 28 November 2015, Yangon, Myanmar.

UNESCAP (2017). Small and Medium Enterprises Financing. 4th High-Level Dialogue on Financing for Development in Asia and the Pacific, April 2017.

SMART ISLAMIC ASSET AND WEALTH MANAGEMENT

Artificial Intelligence (AI) is a highly-evolved area of computer science that strives to create intelligent machines that can replicate certain human behavior without its irrationalities for better predictability and consistency. Advanced AI that utilizes machine learning makes it possible for machines to learn from previous data (experience), adjust to new inputs (instructions), and perform tasks through updated algorithms. Through sophisticated algorithms, modern AI systems can be trained to accomplish specific tasks by processing large amounts of data, and obtaining insights and recognizable patterns in the data to act upon. As such, AI has become a hot topic, with much interest on its advantages to the highly regulated financial services industry.

Similarly, blockchain technology also has the potential to both enrich and improve financial processes and asset management systems, and progressive corporations have invested and devoted resources to utilize and incorporate blockchain into their businesses. The use of distributed ledgers or blockchains has been explored in areas such as compliance and securities settlement, and these technologies could also be used to improve efficiencies in asset management.

In this chapter, we provide a short discussion of AI and blockchain applications in asset management, understand the benefits and the shift in processes, as well as the challenges that need to be overcome for practical applications for AI and blockchain and how to approach such innovations.

Keywords: *Clearing and Settlement, Portfolio Management, Robo-advisory*

JEL Codes: E58, E61, G20

Contents

1. Explosive Artificial Intelligence (AI) Growth Around the World

In the last 60 years, the AI field has experienced curious interest, but in the last five years, it has experienced an explosive growth where governments around the world are competing to create superior AI facilities and research with a view to AI being a lever for greater economic power and influence. According to the Wuzhen Institute Report (2017), 5,154 AI start-ups have been established globally during the past five years, representing a 175% increase relative to the previous 12 years. There are two explanations for this impressive growth. First, exponential advances in computing power have led to declining processing and data storage costs and secondly, the immense data availability has increased, creating more possibilities in the AI field.

Historically, the US has dominated the AI industry, with 3,033 AI start-ups between 2000 and 2016, accounting for 37.41% of the worldwide total (Buchanan, 2019). Between 2012 and 2016, the US invested $18.2 billion into AI compared with $2.6 billion in China and $850 million in the UK.[1] However, the proportion has been decreasing and in 2016, dropped to under 30% for the first time. During the same period, the US received $20.7 billion in funding, accounting for 71.78% of the world's total funding (Wuzhen Institute Report, 2017). In 2017, China surpassed the US for the first time in terms of AI start-up funding (CB Insights, 2018). In 2012, China accounted for 48% of global AI start-up funding and in 2017, the total global AI funding was $15.2 billion. AI equity deals increased 141% relative to the previous year and since 2016, more than 1,100 new AI companies have raised their first round of equity financing. However, the US global AI equity deal share has fallen significantly, from 77% to 50% during the last five years (CB Insights, 2018). China leads the Asian market in terms of AI growth. During the past five years, China accounted for 68.67% of Asian AI start-ups, dominating with 60.22% of corresponding the total Asian AI funding.

With the help of AI, blockchain not only benefits wealth managers but also works on making returns for their clients. In return, AI gets more information and that helps the system's evolutionary process. Furthermore, the more sophisticated the AI, the more it becomes efficient. The innovation of technology and the susceptibility to work in harmony with AI will also improve machine-to-machine interactions. These machines were made to facilitate human actions thus, clustering computer systems together will make processes quicker and simplify complex processes. In fact, the Japanese Government Pension Investment Fund (the world's biggest manager of retirement savings) is considering AI to ultimately replace human fund managers.

---

1   "Britain Urged to Take Ethical Advantage in Artificial Intelligence," John Thornhill, *Financial Times*. 16 April 2018. Available at: https://www.ft.com/content/b21d1fb8-3f3e-11e8-b9f9-de94fa33a81e.

The integration of blockchain and AI into a decentralized intelligence system has profound possibilities to employ data in innovative ways. An effective amalgamation of both technologies will enable faster and seamless data management, validation of transactions, and detection of illegal documents, among others. For the asset and wealth management industry, blockchain will simplify transaction-tracking and reduce costs, as well as produce novel asset structures that can possibly maximise returns to the investor. AI has the ability to update and optimize investment strategies by diligently digesting new market data and consequently using them as inputs to project returns and risks for much attuned advisory and customer-centric service.

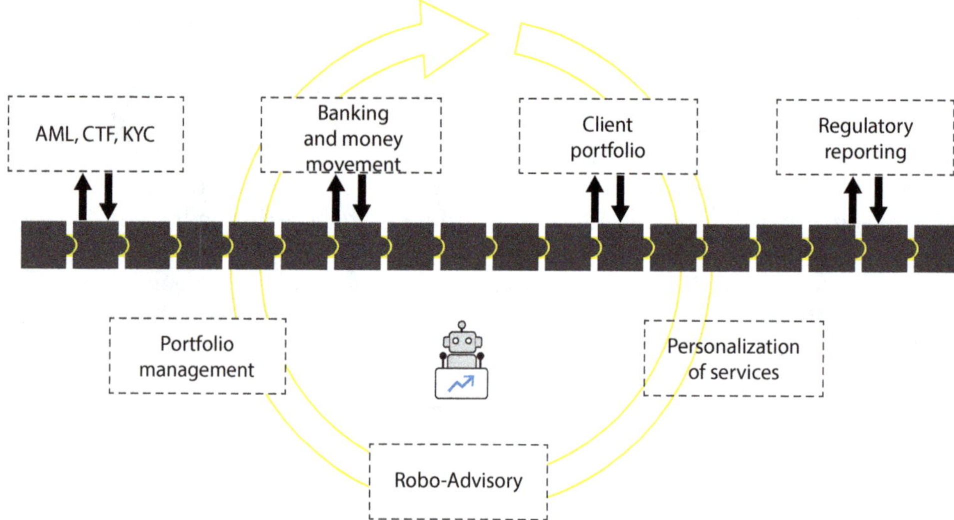

Figure 4.1: Integration of AI and Blockchain in Asset and Wealth Management

2. AI Applications in Asset Management

The term artificial intelligence, or AI, was coined in 1955 by the American computer scientist John McCarthy, based on the idea that "every aspect of learning or any other feature of intelligence can in principle be so precisely described that a machine can be made to simulate it" (McCarthy *et al.*, 1955). Other terms — like machine learning (ML), smart automation, cognitive computing, and self-service analytics — are all closely related to AI. Within the financial services industry, AI applications include algorithmic trading, portfolio composition and optimisation, model validation, back testing, robo-advising, virtual customer assistants, market impact analysis, regulatory compliance, and stress testing.

Much of AI in the 1950s and 1960s did not focus on finance applications. In the 1960s, a substantial body of work on Bayesian statistics was being developed that would later be used in ML (Buchanan, 2019). Neural networks (which would become a cornerstone of deep learning) were developed in the 1960s and grew rapidly. However, due to a lack of sufficiently available electronic data and computing power, it did not progress much further (FSB, 2017). During the 1980s, however, AI made a revival when Japan, the UK, and the US competed heavily in AI funding. Japan invested $400 million through the Japanese Fifth Generation Computer Project (Kaplan, 2016). The UK invested £350 million in the Alvey Program and the U.S. Defence Advanced Research Projects Agency (DARPA) spent over US$1 billion on its Strategic Computing Initiative. In 1982, AI made inroads into the financial services industry when James Simons founded quantitative investment firm Renaissance Technologies. Chase Lincoln First Bank and Arthur D. Little Inc. developed AI systems to carry out investment planning, debt planning, retirement planning, education planning, life-insurance planning, budget recommendations, and income tax planning. Institutional investors also used program trading to capitalise on pricing disparities in the market.

The late 1980s witnessed the rise of IBM and Apple desktop computers, but specialised expert systems became more expensive to maintain. While probabilistic reasoning models dominated the 1960s and 1970s, Bayesian networks gained more acceptance by combining classical AI and neural nets which allowed for learning from experience (Buchanan, 2019). In the 2000s and 2010s, the development of machine learning, deep learning technology, bots and intelligent agents on a powerful cloud computing platform has ushered in a new era of computing. Although there are initial fears of AI taking over human activities, more awareness will shift these perceptions that AI harnesses humanity's collective knowledge and experiences to make better decisions and enrich communications across institutional or consumer omni-channels. For example, large firms like BlackRock, Deutsche Bank, UBS, and Wells Fargo are already using AI engines to analyse consumer digital footprints[2] via their online behaviors, to understand and subsequently predict the products and services most likely to be embraced and used.

2.1. *Personalisation of Services*

With increasingly high levels of client expectations, the need for quick, secure, and highly personalized solutions is vital (PwC, 2018). High-net-worth individuals (HNWIs) and wealth management clients have become accustomed to highly personalized services by their wealth managers, who do so through a support network of connected channels and integrated systems. Contextual insights from massive data analytics can be distributed to wealth managers to help them schedule their daily activities — engage clients in a timely manner and identify opportunities for them whilst all the time remaining compliant to regulations. Peers (2018) believes this enables them to keep up with the "increasing speed, complexity and scale of the financial services industry". As such, they are still able to make every interaction personal and relevant, while "build[ing] long-term rapport and trust by confidently helping clients solve their most important financial challenges".

Some possible situations where Peers suggest that AI can help achieve these are:

- Attaining a holistic evaluation of the client's portfolio and using automated recommendations to advance engagement for further improvements. What can make this possible is through leveraging advanced machine learning algorithms that utilizes client's actions and behaviors from customer relationship management (CRM) systems to better understand unspoken client sentiment whilst generating targeted engagements and relevant conversations across all the channels with full orchestration from these customer insights.
- Retrieving instantaneous client relationships status, preferences, and needs through tools such as sentiments,

---

2   FinTech — How Exponential Technological Progress will affect Asset & Wealth Management. https://finlantern.com/fundforum/wp-content/uploads/2017/12/FACTSET_FinTech-how-exponential-technological-progress-will-affect-Wealth-Mana....pdf.

> market analyses, and sector alerts will enable real-time solutions, and they can produce insights that help to assess timely opportunities for a wealth manager to give their clients a call or visit. Customized engagements delight clients with pertinent information that are relevant to them.

- AI-driven services for wealth management have the capacity to craft new business models, provide incredible insights, and spin off value-added products and services through massive data that can inform decisions better and quickly. This generates quality advice at a much lower cost through an optimal combination of intelligence from data analytics from technology and human assessment.

Certain facets of client engagement within financial services that can increase client relations and meaningful exchange without escalating fees are:

- Chatbots are programmed to answer clients' frequently asked questions (FAQs), or direct them to appropriate channels like appointment bookings, or lead clients to the best resources for further assistance — be it to check portfolio status, find updates on order status or submissions, new financial reports, and market events.
- Secure authentication bots that handle automated verification through reliable channels to conclude financial transactions.
- Transactional bots that answer simple queries and flag events to trigger alerts, such as when a transaction exceeds trigger limits, a deduction is due or when trading authorizations close.

2.2. Portfolio Management

Asset and wealth management firms are studying and testing prospective AI solutions to better their investment decisions through insights gleaned from mammon of historical data.[3] Digital asset management (like an investment portfolio) are ripe for automation through AI, where copious amounts of data

---

3   https://emerj.com/ai-sector-overviews/machine-learning-in-investment-management-and-asset-management/

about the assets (like the historical performance of a particular fund and market movements) are already being monitored. "More and more investors are turning to advisory services augmented with robo-advisors for essential investment needs because of their convenience, ease of use, affordability and transparency. They can provide a range of advisory services, from personalized, automated, algorithm-based portfolio management to sophisticated tax strategies and risk management, all at a markedly lower cost than the traditional advisory model" (Peers, 2018). Applying cognitive technologies and AI to various advisory utilities across the industry value chain[4] by analyzing historical data, market patterns, and market dependencies. While there have been debates like fundamental versus macro, and passive versus active investing in the past, it may be about AI enhancing (or perhaps, replacing) modern portfolio theory with drastically better projections.

2.3. *Chatbots and Robo-Advisory*

Robo-advisors and chatbots are "emerging across the financial services sector, helping consumers choose investments, banking products and insurance policies" (Buchanan, 2018). A "bot" is a software application created to automate certain tasks using AI technology (Future Today Institute, 2017). A robo-advisor is an algorithm based digital platform that offers automated financial advice or investment management services. Robo-advisors have the potential to lower costs and increase the quality and transparency of financial advice for consumers. Rohner and Uhl (2017) see robo-advisory services in three ways: "(1) access to and rebalancing of passive and rule-based investment strategies, (2) cost-efficient implementation of a diversified asset allocation", and (3) overcoming behavioral biases. They find that compared to traditional investment advice, robo-advisors can save costs of up to 4.4% per year.

Banks are also engaging chatbots to improve their self-service interfaces. The Bank of America has launched its AI chatbot *Erica* and it is available through voice or message chat on the bank's mobile app. *Erica*'s AI engine also leverages analytics

---

4   "Artificial intelligence: The Next Frontier for Investment Management Firms," Deloitte, 2019.

to assist in managing personal finance. JP Morgan has invested in *COiN*, an AI technology that reviews documents and extracts data in far less time than a human. *COiN* can review approximately 12,000 documents in a matter of seconds, whereas a human would spend more than 360,000 hours of work on the same number of documents (Brummer and Yadav, 2019).

Chatbots and conversational interfaces are a rapidly expanding area of venture investment and customer service budget. Such chatbots have had to be built with robust natural language processing engines as well as reams of finance-specific customer interactions. Natural language processing is making it increasingly difficult for bank customers to tell whether they are talking to an AI interface or a human. Japan's three megabanks are using AI and robotics to streamline customer questions.[5] For example, the Mizuho Group has a robot that helps answer asset management questions and compiles documents.

2.4. *Financial Prediction*

Advances in technology have been the vanguard of financial services, especially if these solutions can provide strong and viable economic advantages to them. In portfolio management, AI and machine learning tools are being used to recognize new signals on price movements and to generate effective use of vast available data to improve market assessment and decision acumen than with current models. "The key task is to identify signals from data on which predictions relating to price level or volatility can be made, over various time horizons, to generate higher and uncorrelated returns" (FSB, 2017). Portfolio construction with probabilistic (risk) calculations, stochastic modelling, and scenario testing are some of the mathematical models (including option related calculations) that are computationally intensive. Technology again will provide that leap forward with "cloud computing streamlining existing infrastructure and at the same time enabling many new, previously unimaginable or unimplementable, applications. In addition to the currently available near-unlimited, on-demand cloud computing, recent progress in quantum computers could soon provide the

---

5   "Megabanks in Japan Embrace Artificial Intelligence," *Robot Technology*. 30 October 2017. Available at: https://business.inquirer. net/239571/megabanks-japan-embrace-artificial-intelligence-robot-technology.

next disruptive chapter in humanity's unbounded appetite for computational processing" (Buchanan, 2019).

Black swans or extreme events in financial markets have been impossible to predict or time, but historically, most of the profits have been made or lost during these extreme events.[6] It is now possible to not depend on predictive analytics based on existing models and past events. Newer technologies, for example, those that use forward-looking directional market risk forecasting instead of being limited to historical data, are beginning to be adopted by asset managers and other financial institutions globally. Concepts like the efficient market hypothesis (EMH) and portfolio diversification may still be applicable, but these concepts will give birth to new ones, as the financial data gets increasingly processed by the improved algorithm types in the enhanced AI systems for better projections and predictions.

2.5. Algorithm Trading

Algorithmic trading (AT) has become a dominant force in global financial markets. Also called "Automated Trading Systems", AT's origins date back to the 1970s. Kirilenko and Lo (2013) provide a brief survey of the evolution of the AT field. Chakravorty (2016) defines AT as: "Algorithmic trading is about implementing trading rules into a program and using the program to trade, [and AI trading] can be defined as an approach to machine learning that learns the structure of the data, and then tries to predict what will happen". Algorithmic trading now involves the use of complex AI systems to make extremely fast trading decisions. Computers generate 50% to 70% of equity market trades, 60% of futures trades, and 50% of Treasuries (Brummer and Yadav, 2019). Aldridge and Krawciw (2017) estimate the share of market AT to be between 10% to 40%. The benefits of AT include: (1) the ability of trades to be executed at the best possible prices, (2) increased accuracy and a reduced likelihood of mistakes, (3) the ability to automatically and simultaneously check multiple market conditions, and (4) human errors caused by psychological or emotional conditions are likely to be reduced.

---

6   http://mebfaber.com/2011/08/12/where-the-black-swans-hide-andthe-ten-best-days-myth.

Algorithmic trading's target clientele is hedge funds, proprietary trading houses, bank proprietary trading desks, corporates, and the next generation market makers. AT includes making certain trading decisions, submitting orders, and managing those orders after submission. Martinez and Roşu (2013) argue that algorithmic speed should have a positive effect on the informativeness of prices. Hendershott *et al.* (2013) find that AT improves liquidity and enhances the informational content of quotes. On the other hand, AT may also impose higher adverse selection costs on slower trades.

Algorithmic systems often make thousands or millions of trades per day. The term given to this is high-frequency trading (HFT). HFT is the most recognisable form of AT, and uses high-speed communications and algorithms in financial market transactions. HFT has both its supporters and detractors. Since 2013, two-thirds of the top 30 cited papers on HFTs show positive market effects from HFTs (Das, 2017). There are supporting arguments that HFT helps with price discovery and efficiency by trading in the direction of permanent price changes and in the opposite direction of transitory pricing errors (Broggard *et al.*, 2014). These types of trading improve market liquidity. Hendershott and Riordan (2013) find that HFT can provide market stability and Menkveld (2016) finds that HFT reduces trading costs. Hasbrouck and Saar (2013) provide evidence that HFT improves market quality and reduces bid-ask spreads. In fact, HFT is changing the traditional field of market microstructure and will continue to be reinvented through new AI and deep learning (DL) techniques.

Most hedge funds and financial institutions do not openly disclose their AI approaches to trading (for proprietary reasons), but it is believed that machine learning (ML) and DL play an important role in calibrating real-time trading decisions. It also involves neural networks, fuzzy logic, and pattern recognition.

3. Blockchain Applications in Asset Management

Many blockchain experts believe that "distributed ledgers are highly flexible; once implemented, they can be used to remove friction from the client onboarding process, streamline management of model portfolios, speed the clearing and settlement of trades, and ease compliance burdens associated with anti-money laundering (AML) and KYC" (EY, 2017). Blockchain applications bring efficiencies in eliminating redundant functions, reducing operational expenses, and increasing client ease-of-use experience. It may be used to reconcile information across current legacy systems, and subsequently enable new infrastructure for potentially new markets and novel products.

Blockchain experts are sure that it can be used to develop client profiles more efficiently and reliably. "Storing client profile data on a blockchain allows for data points — profile data, behavioral preferences, wealth net worth, personal account information, social media profiles — to be shared as needed, with each individual block of data being stored securely, but permissioned for access by the individual (read, write, edit) as needed" (EY, 2017).

3.1. *Client Onboarding Process*

In the current system, prospective patrons are required to show identification and residency documents, prove marital status, sources of wealth, pronounce business interests and official occupation (and even declare political ties in order to set up certain accounts) for financial transactions. Going through this process, financial institutions may take days or weeks to verify information and conduct due diligence with reliable accuracy. In such cases, the blockchain presents a strong use case for client onboarding in wealth management.

Utilizing the blockchain, it would enable profiles of customers to be stored on a blockchain or distributed ledger, where assigned groups can be granted access to selected information or entire profile based on issuing cryptographic access keys. The system intrinsically embeds an audit trail for tracking any change along the chain of information blocks (hence, the blockchain). As a result, processes requiring information-verification and fact-checking, such as those employed in AML or KYC, can be very much streamlined. In addition, blockchain technologies can be integrated into onboarding and "automated clearinghouse (ACH) and automated customer account transfer (ACAT) systems that traditionally takes multiple days and involve manual processes using multiple systems and databases" (EY, 2017). The blockchain can also enhance transfers of assets between financial institutions with verified derivation of tracked changes.

3.2. Management of Model Portfolios

The propagation of open architecture investment offerings and the availability of third-party investment vehicles have presented significant hurdles for wealth managers. "Distributed ledger technology would allow portfolio managers to instantly communicate portfolio changes to all clients 'subscribed' to the model, as well as enable real-time views of individual account performance, drift outside of tolerances and cash flows" (EY, 2017). Also, smart contracts built on the blockchain would execute trade terms and conditions, including management of fees to be paid by the sponsors, if programmed to take proprietary fees every time the model is used.

Currently, asset managers use legacy platforms operating on archaic data architectures, which inhibits ease of distribution, interfacing, and updating newer third-party models. In some cases, corporations may end up supporting redundant model management systems, and remain stuck in time-consuming processes and frustrating users. However, with the blockchain, investment EY notes that managers can create and maintain a model which "could be transmitted through a blockchain to various subscribed brokers where individual accounts can be invested according to the model". Other account-level constraints or restriction customizations can be implemented conveniently.

3.3. Trade Clearing and Settlement

The last few decades have seen the asset management industry grow remarkably in both size and complexity. The range of fund structures and coverage of underlying asset classes has expanded to meet the investor's demands for a distinct set of products. To service this global set of products, "the industry makes significant use of service companies that act as intermediaries between them and the clearing and settlement infrastructure, currently a complex network of brokers, custodian banks, stock transfer agents, regulators, and depositories" (BIS, 1997). A single transfer can require multiple liaising transactions, and usually takes three days to settle, of which about 20% generate errors, which has to be corrected manually (Mohamed and Ali, 2019).

With a blockchain, two trading parties can read and write to a shared, trusted, and error-free platform.[7] "The transaction could be written in legal language as well as in computer code, so that the data exchange itself is the settlement" (BCG, 2016), which can be made visible to regulators where necessary. "The brokers (as agents of the buyer and seller) could trade on a larger blockchain to remove custodians as intermediaries, thereby reducing total transaction costs. Institutions issuing securities, such as corporations, cities and municipalities, could issue them directly onto the blockchain", thereby removing the need for share registry agents.

The "ability of blockchain distributed ledgers to replace intermediary centralized systems of record has attracted real interest in investment firms given the potential to cut cost, reduce delays, provide more timely and accurate data and enhance reporting accuracy".[8] The blockchain can have a deep bearing on the settlement of securities transactions and offer massive reduction in transactional costs leading to reduced charges for investors.

3.4. *Regulatory Compliance to Shariah Observance*

Blockchainized platforms can be used to address the administration and coordination of identity, privacy, and security across millions of devices by making them autonomous. These decentralized platforms give integrated systems an identity, make and receive payments, enter into complex agreements, and transact without an intermediary (Mohamed and Ali, 2019).

One way to help ease compliance burdens is to build and deploy identity management solutions using blockchain. A blockchain consists of a node and any transaction comprises a chain of blocks that have been accepted by the participating node through a consensus mechanism. One of the most important elements in the blockchain is the identity of a node, and once the node has been identified flawlessly, the entire transaction becomes trustworthy.

---

7   https://www.bcg.com/en-sea/publications/2016/blockchain-thinking-outside-the-blocks.aspx.

8   https://sokodirectory.com/2018/01/blockchain-and-its-impact-to-the-investment-industry/.

An identity management system based on verification cryptography can be built using AML, CTF, and KYC[9] requirements according to the country-specific regulations. The same is stored virtually and a part of this information is released to the counterparty at the time of transaction to suffice the counterparty's requirement. The entire solution is built on the distributed ledger where an enterprise is a node and the platforms developed by asset management companies provide a cryptographic code for each node based on AML, CTF, and KYC requirements.

Islamic asset and wealth investment funds are similar to conventional funds in terms of the common objectives that they share, such as pooled investment, capital preservation, and returns optimization. The distinguishing feature between the two types of funds is that Islamic funds must always comply with Shariah rules and laws in terms of their operations, activities, and investments. Islamic fund management is therefore about the professional management of investors' money in Shariah-compliant securities and assets, in line with Shariah principles to achieve set financial goals. Elements such as the contractual relationship between fund managers and investors, Shariah screening of investments, the role of Shariah boards, Shariah governance mechanisms involving Shariah reviews and audits, purification of impure income, and alms-giving (zakat) calculation are important in the adherence of Islamic funds' activities to Shariah requirements.

Automated reporting, automated audits, and process streamlining are other benefits offered by AI-driven features on blockchainized platforms to address regulatory compliance, where technology is bridging the gap between regulators and the asset management industry.

4. Openness to Adoption and Regulations

While many technologists are able to grasp the decentralized ledger concept and the complex Bayesian algorithms, many business leaders are still fuzzy on how it can benefit their business in a profound way, or where it can disrupt current models for competitive advantage. As blockchain applications may be

---

9   AML refers to anti-money laundering, CTF is counter-terrorism financing, and KYC is know-your-client.

complicated to understand, determining a good business strategy for using it becomes even more difficult.

Establishing an effective framework to identify real business value is critical especially when there are many potential blockchain opportunities. "Firms should focus on those use cases that have the greatest opportunity with minimal risk, and use a framework to properly allocate time and resources" (EY, 2017). In the short-term, there are use cases that can be developed quickly to drive results to win support for long-term solutions that may be slow to show returns. In addition to creating blockchain-specific business solutions, blockchain should be seen as an enabling technology to improve business operations in the areas of data management through transparency and revenue-generating opportunities captured through ease of use.

AI and ML are moving faster than policymakers can understand, to the extent that it is almost outstripping the current legal and regulatory framework. Technology is opaque and fast-moving and regulators find it hard to keep pace, for both the cumulative impact and risks of contagion. Athey and Imbens (2017) and Mullainathan and Spiess (2017) argue that ML methods hold great promise for improving the credibility of policy evaluation. The technology underpinning Fintech is also fuelling a spinoff field known as RegTech, which aims to make compliance and regulatory activities easier, faster, and more efficient. RegTech utilises Big Data and ML. RegTech is an emerging field to reduce costs and increase effectiveness. Alarie, Niblett and Yoon (2016) explore how ML technology can improve regulation of human behavior. They argue that ML techniques can provide fast, accurate, and consistent judgements, and streamline operations with reduced error.

Financial regulators are also exploring the use of AI for better monitoring of financial institutions. The UK Financial Conduct Authority (FCA) is examining "the possibility of making its handbook machine-readable and then fully machine-executable. This would mean that machines can interpret and implement the rules directly" (Citi, 2018). "The Division of Economic and Risk Analysis (DERA) at the SEC is exploring ML to extract actionable insights from massive datasets, helping examiners find cases of potential fraud or misconduct" (Baugess, 2017). "As institutions find algorithms that create uncorrelated profits or returns, there are concerns that these will be manipulated on a suitably wide scale that correlations actually increase, which will only become clear as such advanced technologies are actually adopted". More generally, "greater interconnectedness in the financial system may help to share risks and act as a safety net to potential shocks or contagion effects" (FSB, 2017).

International regulators utilise "AI-supported analytical methods to recognise vulnerability patterns, scan lengthy reports or analyse incoming data" (Buchanan and Cao, 2018). In 2017, the Bank of England (BoE) joined forces with MindBridge to use an AI auditor to help detect anomalies in transactions and reports. In 2018, Chancellor Angela Merkel announced that the German government would spend €3 billion to boost AI capabilities. The Deutsche Bundesbank is already using AI in its risk management area and uses neural networks (NN) to assess financial market soundness.

The European MIFID II50 (which also came into effect in 2018) requires that "firms applying algorithmic models based on AI and ML should have a robust development plan in place. Firms need to ensure that potential risks are included at every stage of the process" (Wuermaling, 2018). In February 2018, the FCA and Prudential Regulatory Authority released consultation papers on algorithmic trading that lists key areas of supervisory focus in relation to MIFID II.

5. Conclusion

Along with Big Data, AI is viewed in the financial services sector as a technique that has the potential to deliver huge analytical power. Yet, many risks still need to be addressed. Many AI + Blockchain techniques remain untested in financial crisis scenarios. There have been several instances in which the algorithms implemented by financial firms appeared to act in ways quite unforeseen by their developers, leading to errors and flash crashes (notably the pound's flash crash following the Brexit referendum in 2016). More robust technology capable of adapting to human idiosyncrasies is necessary so that users can employ these tools safely, effectively, and effortlessly.

In the asset management industry, advanced AI technology supported by blockchain applications will help us automate existing processes and realize new revenue streams and business models. In the distributions space, we use AI + Blockchain technology to help us predict customer journeys

throughout the life cycle of their engagement with the company —
from onboarding to redemption — and explore ways consumers
can be better served by offering products better suited to their
investment style at certain stages in their customer journey. On
the product management front, AI + Blockchain technology help
our portfolio managers make the smartest possible investment
decisions at a given point in time using sophisticated analytics.
Other emerging technologies and approaches to be adopted in the
financial space — such as virtual reality (VR) and integrating the
Internet of Things (IoT) to create holistic solutions.

Bibliography

Alarie, B., Niblett, A., & Yoon, A.H. (2016). Using Machine Learning
to Predict Outcomes in Tax Law. Canadian Business Law
Journal 58 (3): 231–254.

Aldridge, I. and Krawciw, S. (2017). Real-Time Risk: What Investors
Should Know About FinTech, in High-Frequency Trading,
and Flash Crashes, John Wiley & Sons, Inc., Hoboken, NJ,
USA.

Athey, S., and Imbens, G. W. (2017). The State of Applied
Econometrics: Causality and Policy Evaluation. Journal
of Economic Perspectives, 31(2), pp. 3–32.

Bauguess, S. W (2017) The Role of Big Data, Machine Learning,
and AI in Assessing Risks: A Regulatory Perspective,
Keynote Address: OpRisk North America.

Bank for International Settlements (1997): Real-time Gross
Settlement Systems, Basel, March.

Boston Consulting Group (2016). Thinking Outside the Blocks.
1st December 2016. https://www.bcg.com/en-co/
publications/2016/blockchain-thinking-outside-the-blocks

Brogaard, J., Hendershott, T. and Riordan, R. (2014). High-
frequency trading and price discovery. The Review of
Financial Studies, 27(8), pp. 2,267–2,306.

Brummer, C., and Yadav, Y. (2019). The Fintech Trilemma.
Georgetown Law Journal, 107, pp. 235–307.

Buchanan, B and C. Cao (2018) Quo Vadis? Fintech in China
Versus the West. Working Paper. Available at: https://
swiftinstitute.org/wp-content/uploads/2018/10/SIWP-
2017-002-_Fntech_China_West_BuchCao_FINAL.pdf.

Buchanan, B. (2019). Artificial Intelligence in Finance. Seattle University with funding from The Alan Turing Institute. https://doi.org/10.5281/zenodo.2612537.

CB Insights (2018). Top AI Trends to Watch in 2018. https://www.bastagroup.nl/wp-content/uploads/2019/01/CB-Insights_State-of-Artificial-Intelligence-2018.pdf

Chakravorty, G. (2016) What is the Difference between AI and Algo Trading? Available: https://www.quora.com/What-is-the-difference-between-AI-trading-and-algo-trading.

Citi (2018) Bank of the Future: the ABCs of Digital Disruption in Finance. CitiReport March 2018.

Culkin, R. and S. Das (2017) Machine Learning in Finance: The Case of Deep Learning in Option Pricing. Working Paper.

Dawson, R. (2014) "The New Layer of the Economy Enabled by M2M Payments in the Internet of Things." *Trends in the Living Networks*, September 16, 2014.

Das, S. R. (2017) The Future of FinTech. Available at: https://srdas.github.io/Papers/fintech.pdf.

Ernst and Young (2017). *Blockchain Innovation in Wealth and Asset Management: Benefits and Key Challenges to Adopting This Technology.*

Financial Stability Board (2017). Artificial Intelligence and Machine Learning in Financial Services: Market Developments and Financial Stability Implications. 1 November 2017.

Future Today Institute (2017) Tech Trends Annual Report. Available at: https://futuretodayinstitute.com/2017-tech-trends/.

Golmohammadi, K., and Zaiane, O. R. (2012). Data Mining Applications for Fraud Detection in Securities Market. In Intelligence and Security Informatics Conference (EISIC), 2012 European (pp. 107–114). IEEE.

Hasbrouck, J., and G. Saar. (2013). Low Latency Trading. *Journal of Financial Markets*, 16: 646–679.

Heaton, J. B., Polson, N. G., and Witte, J. H. (2017). Deep Learning for Finance: Deep Portfolios. *Applied Stochastic Models in Business and Industry*, 33(1), pp. 3–12.

Hendershott, Terrence, Charles M. Jones and Albert J. Menkveld, 2011, Does Algorithmic Trading Improve Liquidity?, Journal of Finance, 66, 1–33.

Hendershott, T., and Riordan, R. (2013). Algorithmic Trading and the Market for Liquidity. *Journal of Financial and Quantitative Analysis*, 48(4), pp. 1,001–1,024.

Kaplan, J. (2016). *Artificial Intelligence: What Everyone Needs to Know*. Oxford University Press.

Kirilenko, A. A., and Lo, A. W. (2013). Moore's Law versus Murphy's Law: Algorithmic Trading and its Discontents. *Journal of Economic Perspectives*, 27(2), pp. 51–72.

Martinez, V. H., and Rosu, I. (2013). High Frequency Traders, News and Volatility. In AFA 2013 San Diego Meetings Paper.

McCarthy, J., Minsky, M., Rochester, N. and Shannon, C. (1955). *A Proposal for the Dartmouth Summer Research Project on Artificial Intelligence.*

Menkveld, Albert J. (2013). High Frequency Trading and the New Market Makers. *Journal of Financial Markets* 16, No. 4: 712–740.

Menkveld, Albert J. (2016) The Economics of High-Frequency Trading: Taking Stock. *Annual Review of Financial Economics*, 8: 1–24.

Mohamed, Hazik and Ali, Hassnian (2019). *Blockchain, Fintech and Islamic Finance — Building the Future of the New Islamic Digital Economy*. De I G Press, Boston/Berlin.

Mullainathan S, Spiess J. 2017. Machine Learning: An Applied Econometric Approach. J. Econ. Perspect. 31: 87–106.

Omohundro, S. (2014). Cryptocurrencies, Smart Contracts, and Artificial Intelligence. Submitted to AI Matters (Association for Computing Machinery), October 22, 2014.

Peers, R. (2018). Digital Super Powers — The Role of Artificial Intelligence in Wealth Management. In Chishti, S. and Puschmann, T. (Editors). *The WEALTHTECH Book: The Fintech Handbook for Investors, Entrepreneurs and Finance Visionaries*. Hoboken: Wiley, 2018.

Rohner, P. and Uhl, M. (2017). Robo-Advisors vs. Traditional Investment Advisors — An Unequal Game. *Journal of Wealth Management*, 21(1), pp. 44–50.

Schneider, J., Blostein, A., Lee, B., Kent, S., Groer, I. and Beardsley, E. (2016). *Profiles in Innovation — BlockChain: Putting theory into Practice*. Goldman Sachs.

Wuermaling, J. (2018) Artificial Intelligence in Finance: Six Warnings from a Central Banker. Intervention at the 2nd Annual Fintech Conference. Brussels.

Wuzhen Institute. (2017). Global AI Development Report. August 2017, http://sike.news.cn/hot/pdf/25.pdf; www.iwuzhen.org.

DIGITALIZED TAKĀFUL CLAIMS PROCESSING

The takāful and insurance industry is an evolving process of safeguarding the assets of people from loss and uncertainty. It may be described as a social device to reduce or eliminate risk of loss to life and property. Insurance offers financial protection to both individuals and business, in the risks of a loss and as such, plays an essential role in mitigating risks through risk-sharing in uncertain but potentially injurious episodes. The risk landscape is continually evolving, and in order to keep up, the insurance industry needs to trace and provide customized insurance policies that can serve specific indemnity needs of the new economy. The insurers have to possess full understanding of every risk covered in their policies and when disaster hits, compensation and claims will be done in a timely and judicious manner.

Latest developments in FinTech promises more efficiency and reduced costs causing significant shifts in the financial landscape, and the impending disruption in the insurance industry is inevitable. Blockchain today is something like where the Internet was in the 1990s — on the strategic interest of forward-looking companies, but still a while from extensive implementation. Therefore, the question for most insurance companies is not whether they will adopt blockchain, but rather, what to start with and how to test and prove the value proposition.

In this chapter, we provide a strategic discourse on how blockchain can provide additional value to the insurance and takāful industries, understand the change in processes, issues that need to be overcome, and efficiency benefits, projected cost-saving, and risk management.

Keywords: *Digital Disruption, Distributed Ledgers, Smart Contracts.*

Contents

1. Introduction

The takāful and insurance is an evolving process of preserving individuals and businesses from loss and uncertainty. It can be described as a financial product to decrease or eradicate risk of loss and protection, be it life or property. Insurance offers financial protection to both individuals and business, in the risk of loss hence playing a vital function in reducing risks through risk-sharing in the face of uncertain but likely losses or damages. Insurance and takāful companies take on risk dangers of individuals and businesses so that they can survive such events to develop in a sustainable way.

The risk landscape is continually evolving, and in order to keep up, the insurance industry needs to trace and provide customized insurance policies that can serve specific indemnity needs of the new economy. The insurers have to possess full understanding of every risk covered in their policies and when disaster hits, compensation and claims will be done in a sensible and timely manner.

Latest developments in FinTech promises more efficiency and reduced costs causing significant shifts in the financial landscape, and the impending disruption in the insurance industry is inevitable. Blockchain today is something like where the internet was in the 1990s — on the strategic interest of forward-looking companies, but still a while from extensive implementation. For that reason, the question is not whether should one accept the blockchain revolution, but instead, when and what to start with.

In this chapter, we provide a strategic discussion of how blockchain can provide additional value to the insurance and takāful industries, understand the change in processes, issues that need to be overcome, and efficiency benefits, projected cost-saving and risk management.

1.1. *Market Size and Segments of the Takāful (Islamic Insurance) Business*

As a niche section of the insurance sector, the takāful segment is significantly interrelated with disruptions occurring in the insurance sector. The global insurance market had a reasonable growth rate, with global real premium growth rates of 2.9% in the advanced economies and 7.4% in the emerging and developing countries in 2014, an improvement over the 2012 and 2013 rates (IFSB, 2016). Likewise, the growth rate of gross contributions in the takāful sector demonstrated a recovery in 2014 from 2013, when the growth rate of premiums was by far the lowest historically.

In its Islamic Financial Services Industry (IFSI) Stability 2016 report, Islamic Financial Services Board (IFSB) observed that the reinvigorated gross contributions of the takāful sector reached US$22.1 billion in 2014, up from only around US$5 billion in 2006. The biggest share of the takāful sector belonged to the Gulf Cooperation Council (or the GCC) countries, followed by Iran and the East Asia and Pacific region. The other three regions (Africa, South Asia, and the Levant) had a very much lesser share in total. As takāful's share of the insurance sector is only 1%, there is a long way to go for the takāful sector. Indeed, the low penetration rates in certain countries in which the takāful industry operates indicate an available market for the takāful sector. Since many of the target markets like Turkey, Saudi Arabia, Pakistan, Qatar, and Egypt, have a growing middle-class and young populations with solid growth prospects, there is promise for the takāful sector to grow further.

Three jurisdictions account for 84% of the global takāful contributions: (1) Saudi Arabia (37%), (2) Iran (34%) and (3) Malaysia (14%). However, the types of takāful provision are different for different jurisdictions; for example, in Malaysia, nearly two-thirds of the takāful contributions are for family takāful (which features a strong savings/investment component). In Saudi Arabia and Iran, insurance such as medical/healthcare or motor takāful is prevailing. The current low diffusion of takāful services indicate there is ample opportunity for further growth of the insurance/takāful industry, combined with high population growth and a growing middle class.

Also, the IFSI report revealed that the business profiles of takāful operators differ among the countries to a great extent. They found that in Malaysia, family takāful is 68.1% of the total business line, which is the highest number in the sample. The combination of a relatively young population, a high percentage of working population, a vibrant social security system, and saving incentives for retirement, play a part in the high proportion of life insurance in its society, including family takāful. Behind Malaysia is Pakistan and the UAE, which comprise a reasonable share of family takāful — around 30%. This is not so in Saudi Arabia, where health coverage is compulsory and a tradition of long-term saving using insurance/takāful products is non-existent. Other countries with low shares of family takāful are Kuwait (at 8.6%), and Bangladesh and Qatar (both at 0%). From the rising trends of births and the middle class, policies geared towards increasing public awareness on such services as well as those encouraging long-term savings such as unit-linked instruments could grow the family takāful business.

Motor takāful is the second-most important business line in the sample countries of the IFSI report, with an average of 27.7% over the entire sample of countries. Kuwait has the highest share of motor takāful, followed by Sri Lanka, Pakistan, and Qatar.

The third-most important business line for takāful was Fire, Property and Accidents, with the highest levels of domestic markets in Qatar and Bangladesh. Other business lines in the takāful sector, include Workmen's Compensation and Energy Takāful, which has a considerable traction in the UAE and Sri Lanka.

2. Blockchain-based Takāful

Smart contracts deployed through the blockchain will provide customers and takāful (insurance) companies a system to manage claims in a transparent, quick, and indisputable manner (Mohamed, 2019). Takāful policies, along with its terms and conditions and potential claims, can be recorded onto the blockchain and validated by the network, ensuring valid claims are dispensed and rejecting false claims.[1] For example, the blockchain will reject multiple claims for one accident because the network would know that a claim has already been made. Smart contracts would also process claims efficiently, by triggering payments automatically when certain conditions are met and validated. To more effectively detect identity fraud and falsified injury or damage reports, etc., blockchain can be used as a cross-industry, distributed registry with external and customer data to:

- Confirm authenticity, ownership, and origin of goods as well as legitimacy of documents (e.g., medical reports)
- Check for police reports indicating theft, claims history, as well as a person's verified identity, and expose patterns of deception related to a particular person or identity
- Proof of date and time stamps of policy issuance or purchase of a product/asset
- Validate ownership and site changes

Still, to attain full blockchain-specific benefits from these applications above what is achievable with traditional solutions and other current types of cooperation, e.g. via industry associations, broad cooperation between insurers, customers, manufacturers, and other stakeholders is needed. This is an example of an ecosystem growing beyond the traditional industry practice in the Sharing Economy of the digital era. Emerging

---

1   An estimated 5% to 10% of all claims are fraudulent. According to the estimated global size of the takāful industry, this costs takāful operators more than US$2 billion per year.

blockchain applications and four key areas where we see the most potential for evolution and transformation are covered next.

2.1. *Fraud Detection and Risk Mitigation*

The blockchain has the potential to eradicate mistakes and detect deceptive activity because of its ability to be a public ledger across multiple unknown parties. A distributed digital depot can autonomously confirm the legitimacy of customers, policies, and transactions (such as claims) by presenting a comprehensive historical record. As such, insurers would be able to spot fake or counterfeit transactions involving doubtful people and suspect entities.

First-movers insurers are already evaluating the use of blockchain to mitigate scams and risks related to cross-border payments and transactions linking multiple currencies. In forte insurance and reinsurance segments, where insurers are often disconnected from the clients, blockchain may be used to tackle the significant inefficiencies, disparities, and errors caused by bad data quality from the front and back offices. In the US, health insurers and regulators view blockchain as a powerful tool for fighting Medicare deceit. Validation and verification form the nucleus of the blockchain business case, which can improve many insurance processes.

Blockchain will lessen administrative and operational costs through automated verification of policyholder identity and contract validity, auditable record of claims and information from third parties (e.g., encrypted patient data between doctor and injured party manageable by insurer to authenticate payment), and disbursement for claims through a blockchain-based payments infrastructure or smart contracts-linked escrow account. Providing the reinsurers controlled access to claims and claims histories recorded on the blockchain increases transparency for the reinsurer in an automated yet auditable manner.

2.2. *Claims Processing and Management*

Besides mobile and digital technologies, blockchain is essential to establishing an efficient, transparent, and customer-focused claims model based on higher degrees of trust through transparency. Within claims management, new data streams can enhance the risk selection process by combining location, external risk, and data analytics. A distributed ledger integrated to existing systems can enable the insurer and various third parties to easily and instantly access and update relevant information (e.g., claim forms, photo evidence, police reports and eye-witness, or third-party accounts).

The application of data from a mobile phone can simplify claims submission, reduce loss adjustment costs, and increase client satisfaction, with blockchain systems connecting communications to all parties.

Correspondingly, the use of mobile technologies, satellite imagery, sensor data, and blockchain could facilitate claims payments and rescue services when natural disasters occur in remote areas. Information collected from weather stations could establish claims sum based on actual climate readings, with blockchain facilitating more efficient data sharing and stronger protection against fraud.

In addition, advanced technology will be able to work effortlessly through the concept of Internet of Things (IoT), where massive devices are linked via the internet. For example, accident claims can be made through an app provided by the insurer by taking pictures or sending videos of accidents which are time-stamped. Together with blockchain solutions for know-your-client (KYC) data, a client can send the verified identity data to other companies for confirmation with the same app, avoiding the need to repeat the verification process, thus expediting efficiency in the on-boarding of new users.

2.3. New Distribution and Payment Models

Some international insurers are already developing partnerships and exploring new payment systems and business models (cryptocurrencies and digital wallets) to achieve capital efficiencies through a truly public global ledger system. Increased computerization to acquire risk information in contracts also suggest new opportunities to build market intelligence, simplify payments, and build financing risk. At the very least, global insurers can use the blockchain to remove asset management costs or hedging fees required for mitigating currency fluctuations in cross-border and international transactions.

In the new business model, the focus of the insurers would be on matching supply and demand and to risk calculation research, instead of asset management. The insurer could create a marketplace-like platform where customers can post their insurance demand, which could be either a standardized product or even a specific demand. The insurer then would use its risk models along with 'risk assessment intelligence', based on available historical information, to perform a premium calculation for the expected return. With this expected return, interested investors can bid or subscribe to the demanded insurance.

With the use of smart contracts and records on a decentralized ledger, the payment from the investor to the customer in the event of an insurance claim become cheaper, transparent, and more efficient than long-established ways. In addition, the investors know their maximum exposure as the amount defined in the smart contracts.

The insurer can also now play the role of assessor of the damage to validate the authenticity of the insurance claim. However, this could as easily be outsourced to a third party and by connecting the blockchain to other ledgers where verification can be done automatically.

2.4. Reinsurance

Property and casualty insurers seeking clearer visibility into their reinsurance contracts and risk exposures may gain it through blockchain. Consider the case of an insurer seeking to offload an equal amount of risk to two separate reinsurers. A blockchain ledger could provide insight and notification if one of those reinsurers then tried to offload some of its portion to a subsidiary of the other reinsurer. It also would help insurers gain confidence that, as they pay out claims, they are appropriately rebalancing their capital exposures against specific risks.

Within reinsurance, the benefits of blockchain include more accurate reserve calculations based on actual participating contracts and automatic calculation updates once the primary information and data are updated. On top of that, insurers obtain more room to move capital and improve transparency into known risks, capital productivity, and compliance. Operationally, the process of audit trails become simpler to chart, modelling requirements are significantly reduced, and there is less coordination required between the finance and IT functions.

3. Enhanced Claims Processing and Management

Besides mobile and digital technologies, blockchain is essential to establishing an efficient, transparent, and customer-focused claims model based on higher degrees of trust through transparency. Within claims management, new data streams can enhance the risk selection process by combining location, external risk, and data analytics. Figure 5.1 shows a distributed ledger integrated to existing systems can enable the insurer and various third parties to easily and instantly access and update relevant information (e.g., claim forms, photo evidence, police reports, and eye-witness or third-party accounts).

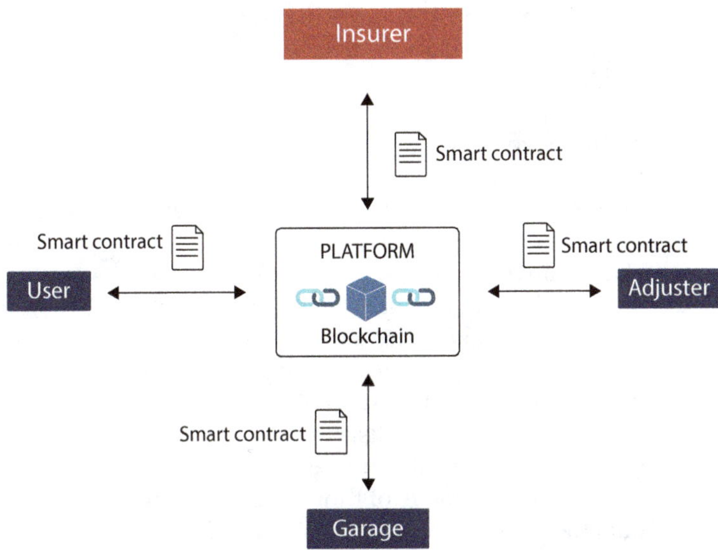

Figure 5.1: Private (Centralized) Blockchain System for Claims Processing

Figure 5.2 illustrates the process flows of the claims processing on the blockchain via smart contracts. The main processes are claims submission, loss assessment, and finally claims approval.

1. Through an app that has been developed for the users, the insurer enables the insured to submit claims efficiently

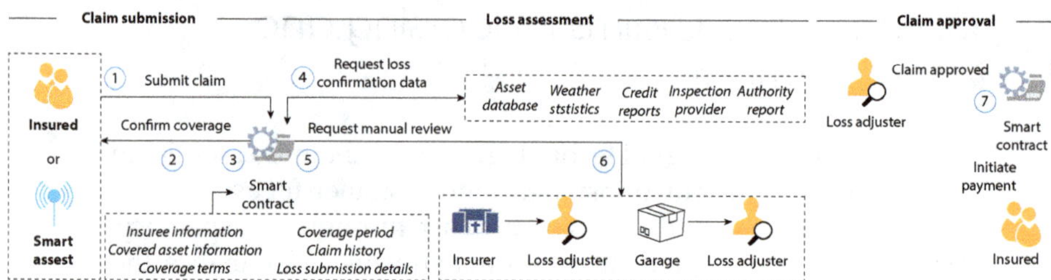

Figure 5.2: Process flow of Claims Processing via Smart Contracts deployed on the Blockchain

without having to fill laborious paperwork or make their way down to meet insurers in order to make a claim.

2. Once the app is launched, it first checks if the insured has a valid insurance coverage, i.e., still active or expired.

3. Based on the policy details of the insured, the smart platform verifies the coverage terms against the insured identity and claims history.

4. Further information pertaining to the claim, like weather conditions, accident reports, etc., are also processed as the claims move into the loss assessment phase.

5. This single database that collates all necessary information required to make a decision on the insurance claims are accessible to the insurer, loss adjuster, garage, workshop or mechanic, and insured. This makes the process transparent to reduce disputes and fraud.

6. To some extent, it will automate claims processing replaces the exchange of thousands of emails and massive data files. The more efficient steps will not only save costs but also save time and eliminate unnecessary procedural and operational delays.

7. Once the loss adjusters are ready to make a decision on the claim, their approval triggers payment to the awardee accordingly based on the amount determined via instant payment systems connected to the smart contract platform.

This new system will make a better and more efficient flows to existing cumbersome processes. Since there is an existing system with contracts attached to them that are still running, the new system will only start to onboard new insurance/takāful contracts. The existing customers will only be onboarded when their current contract expires, and onboarded on the new system when they renew their contracts.

As for claims that are minor, e.g. cracked windscreens, the process will be much faster as shown in Figure 5.3.

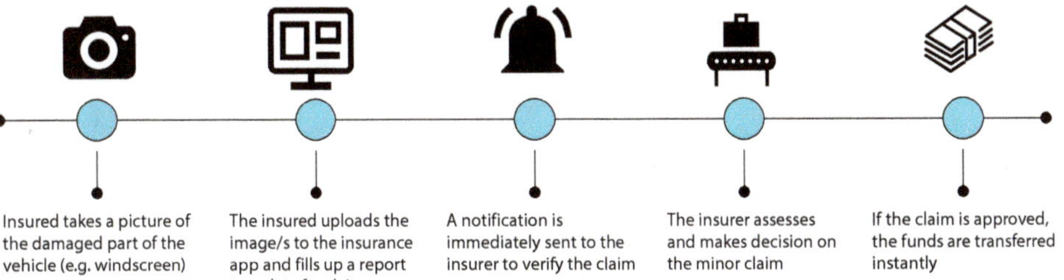

Figure 5.3: The Process for Minor Claims

The main processes for minor claims are:

1. Through the same app, the user uses the camera function to take snapshots of the damage at different angles.
2. The images are time-stamped and uploaded with details of the insured through his policy details, pre-loaded from the profile of the app user.
3. The smart platform alerts the insurer of this claim and thus triggers the insurer to validate and verify the minor claim.
4. For this minor claim, verification software is used to ensure that the images are not doctored or have been tampered with to sieve out fraudulent claims.
5. The insurer decides on the claim and if approved, transfers the corresponding funds claimed to the insured's account.

4. Benefits of Blockchainized Intelligent Takāful Claims System

The projected cost and time savings can be depicted in the chart below (Figure 5.4):

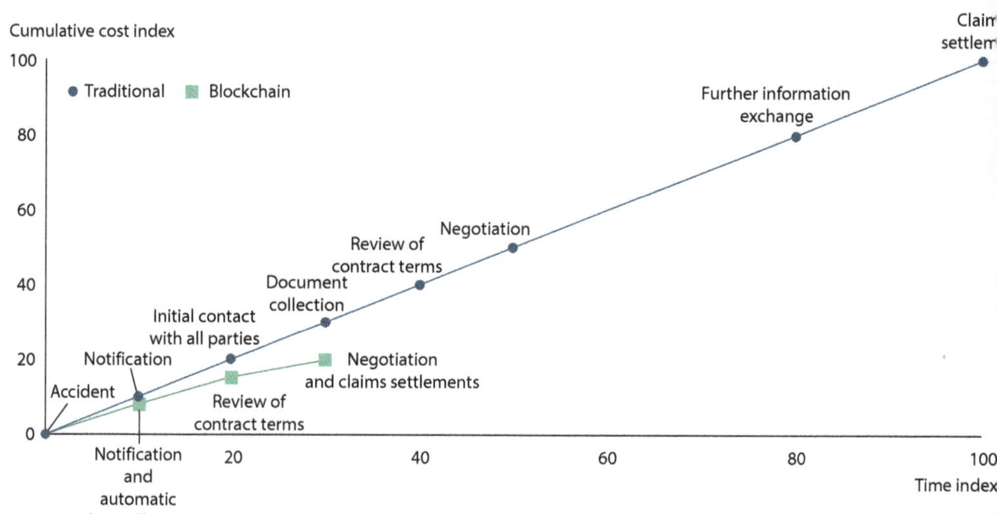

Figure 5.4: Projected cost and time savings

A study by Boston Consulting Group showed that time can be saved by 70% and costs by about 80%. Automated claims processing replaces the laborious exchange of thousands of emails and massive data files, going back-and-forth between claimants, loss adjusters of the insurers, and workshops.

So, the three main benefits to the intelligent claims system are:

1. Simplicity and Speed of Execution
   a. Increased backend efficiency and usability for insurers
   b. Also lead to a superior user experience (UX) for customers
2. Obvious and Significant Cost Efficiencies
   a. Automated claims processing replaces the exchange of thousands of emails and massive data files with reduced steps will not only save costs but also save time and eliminate unnecessary procedural and operational delays
3. Transparency and Scalability
   a. All related parties can access the necessary information through the private blockchain system to verify and process claims

    b. Since the system is efficient with less repeating steps, the usability and ability to onboard new customers can increase tremendously

5. Moving Forward

Blockchain functions as a distributed system and, thus, its value will mostly depend on collaboration with all actors in the value chain like customers, service providers, payment systems, and regulators. Blockchain is an IT investment with a perspective of presumably five years until full realization of benefits. In application areas that do not strongly rely on blockchain's distributed mechanisms, alternative solutions can provide similar benefits much sooner. For the industry as a whole, this means starting to work with consortia, technology experts and start-ups, regulators, and other market participants to identify the challenges around and leverage upon blockchain's open and decentralized nature. Among these challenges are technology limitations as well as market, legal or regulatory (who regulates in the absence of an intermediary or in cross-border transactions), and operational requirements regarding, for example, data protection and standardization.

Individual takāful companies should start with a holistic understanding of customer engagement needs and their own pain points to assess where the most promising blockchain use cases exist. As an innovative technology, blockchain presents a threat for incumbents in the form of innovative business models and/or cost advantages. However, there is a range of options to counteract this threat by adopting the way of working of start-ups, partnering with, or acquiring them. The key to shaping the future of the blockchain takāful ecosystem is getting involved in partnerships and industry activities early on.

6. Conclusion

The use of distributed ledgers to exchange data related to transfer of goods and information could also enable more granular payments along the supply chain. Enabling all actors in the supply chain to directly input information into a distributed ledger means there is more visibility of each step along the supply chain.

These events could facilitate smaller portions of financing to be released, thereby unlocking liquidity and reducing the risk of non-payment.

In an era of "point innovations" such as mobile apps and robo-advisory models, blockchain stands out as a more foundational or architectural development. In that sense, blockchain may support, and subsequently drive the increased use and broader adoption of the many other digital innovations that have helped reshape the insurance landscape.

Takāful operations management should recognize how the blockchain can increase trust and transparency, which speaks to the heart of the insurance business. After all, the industry's inherent bond of trust and "promise to pay" are based on disclosure of accurate personal data describing the insurable interests of the client, the agreement to a contract between two parties and timely exchange of payment. Blockchain can help remove friction, errors and risks from all of these essential steps. There is substance behind the hype, but the insurance industry must make investments now to be in a position to take advantage of efficiencies and opportunities blockchain technology can deliver long term.

It is vital that the Islamic economic actors surmount current and future challenges related to insurance by manifesting the objectives of the Shariah. One of the most fundamental functions of takāful is to provide the efficient compliance to settlements of claims according to agreed contractual stipulations and timely payouts of those genuine claims. The development of a blockchain-based insurance system would help to propel the Islamic takāful industry into a competitive one through cost-efficient processes, faster verifications, and better fraud detection capabilities. This way, the takāful operators shows nimbleness by adjusting to changing trends and landscapes, and after all, mitigating risks through takāful insurance is perceived as protecting one's lifestyle and livelihood.

Bibliography

Antonopoulos, A.M. (2014). *Mastering Bitcoin: Unlocking Digital Crypto-Currencies.* Sebastopol, CA: O'Reilly Media, 2014.
Back, Adam, *et al.* (2014). *Enabling Blockchain Innovations with Pegged Sidechains.* White paper, Blockstream, pp. 1–25.

Boston Consulting Group (2020). Ten Digital Moves for a Quick Performance Boost. 19th March 2020. https://www.bcg.com/publications/2020/ten-digital-moves-for-quick-performance-boost

Buterin, Vitalik. *Ethereum White Paper: A Next Generation Smart Contract & Decentralized Application Platform*. White Paper, Ethereum, Ethereum.

daCosta, F. (2013). *Rethinking the Internet of Things: A Scalable Approach to Connecting Everything*. New York: Apress, 2013.

Dawson, R. (2014). "The New Layer of the Economy Enabled by M2M Payments in the Internet of Things." Trends in the Living Networks, September 16, 2014. http://rossdawsonblog.com/weblog/archives/2014/09/new-layer-economy-enabled-m2mpayments-internet-things.html.

Ernst and Young (2017). Blockchain in Insurance: Applications and Pursuing a Path to Adoption. https://webforms.ey.com/Publication/vwLUAssets/EY-blockhain-in-insurance/$FILE/EY-blockhain-in-insurance.pdf

Evans, P., Aré, L., Forth, P., Harlé, N. and Portincaso, M. (2016). *Thinking Outside the Blocks: A Strategic Perspective on Blockchain and Digital Tokens*. Boston Consulting Group. December 1.

GitHub. *Blockchain Based Proof of Work*. GitHub. March 2014.

Islamic Financial Services Board (IFSB), Islamic Financial Services Industry Stability Report 2016, https://www.ifsb.org/docs/IFSI%20Stability%20Report%202016%20(final).pdf

Mohamed, H. (2019). Takāful (Islamic Insurance) on the Blockchain. In *The Growth of Islamic Finance and Banking: Innovation, Governance and Risk Mitigation, 1st Edition*. Chapter 4, pp 45–67. Routledge, U.K.

Nakamoto, Satoshi. (2009). *Bitcoin: A Peer-to-Peer Electronic Cash System*. White paper, 2009, pp. 1–9.

Omohundro, S. (2014). *Cryptocurrencies, Smart Contracts, and Artificial Intelligence*. Submitted to AI Matters (Association for Computing Machinery), October 22, 2014. http://steveomohundro.com/2014/10/22/cryptocurrencies-smart-contracts-andartificial-intelligence/

Swan, Melanie (2015). *Blockchain: Blueprint for a New Economy*. O'Reilly Media, Inc.

Szabo, Nick. (1996). *Smart Contracts: Building Blocks for Digital Markets*. Extropy, No. 16.

DIGITIZING MEDICAL RECORDS AND HEALTHCARE MANAGEMENT

The healthcare industry faces a critical need for digital innovation, as personalization and data science prompt patients to engage in the details of their healthcare and restore agency over their medical data.

In this chapter, we discuss ways as to how technologies like the blockchain can primarily secure personal and confidential patient data giving permissioned-access approved by the patient herself/himself to related parties like healthcare providers, pharmacies, and healthcare or medical insurers. Patients do not transfer the data to the parties requesting it, but he/she is merely giving them access to view it to enable their work. This protects the privacy of the patients.

Keywords: *Distributed Digital Ledgers, Permissioned-based Access, Smart Contracts.*

Contents

1. Introduction

Healthcare is at a crisis globally, with global demand for medical services outpacing the ability to pay for it. As the world population ages, the ratio of elderly people to working age people is rapidly growing. The result is a greater need for healthcare services by the elderly, with fewer working age people to provide financial support for medical insurance. In addition, the cost of providing medical care continues to outpace inflation, with the average global rise in medical care projected to be 7.8% in 2017, up from 7.3% in 2016 and 7.5% in 2015 (WTW, 2017).

An aging population with fewer working age people to pay for their medical costs, along with steadily increasing costs of medical care, are creating an enormous pressure on governments and businesses to find innovative ways to make the delivery of healthcare more efficient and less costly. Advances in technology to control the bureaucratic burden of medical care will provide a means to accomplish these goals.

Electronic Health Records (EHRs) were never designed to manage the complexities of multi-institutional, lifetime medical records. As patients move between providers, their data becomes scattered across different organizations, losing easy access to past records. As providers — not patients — are the primary stewards of EHRs, patients face significant hurdles in viewing their reports, correcting erroneous data, and distributing the information. The situation is much like consumer finance, where an individual may have several bank accounts, credit cards, loans, and assets, but no unified way to access and control them. In the case of finance, however, there is an infrastructure in place that greases the wheels — currency.

EHR is the combination of a social need with a technological enabler — a system that prioritizes patient agency, giving a transparent and accessible view of medical history. To continue the banking analogy, financial systems may contain multiple different depositories of currency, perhaps one for each provider network. The problem is that health records are not fungible; each is an individual's unique imprint. There is no like for like trade possible as we can do with money. While competition and multiplicity often result in lower consumer costs, here it risks a mass of incompatible or inaccessible barriers to interchange and control. We propose an alternative — a distributed access and validation system using the blockchain to replace centralized intermediaries. The healthcare industry faces a critical need for such innovation, as personalization and data science prompt patients to engage in the details of their healthcare and restore agency over their medical data. Blockchain used in healthcare systems will provide control, supervision, accessibility, auditability, and interoperability over large-scale data management systems using a comprehensive log. It is expected to revolutionize and drive the digitalization of healthcare economics because it is secure, fast, trustworthy, immutable, and provides public and private transparent solutions.

In this chapter, how technologies like the blockchain can primarily secure personal and confidential patient data giving permissioned-access approved by the patient herself/himself to related parties like healthcare providers, pharmacies, and health/ medical insurers will be discussed. Patients do not transfer the data to the parties requesting it, but he/she is merely giving them access to view it to enable their work. Thus, this paradigm shift enables the emergence of data economics, supplying big data to empower researchers while engaging patients and providers in the choice to release metadata.

2. Benefits of Digitalized Processes for Medical Records-keeping

Electronic records are superior to paper records because they decrease error due to handwriting problems and also ease physical storage requirements. Additionally, electronic records simultaneously leverage other error-reducing technologies and render them coherent. EHR models present significant additional advantages because of their potential to deliver a longitudinal record that tracks all medical interactions by a particular patient and provide comprehensive data across populations.

On top of error reduction, business concerns and structural changes in healthcare delivery will drive EHR adoption. First, the shift from in-patient to ambulatory care (and other episodic models) has accelerated the need for accurate and efficient flow of patient medical and billing information between organizationally and geographically distinct providers. Second, the operational aspects of managed care, such as the data needs of "gate-keeping" physicians, demands by payers for performance "report cards", and system administrators' increasing needs for sophisticated utilization review and risk management tools, have increased the need for data transparency. Third, the growth of "shared care", whereby the patient both shares responsibility with the provider for care and is likely to have increasingly fragmented or episodic relationships with multiple providers, requires that patients must have access to health data to information in their record (Rassbass, 2001). Furthermore, it requires that providers have transparent access to other occasions of treatment. Finally, both patients and regulators are demanding increasing amounts of data regarding errors or near misses and outcomes in populations — data that is difficult to capture without access or voluntary reporting and nearly impossible to analyze without complex, comprehensive database systems.

Using the blockchain to store medical records has the potential to make private healthcare data more tamper-proof, secure, and scalable. The distributed nature of the blockchain can ease the sharing of data among authorized parties and bridge traditional data silos, dramatically increasing efficiencies and improve coordination of care (DeMeijer, 2017). Costs of medical care can be decreased through better insurance claim coordination with treatment rendered. Data auditing is improved through the immutable records maintained by the blockchain. The costs associated with blockchain mining can even be offset by offering anonymized metadata rewards for medical researchers (Ekblaw *et al.*, 2016).

The success of the digital medical record blockchain initiative will depend upon its ability to keep medical records private while at the same time widely available to medical providers and insurance companies. Scaling a national blockchain-based electronic medical record to the global community will require broad acceptance of protocols for the coding of medical information and interoperability of data exchange across systems.

3. Utilizing Technology for Medical Records-keeping

Among the different applications that use blockchain, healthcare is one of the most interesting fields in current blockchain-based research. Since healthcare is one of the most regulated industries, blockchain can have a positive impact on the healthcare domain. Blockchain technology has led to tremendous solutions for traditional healthcare domain issues (Angraal *et al.*, 2017), such as providing a secure infrastructure and integrated private health records (Zhang *et al.*, 2016). Blockchain can be used to provide secure communication among stakeholders and deliver clinical reports efficiently (Rabah, 2017).

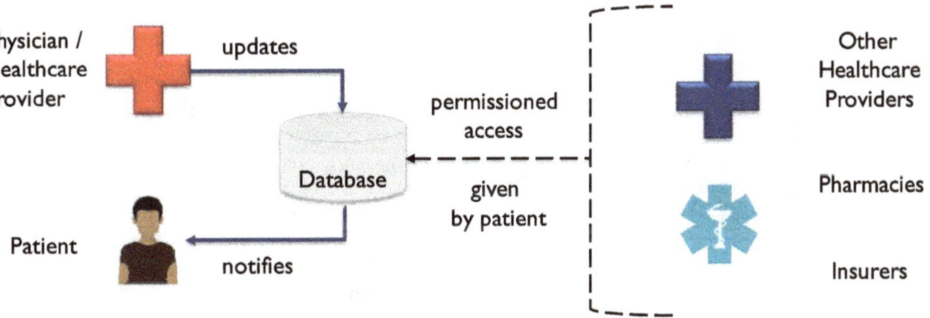

Figure 6.1: A Permissioned-based Access to Medical Records

Blockchain allows sharing an EHR in a secure manner since blockchain technology can be extended as a standard for stakeholders (Esposito *et al.*, 2018). Using blockchain for EHR provides many advantages, such as preserving patient's privacy (Raseena and Harikrishnan, 2013) and improving the quality of medical care (Omar *et al.*, 2017). The need for patient-centric services and connecting disparate systems have triggered the usage of a shared decentralized platform built on the blockchain.

Blockchain provides patients full control over their medical records. Patient information is very sensitive and should be kept in a secure and confidential system with controlled access. As such, it has become a prime target for malicious attacks, such as Denial of Service (DoS), Storage Attacks, and so on (Dwivedi *et al.*, 2019). Blockchain may provide a secure and robust platform for healthcare against failures and attacks because it contains different mechanisms of access control.

4. Record Management System

An effective Electronic Medical Records Management (EMRM) system has to address several major issues related to healthcare, namely data quantity and quality, system interoperability, fragmented medical data, patient agency, and slow access to medical data. In order to provide interoperability, a set of APIs has to be built for provider database integration. Smart contracts can be used for data retrieval instructions and viewing permissions using a log of medical relationships between patients and providers. To ensure that the data are not tampered with, a cryptographic hash can be used to guarantee data integrity. Participating parties control their records by accepting or rejecting new information.

A DNS-like implementation is used for identity confirmation by linking a specific Ethereum address to a specific patient's ID. Handling off-chain data exchange between the provider and patient's database is implemented by a syncing algorithm. A database authentication server is used to confirm permissions on the blockchain. The proposed system provides patients with easy access, an immutable medical history log, and comprehensive services to medical information across treatment sites and providers. An EMRM system allows data sharing, confidentiality, authentication, and accountability for sensitive information. An EMRM system will rely on multiple participants to avoid a single point of failure. Also, it has to include contract encryption and preserving auditability while improving complexity faced in the existing systems. Scalability is an open issue in an EMRM system, and such a system needs to be extended for complex scenarios regarding healthcare data since it only validates the medical records.

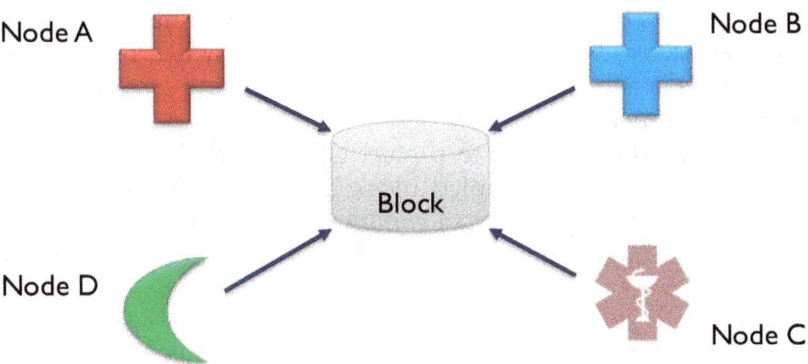

Figure 6.2: Defining Appropriate Nodes for Validation of New Information

4.1. Privacy Preserving Systems and Data Exchange

A privacy-preserving framework should offer efficient access, interoperability, and security for medical records for third parties, providers, and patients. A proposed framework should be able to preserve patients' privacy and security using cryptographic techniques and allows access control and data by utilizing blockchain-based databases and smart contracts to optimize patients' experience, minimizing any interaction between contracts and patients, and reduce privacy threats. These permission-based processes allow patients to manage control of the privacy of their own medical records, whose integrity can be confirmed using query links and cryptographic hashes. Multi-signature contracts are utilised to control and administrate activity of a specific account, by establishing powers and rights to that specific account. Multi-signature contracts also allow for the use of multiple keys to edit the medical data on the chain; thus, the entities that hold all the keys are allowed to edit the information, while others can only read or initiate transactions from the ledger. The data are not stored on the blockchain, but rather stored in a decentralized repository called a 'data lake'. A data lake can store various types of data, and is highly scalable due to interoperability. Only encrypted data are stored in the data lake, and as illustrated in Figure 6.1, only the patient holds the right to give access to his/her medical records data. This approach provides two main advantages: (1) it allows patients to manage and control their own medical records; and

(2) it also enables cross-institutional sharing with many types of devices such as home devices, and is particularly helpful for data access (such as historical assessment, etc.) during emergency or urgent treatments.

Another method to protect data privacy is through the utilization of loosely-coupled blockchains. In order to enhance the privacy, the platform can combine on-chain verification and off-chain storage. Some models use "the distributed databases of hospitals to ensure off-chain storage, while the hash value of medical records is used in a transaction for on-chain verification" (Jiang *et al.*, 2018). Other architectures use context blockchains, off-chain storage, and exchange reference pointers on-chain, token-based permission model and Model-View-Controller (MVC) pattern to provide a comprehensive solution. They use public key cryptography to create and manage health identities.

To guarantee the encapsulated EHR validity, an attribute-based signature scheme can be used for multiple authorities (Guo *et al.*, 2018) on the blockchain for EHR. In this approach, patients will endorse messages based on specific attributes without disclosing other information. The only parameter needed to access the messages is providing evidence to the verifier. Distributing the patient's public and private keys is done without the need for a central or single authority. Multiple authorities are responsible for this task. This conforms to distributed data storage mode in the blockchain, which can avoid escrow problems. Patients' information such as insurance records, consumption records, and EHRs is encapsulated in a single block when treatment is finished. When a patient goes to another healthcare service provider, the new entity needs to authenticate the patient's identity and he/she gives access to the required information.

5. Mobile Application Architecture

A blockchain-based mobile application is designed to manage healthcare data. It collects data from patients in a secure manner, then synchronizes it with cloud services and shares the data with healthcare entities and insurance providers. Cloud security is the main area that many previous works have examined and evaluated for the implementation of blockchain technology in it, or any cloud-based or online application for that matter. However, mobile-based (or DApps) should provide health data and medical records sharing solutions through user-centric models. Some prototypes and designed mobile applications have used "membership service (supported by blockchain) and a channel formation scheme to enhance identity management service and privacy protection by utilizing permissioned blockchain characteristics" (Liang *et al.,* 2017). In such DApps, the mobile architectures utilize medical devices, manual input, and wearable devices to collect patient information. The data are shared with healthcare institutions by synchronizing them with a cloud database. Proof of integrity and validation are permanently retrievable to ensure health data integrity. Batching and tree-based data processing methods are used to ensure scalable and performance stability and handle a large amount of medical data uploaded and collected by the mobile platforms or synced wearables.

For example, patients decide when they need to see their doctor, generally only once visible symptoms have appeared, or an accident has occurred. They have to schedule an appointment, and often, they must remember the pertinent details of their medical history. Human beings, of course, are fallible and forgetful. Instead, with interoperability of information and systems, we can imagine a nation of sensor-equipped patients. Machine learning monitors IoT sensor data built in the patient's home or domicile consolidated via a DApp, and can determine — at an early stage — when something has gone wrong. The patient's virtual assistant can cross-reference their calendar with their doctor's, and schedule an appointment automatically. When the patient arrives, doctors who want to record a patient visit have external apps that pull demographic information from the shared patient's medical record (EHR). These DApps can also book appointments and notify of visits through the clinicians' schedule, typically maintained in the EMRM. When exchanging more clinically related data, interoperability between DApps with EMRMs will have to be resolved. Structured and often codified information such as the patient's problems, procedures, medications, and allergies are shared. Some of these semantic interoperability issues can be resolved through standard coding terminologies. Likewise, when DApps want to extract a patient's drug allergies and use it to alert of potential drug allergy reactions for a prescription, the drug allergies need to be coded using the same proprietary terminology or appropriately mapped to each other.

A diagnosis recorded during other medical encounters can be codified and sent back into an EMRM system, which is shared onto a cloud-based personal EHR. Similarly, lab and radiology reports can be codified for personalized-EHR medical records and shared whenever required across systems where permission is enabled only by the patient.

6. EHR in the Context of National Healthcare Policy

EHR systems present a valuable opportunity to improve health surveillance and evaluate service provision potentially leading to improvements in the management and the promotion of public health (Danciu *et al.*, 2014). Public health research includes preparedness for pandemics (e.g., bird flu and swine flu outbreaks), cancer, maternal health, infectious diseases such as leprosy, and sexual health. It also incorporates evaluations of systems already in place in urban and/or rural regions, ranging from primary to tertiary care as well as across different healthcare providers, such as non-governmental organizations.

A key consideration of public health in national healthcare policy is the utilisation of EHR for disease surveillance and outbreak monitoring systems. EHRs have the ability to help identify and predict seasonal outbreaks and high-risk areas and prevent infections or diseases as well as assisting in the coordination of demographic information and community profiles, which are invaluable in the current public health climate due to the ease of mobility.

Table 6.1: Role and Benefits of National EHR Systems to Public Health

National EHR Policy	
Disease Surveillance and Outbreak Monitoring	**Healthcare System Continuous Improvement**
<ul><li>Monitor trends</li><li>Planning for outbreaks</li><li>Identify transmissions and action plans</li><li>Action plan accountability (closed-loop governance)</li></ul>	<ul><li>Data sharing or transfer between hospitals and systems</li><li>Alerts to improve clinical decision making and patient safety</li><li>Updated records for interoperability with DApps and wearables</li></ul>

Another key utilisation of EHR (as shown in Table 6.1) is their implementation to improve healthcare systems. The identification of risk factors through electronic health systems allows health professionals to recognize and track them over time, helping in clinical decision-making, planning for outbreaks, and identifying transmission of diseases (Chang *et al.*, 2015; Jo, 2016). For example, a study of cancer patients allowed the tracking and analysis of diagnostic patterns, the number of investigations completed by physicians, and transfer of information as well as factors for the diagnoses (Lee *et al.*, 2015).

7. Conclusion

Electronic digitized records are superior to traditional paper records because they decrease consolidation efforts, errors from handwritten records, and bulky physical storage requirements. EHR models present significant additional advantages because of their potential to deliver a better record-keeping that tracks all medical interactions by a particular patient and provide comprehensive data across populations. Thus, a national healthcare authority should envision a decentralized compendium of digital healthcare data of individuals and populations as supporting data into error-free medical records, up-to-date healthcare systems, and enhanced disease surveillance and monitoring.

Most EMRM initiatives are national in scope and frequently government-initiated or funded. EMRM initiatives are typically hospital- or system-wide, yet are being designed with an eye to broader push or pull systems that will make wide-area use of such institutional data. However, this chapter discussed a personal EHR model which is conceptually different, and assumes that individual patients will aggregate their diverse records and then make them selectively available to new or emergency providers for personal data protection and privacy controls.

As more sophisticated EHR progress continues, leading solution-providers will converge and a preferred EHR model will emerge — be it a shared summary system or a full interpretational longitudinal base of EHRs. The ideal system would probably provide flexibility for patients and providers which health information is shared across systems, and the interactivity of a permission-based EHR protocol would likely increase patient interest and involvement in their own care. Ultimately, the technology should overcome the technical problems they pose — security and privacy costs — and bottlenecks from legacy systems already identified. To reach large-scale adoption, EHRs should deliver lower costs and higher quality, while promoting the continued industrialization of healthcare delivery through patient autonomy and upholding professional ideals. It is indeed ever more important for service and solution providers to be aware of emerging technology, to comprehend the tension between improved care and the preservation of patient privacy and autonomy in the era of the fourth industrial revolution (IR4.0).

Bibliography

Angraal, S.; Krumholz, H.M.; Schulz, W.L. (2017). *Blockchain technology: Applications in Healthcare, Circulation: Cardiovascular Quality and Outcomes.* arXiv 2017, arXiv:1706.03700.

Azaria, A.; Ekblaw, A.; Vieira, T.; Lippman, A. (2016). MedRec: Using Blockchain for Medical Data Access and Permission Management. In Proceedings of the 2016 2nd International Conference on Open Big Data, OBD 2016, Vienna, Austria, 22–24 August 2016; pp. 25–30.

Chang, N.; Dai, H.; Jonnagaddala, J.; Chen, C.; Tsai, R. T.; Hsu, W. (2015). A Context-aware Approach for Progression Tracking of Medical Concepts in Electronic Medical Records, *Journal of Biomedical Informatics*, vol. 58, pp. S150–S157.

Cichosz, S.L.; Stausholm, M.N.; Kronborg, T.; Vestergaard, P.; Hejlesen, O. (2018). How to Use Blockchain for Diabetes Health Care Data and Access Management: An Operational Concept. *Journal of Diabetes Science and Technology.* 2018, 13, pp. 248–253.

Conceiçao, A.F.; da Silva, F.S.C.; Rocha, V.; Locoro, A.; Barguil, J.M. (2018). *Electronic Health Records using Blockchain Technology.* arXiv:1804.10078

Dagher, G.G.; Mohler, J.; Milojkovic, M.; Marella, P.B. (2018). Ancile: Privacy-preserving framework for access control and interoperability of electronic health records using blockchain technology. *Sustainable Cities and Society.* 2018, 39, pp. 283–297.

Danciu, I.; Cowan, J. D.; Basford, M. (2014). Secondary use of Clinical Data: The Vanderbilt Approach, *Journal of Biomedical Informatics*, vol. 52, pp. 28–35.

DeMeijer, C.R. (2017). *Blockchain in Healthcare: Make the Industry Better*. Finextra Research. 2017. Available from: https://www.finextra.com/blogposting/13801/blockchain-in-healthcare-make-the-industry-better.

Dubovitskaya, A.; Xu, Z.; Ryu, S.; Schumacher, M.; Wang, F. (2018). Secure and Trustable Electronic Medical Records Sharing using Blockchain. *Journal of the American Medical Informatics Association*. 2018, 2017, pp. 650–659.

Dwivedi, A.D.; Srivastava, G.; Dhar, S.; Singh, R. (2019). A Decentralized Privacy-Preserving Healthcare Blockchain for IoT. Sensors 2019, 19, p. 326.

Ekblaw, A., Azaria, A. (2016). MedRec: *Medical Data Management on the Blockchain*. PubPub.2016. Available from: https://www.pubpub.org/pub/medrec

Esposito, C.; Santis, A.D.; Tortora, G.; Chang, H.; Choo, K.K.R. (2018). Blockchain: A Panacea for Healthcare Cloud-Based Data Security and Privacy? *IEEE Cloud Computing*. 5, pp. 31–37.

Fan, K.; Wang, S.; Ren, Y.; Li, H.; Yang, Y. (2018). MedBlock: Efficient and Secure Medical Data Sharing Via Blockchain. *Journal of Medical Systems*. 2018, 42, pp. 1–11.

Guo, R.; Shi, H.; Zhao, Q.; Zheng, D. (2018). Secure Attribute-Based Signature Scheme with Multiple Authorities for Blockchain in Electronic Health Records Systems. *IEEE Access* 2018, 6, pp. 11,676–11,686.

Jiang, S.; Cao, J.; Wu, H.; Yang, Y.; Ma, M.; He, J. (2018). Blochie: A blockchain-based platform for healthcare information exchange. In Proceedings of the SMARTCOMP 2018: The 4th IEEE International Conference on Smart Computing, Sicily, Italy, 18–20 June 2018; pp. 49–56.

Jo, E. (2016). The Automated Alert System for the Hospital Infection Control and the Safety of Medical Staff based on EMR data, *Nursing Informatics*. 225: 852–853.

Kumar, T.; Ramani, V.; Ahmad, I.; Braeken, A.; Harjula, E.; Ylianttila, M. (2018). Blockchain Utilization in Healthcare: Key Requirements and Challenges. In Proceedings of the IEEE 20th International Conference on e-Health Networking, Applications and Services, Ostrava, Czech Republic, 17–20 September 2018.

Kuo, T.; Ohno-Nachado, L. (2018). *ModelChain: Decentralized Privacy-Preserving Healthcare Predictive Modeling Framework on Private Blockchain Networks*. arXiv 2018, arXiv:1802.01746.

Lee, Y.; Shin, S.-Y.; Ahn, S.-M.; Lee, J.-H.; Kim, W.-S. (2015). Validation for Accuracy of Cancer Diagnosis in Electronic Medical Records using a Text Mining Method. *Studies in Health Technology and Informatics*, 216: 882.

Liang, X.; Zhao, J.; Shetty, S.; Liu, J.; Li, D. (2017). Integrating Blockchain for Data Sharing and Collaboration in Mobile Healthcare Applications. In Proceedings of the PIMRC 2017: 28th Annual IEEE International Symposium on Personal, Indoor and Mobile Radio Communications, Montreal, QC, Canada, 8–13 October 2017.

Omar, A.A.; Rahman, M.S.; Kiyomoto, A.B. (2017). MediBchain — A Blockchain Based Privacy Preserving Platform for Healthcare Data. In Proceedings of the International Conference on Security, Privacy and Anonymity in Computation, Communication and Storage, Guangzhou, China, 12–15 December 2017.

Rabah, K. (2017). Challenges and Opportunities for Blockchain-powered Healthcare Systems: A Review. *Mara Research Journal of Medicine & Health Science* 2017, 1, pp. 45–52.

Raseena, M.; Harikrishnan, G.R. (2013). Secure Sharing of Personal Health Records in Cloud Computing Using Attribute-Based Broadcast Encryption. *International Journal of Scientific and Engineering Research*. 2013, 1, pp. 323–325.

Rashbass J. (2001). The Patient-owned, Population-based Electronic Medical Record: A Revolutionary Resource for Clinical Medicine. JAMA. 4 April 2001; 285(13): 1769. doi: 10.1001/jama.285.13.1769-a.jms0404-7.

Salahuddin, M.A.; Al-Fuqaha, A.; Guizani, M.; Shuaib, K.; Sallabi, F. (2017). Softwarization of Internet of Things Infrastructure for Secure and Smart Healthcare. *IEEE Computing Magazine*. 2017, 50, pp. 74–79.

World Health Organization (2016). Electronic Health Records. From Innovation to Implementation-eHealth in the WHO European Region. Denmark: World Health Organization;2016.p.22.Availablefrom:http://www.euro.who.int/en/publications/abstracts/frominnovation-to-implementation-ehealth-in-the-hoeuropean-region-2016.

Willis Towers Watson. (2017). Global Medical Trends Survey Report. Willis Towers Watson. 2017. Available from: https://www.willistowerswatson.com/en/insights/2017/05/2017-global-medical-rends-survey-report.

Xia, Q.; Sifah, E.B.; Asamoah, K.O.; Gao, J.; Du, X.; Guizani, M. (2017). MeDShare: Trust-Less Medical Data Sharing among Cloud Service Providers via Blockchain. *IEEE Access* 2017, 5, pp. 14,757–14,767.

Yue, X.; Wang, H.; Jin, D.; Li, M.; Jiang, W. (2016). Healthcare Data Gateways: Found Healthcare Intelligence on Blockchain with Novel Privacy Risk Control. *Journal of Medical Systems*, 2016, 40, p. 218.

Zhang, P.; White, J.; Schmidt, D.C.; Lenz, G. (2015). Design of Blockchain-Based Apps Using Familiar Software Patterns to Address Interoperability Challenges in Healthcare; 2015. Available online: https://www.dre.vanderbilt.edu/~schmidt/PDF/PLoP-2017-blockchain.pdf (accessed on 20 November 2019).

Zhang, P.; White, J.; Schmidt, D.C.; Lenz, G.; Rosenbloom, S.T. (2018). FHIRChain: Applying Blockchain to Securely and Scalably Share Clinical Data. *Computational and Structural Biotechnology Journal*. 2018, 16, pp. 267–278.

Zhang, J.; Xue, N.; Huang, X. (2016). A Secure System for Pervasive Social Network-based Healthcare. *IEEE Access* 2016, 4, pp. 9,239–9,250.

RETHINKING SUPPLY CHAIN MANAGEMENT THROUGH NEW DIGITAL APPLICATIONS

Globalization has created complex supply chains to support free trade. The goods move across production facilities and supply chains, connecting markets involving numerous players along the way, while being subjected to different legal standards and quality requirements across multiple jurisdictions. By generating digital versions of real-world assets and tracking their pertinent data as a distributed, shared source of information, significant efficiencies and process improvements can be achieved. The use of distributed ledgers or blockchains to track goods as they move along the supply chain, makes for transparency and accuracy in the location of the goods at any point of time, in real-time. In this chapter, we provide a short discussion of artificial intelligence (AI), blockchain, and IoT applications in supply chain management and understand the benefits and the shift in the processes, in digital applications.

Keywords: *Fleet Management, Interoperability, Real-time Monitoring, Supply Integrity.*

Content

1. Introduction

There is a big loophole in the current state of supply chain management— the infrastructure is fragmented into offline and online components. As a result, this has led to misplacement of product and mismanagement of inventory; the supply chain management system is neither a single entity nor transparent.

The supply chain passes through millions of people along the way from harvesting the resource, distribution of the products and shelving the products for sales. When there are defects in a product, it becomes difficult for the manufacturer to trace the root of the problem. Another issue stems from unethical supply chain management to achieve cost savings. For example, as globalization starts to pick up pace, brand-named textile manufacturers became exposed as evil, greedy corporations preying on cheap labor. In order to reduce cost, brand-named companies would outsource production to low-cost suppliers situated in developing countries, where the outsourced supplier in turn leverages on cheap, underaged laborers to make some profit. Often, the supply chain is unaware of how many trading partners are really involved, and the initial textile manufacturer knows nothing about the working conditions of the remote contracted laborers. When exposed by wage-gap activists and the media, they are subjected to reputational damage due to the ignorance perpetuated by opaque supply chains. In theory, organizations should know all parties in their supply chain network (within the broader business ecosystem) and trust them — but this is far from today's reality.

The artificial intelligence (AI), blockchain, and Internet of Things (IoT) represent an extraordinary opportunity for all enterprises along the supply chain. Any organization capable of utilizing these technologies will create opportunities for themselves in streamlining and enhancing existing processes, build new business models, and expound innovation as new products and services for its clients. According to Gartner,[1] the enterprise software solutions for the Supply Chain Management market is projected to grow from US$12.2 billion in 2017 to US$20.4 billion in 2022, achieving a 10.7% Compound Annual Growth Rate (CAGR). By 2023, blockchain will support the global movement and tracking of US$2 trillion of goods and services annually.

In this chapter, three specific technological entities which are playing crucial roles in transforming our economy will be discussed. We also propose that for supply chain management and its industry to adopt them as a combined solution in order to fully harness the exponential benefits once used together. In the following sections, future applications and provide use cases that are already being implemented in the industry are also discussed.

1.1. AI on the Blockchain: Decentralized Intelligence?

Modern-day business depends on an intricate web of supply chains, with products, parts, and materials often shipped in thousands across great distances and from numerous places around the world. With the help of blockchain, AI-enabled environments can potentially have major impacts in virtually any industry. These impacts are dependent on both parties (AI and blockchain) providing efficient ways of procuring energy, improved scalability, security, privacy, hardware automation, proper governance, and data regulation.

---

1   https://www.gartner.com/doc/3879064

AI requires data or information to pick out trends and develop itself through deep learning. Interestingly, blockchains requires power and energy to cluster computer systems and run processes quicker. This established relationship creates a dependability between both these parties, which ultimately result in a technological breakthrough or a catastrophic consequence.

With the help of AI, blockchain not only benefits but also provides returns. In return, AI gets more information and that helps the system's evolutionary process. Furthermore, the more sophisticated the AI becomes, the more efficient it will be. The innovation of technology and the susceptibility to work in harmony with AI will also improve machine to machine interactions. These machines were made to facilitate human actions thus, clustering computer systems together will make processes quicker and simplify complex processes.

The integration of blockchain and AI into a decentralized intelligence system has profound possibilities to employ data in innovative ways. An effective amalgamation of both technologies will enable faster and seamless data management, validation of transactions, and detection of illegal documents, among others.

1.2. *The Internet of Things (IoT) and Decentralized Intelligence (AI + Blockchain)*

The Internet of Things (IoT) is a system of integrated devices that has the ability to share data between them. This offers the ability to track and monitor transactions of goods physically in the real world with greater transparency to its movements, and this presents a range of advantages for supply chain and logistics. The operational efficiencies possible with IoT, more than anything else, enable companies to get a real-time visibility of their deliveries and supply lines, allowing them to more efficiently allocate resources or respond to adverse occurrences immediately or as soon as practically possible.

In day-to-day transactions, the utilization of IoT sensors attached to shipments can help shipping or delivery companies to track its loads and monitor their progress, while updating clients' expectations accordingly. Amazon uses Wi-Fi robots in its distribution warehouses to get an instant snapshot of the traffic of its supply chain at any given time.[2] Bottlenecks, backlogs, or unforeseen emergencies can be detected, and efforts to restore, including alerting the necessary authorities, can be done immediately. In an industry that needs to be lean and responsive, RFID, NFC,[3] and other tracking technologies are becoming more and more crucial to the point of being indispensable.

From the fleet management perspective, it is impossible to plan all deliveries in microscopic detail in advance due to external factors beyond our control such as the weather and other trade traffic. With a more data-oriented view of a fleet enhanced by IoT, companies can leverage on various analytics recorded by IoT devices along the supply chain to make better decisions about managing the day-to-day transportation and deliveries. The IoT sensor network of billions of smart devices that connect people, systems, and other applications to collect and share data will improve the logistics industry, by alleviating trade traffic congestion, conserve energy, and monitor and address logistical concerns to authorities. In emergencies, first responders' response times can be optimized by providing the fastest routes to a location.

2. What is a Truly Halal Supply Chain?

The term 'halal' generally depicts lawfulness or permissibility by Islamic laws (or the Shariah). As such, the specific motives of deeming something haram in Islam are to preserve the purity of religion to safeguard against the consumption of impure or unsafe food, goods, or services, which will have detrimental effects on the consumer. By extension, the concept of 'halalan toyyiban' broadens the safeguarding of purity beyond the mere consumption of products (Arif and Sidek, 2015). It is meant to underline the commitment to the Shariah law, to ensure that the consumers are provided with the assurance that such purity from 'farm to fork' or 'beginning-to-end'. In addition, the concept of 'halal toyyib' goes beyond food sectors, and now include all other aspects of the halal economy, such as

---

2   Transforming the Supply Chain with AI, IoT & Blockchain: https:// www.technative.io/transforming-the-supply-chain-with-ai-iot-blockchain/
3   NFC stands for near field communication, while RFID means radio frequency identification.

non-food sectors like cosmetics, financial services, pharmaceuticals, and also other services that support the halal supply chain.

So, a truly halal approach is a holistic concept that have come to include the slaughtering, procurement, production, packaging, labelling, logistics, retailing, and dispensation of goods and services. The assurance of halal integrity to the end customer in the global Islamic market has become increasingly important for its consumers. The requirement of pure, quality, safe, and free from unlawful practices along the supply chain — from farm to fork, that goes beyond proper slaughtering and preparation procedures. Halal now includes riba-free financing, legally-approved labor, integrity of the material, production process, information transparency, and legally-earned capital associated with the goods and services at all levels (and their vendors) along the supply chain.

For the successful management of a halal supply chain, what is required is a 'farm to fork approach' as the halal supply chain has strict requirements to ensure its halal integrity (Manzouri *et al.*, 2013; Tieman *et al.*, 2012). Weak links along the supply chain and their vulnerabilities may cause the halal-ness, due its interconnectedness, to break down and become non-halal. Hence, the management of a truly halal supply chain needs to involve the coordination and close collaboration among suppliers and their vendors to uphold Shariah-compliance to its highest standards.

Such high standards also include the reduction of waste to ensure long-term sustainability, which includes resources other than raw and production materials, such as costs, efficiencies, and cycle times. The use of technologies like AI, blockchain, and IoT which utilizes shared data and information, provides for significant efficiencies and process improvements that enables the reduction of such waste, and become enablers of halal toyyib.

3. Digitalized Halal Supply Chain Management

It is often identified that supply chains are opaque to consumers, with it becoming increasingly difficult to identify where products originated and where they travelled to. Figure 7.1 depicts the information flows within a network of multiple parties in a supply chain. Blockchain could be used in this instance as a transparent ledger that is available on each node and would create a formal log of tracking products in the supply chain (Pilkington, 2015; Iansiti and Lakhani, 2017). This idea of supply chain management (SCM) through blockchain has been conceptualised by Walmart, who are employing the technology to track occurrences of bacteria in food and be aptly able to identify the source and limit the number of items needing to be recalled (Nofer *et al.*, 2017). It has also been implemented in the diamond industry to end unethical behavior (Nofer *et al.*, 2017; Underwood, 2016).

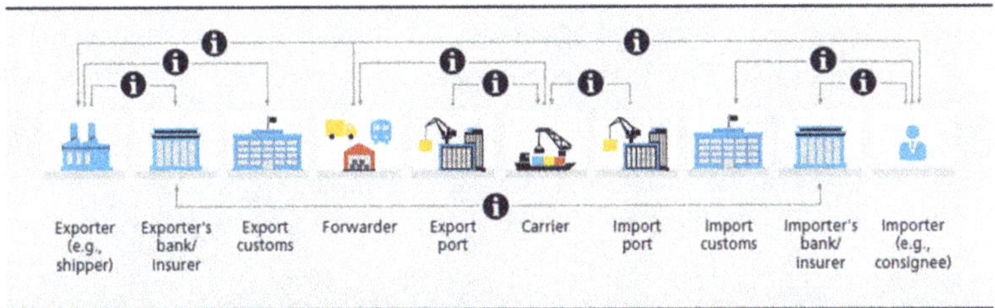

Figure 7.1: Information flows in a supply chain, involving many parties (Source: Accenture in DHL, 2018)

Blockchain provides enterprises with benefits such as immutability (Pilkington, 2015), transparency (Kosba *et al.*, 2016), and higher levels of security. In 2018, the global blockchain technology market is predicted to reach US$548 million in size and is forecast to grow to US$2.3 billion by 2021 (Mehta and Striapunia, 2017).

3.1. *Buyer and Supplier Onboarding Process*

For a large organization, bringing new suppliers onto the roster can be a surprisingly complex series of tasks. It is not unusual for a major corporation to source from more than 100,000 suppliers.[4] With limited resources and busy buyer schedules, individual suppliers will receive little attention. Despite these constraints, companies are expected to possess a deeper understanding of supplier activities. Governments are legislating for increasingly more stringent laws which expect corporations to police their supply chains for sustainability, corruption, forced labor, and many other ethical issues.

---

4   https://www.forbes.com/sites/jwebb/2018/04/30/how-to-onboard-a-new-supplier/#3e79a1d76213.

The solution to these issues starts with ensuring that the right suppliers are brought onboard to service company needs. This supplier onboarding process can also be automated via a Know-Your-Supplier (KYS) process. The steps to create this process are as follows:

a. Supplier Checklist

From there, buyers need to ensure that suppliers are checked before progressed. This requires an easy-to-use checklist. These are comprised of varied items, but consist of risk-focused checks, such as:

- The supplier has strong credentials.
- The supplier is not duplicating the work of a pre-existing vendor.
- The supplier can deliver promised goods or services.
- The supplier is not owned or administered by politically-exposed people.
- The supplier is not on any international sanction lists.

The ability to verify the credibility and performance of suppliers will provide buyers with reliable records which will streamline the process and reduce risk exposure to the company.

b. Develop Strategic Governance

Developing strategic governance requires additional KYS steps for all new suppliers, above a certain monetary threshold. Requiring special procurement sign-off is an example of greater risk management. New suppliers are subject to further checks, as will companies that are assigned large proportions of spend and possess a degree of criticality to the company.

3.2. Fleet Management

The logistics industry is inherently messy, with many touch points, stakeholders, and intermediaries where data points are not verified in real time by decentralized sources. The nature of logistics and transportation as a traditional process is underlined with manual communications (phone, email, fax, and others). In addition, the freight logistics processes involve the challenge of contract terms validation, rate negotiation, changes to agreed contracts certification, and settlement, where contracts need to be modified due to issues such as damage, late fees, loss, or cancellation.

Integrating blockchain to AI and IoT platforms, complex processes can be automated by a framework of automation, trusted data sets, and support system integration. Multi-party stakeholders can work from a unified platform that covers the majority of logistical processes and can enable instant financial transactions, freight, and fleet visibilities, and even unlock funds frozen in traditional contractual disputes.[5]

If adopted globally, it will add billions of data points to the supply chain, benefiting all value-add parties within the entire process and value chain. Bringing decentralized, immutable blockchain technologies with billions of live, verified data points to the logistics and transportation industry, it will add significant value and transparency to the industry's supply chain and its main stakeholders.

Finally, IoT aids supply chain integrity by providing a complete picture of the health of fleet or machinery hardware at any given time, notifying companies in advance if they need to repair their machinery.

3.3. *Warehousing and Distribution*

AI is critical for optimizing these international routes, but also for improving the efficiency of transportation in the "last mile" of delivery — and even in the warehouse itself. Using AI algorithms enables businesses to leverage historic trip sheets and real-time data to estimate time of delivery, and to optimize vehicle routes and sequence deliveries using information on local conditions such as traffic and weather. Data-driven dashboards also provide valuable insight into the performance of drivers, facilities, and operations, enabling organizations to examine key performance indicators such as total travel time, helping to benchmark and improve service planning.

With retailers under pressure to optimize delivery times and competing with each other to provide next day or even same-day delivery, these principles are also being used to improve warehouse operations. AI-powered systems can instantly map capacity and

---

5   https://www.ibm.com/blogs/blockchain/2018/07/creating-solutions-for-freight-management-with-ai-iot-and-blockchain/.

availability of goods within the warehouse, and match available manpower most effectively with current levels of demand.

Other uses include the ability to consolidate shipments more effectively by grouping items by location, customer, season, mode of freight, delivery timelines, and transport prerequisites, such as optimum ambient temperature and humidity. Operators can also gain critical insight into problems such as damage claims, helping them analyze problems in the supply chain, enhance damage mitigation approaches, or to inform the rates they charge for high-risk cargo.

3.4. *Real-time Monitoring and Tracking*

Consumers and regulators need to know that manufacturers have followed the rules surrounding ethical sourcing, counterfeiting, and illegal trafficking. Unfortunately, the complexity of supply chains often makes it difficult for retailers and manufacturers to verify this information and determine its initial point of entry.

This is where blockchain can have a transformational effect upon the logistics, manufacturing, and retail industries. The same technology that is used to log and record bitcoin and other cryptocurrency transactions can be applied to the supply chain.

One effective use case is to catalogue the transactions of goods between two counterparties on the blockchain. The recorded information of the transaction can include critical supply chain information such as origin, manufacturing or production date, cost price, and order quantity, which would be readily obtainable from the distributed ledgers. This allows for those involved in this transaction — including regulatory or other authorities — to re-trace every ingredient or element to its place of origin for whatever reason. The decentralized ledger makes it impossible for anyone to manipulate this data, giving regulators such as food standards agencies or drugs regulators the ability to determine who is responsible for contamination or other breaches of compliance.

Integrating IoT's real-time monitoring ability through its devices with blockchain's permission-based distributed ledger fortifies security and trackability accuracy and complexity, resulting in improvements across supply chains.[6] Enabling

---

6   https://www.forbes.com/sites/louiscolumbus/2019/01/13/top-10-ways-internet-of-things-and-blockchain-strengthen-supply-chains/#21cf78e05e4e

transparency reduces the need for cushion inventory by affording real-time visibility of stock levels and shipments. Urgent orders can also be expedited and rerouted, minimizing disruptions to production schedules and customer shipments. The combination of blockchain and IoT sensors is showing potential to revolutionize food supply chains, where sensors are used to track the freshness, quality, and safety of perishable foods.

In a specific use case, one major diamond producer, De Beers, has utilized the blockchain to track its precious stones from their mining point all the way to the point when they are finally cut and sold to consumers worldwide.[7] By doing so, the company ensures that it avoids 'blood diamonds' or stones obtained from war-torn regions, and assures that the consumers are buying from non-conflict areas and that they are in fact genuine precious stones. In another example, the world's largest mining firm, BHP (Australia), will also use the blockchain to improve its tracking throughout the mining process, and will be able to communicate that data with its vendors. This will increase efficiency internally, but it will also enable more transparency with its partners.

3.5. *Financing and Payments of Trades*

As one major sector of the trade and supply chain industry, financing would reap huge benefits from emerging technologies. According to a report[8] by World Economic Forum (WEF, in collaboration with Bain & Company, 2018), it is estimated that demand for financing transactions is projected to expand by 5% to 15% a year in the Americas and Western Europe, and 10% to 25% in Asia, with food and retail among the most active industries. However, it appears that much of that demand remains unmet and SMEs remain the most underserved. The Asian Development Bank (ADB) estimated a global trade finance gap of US$1.5 trillion in 2016, with most of the underserved businesses being in East Asia and the Pacific. The gap stems largely from hugely underserved small- and medium-sized enterprises (SMEs), combined with the considerable amount of paperwork required for communication among customs brokers,

---

7   https://www.forbes.com/sites/bernardmarr/2018/03/23/how-blockchain-will-transform-the-supply-chain-and-logistics-industry/#24945f2a5fec

8   Trade Tech – A New Age for Trade and Supply Chain Finance, http://www3.weforum.org/docs/WEF_White_Paper_Trade_Tech_.pdf

freight forwarders, transportation carriers, and a multitude of government agencies. Archaic paper-based and manual processes contribute to the complexity and procedural delays, introduce human errors and consequential risks, and impede reliable, real-time information gathering and tracking required for credible financing decisions (Mohamed and Ali, 2019).

Traditional trade and supply chain flows involve different channels which are opaque and have many types of loosely connected participants, which makes authenticating and verifying information very difficult. Distributed ledgers, by contrast, operate as secure, shared databases, where each participant has a copy of the stored data. When a transfer of funds or information about a shipment is recorded, it is validated, made transparent and available to all counterparties, and updated across the network almost immediately. Counterparties can initiate transactions by using encrypted digital signatures, which underpin "smart contracts", a digital protocol that verifies and enforces a contract without third parties.

Bain & Company[9] estimates that distributed ledger technology, if adopted the right way by all participants in the trade ecosystem, could reduce trade finance operating costs up to 70% and improve turnaround up to 80%, depending on the trade finance product involved.[10]

Depending on the product, the supply chain can extend over hundreds of layers, multiple geographical (international) locations, a multitude of invoices and payments, have several individuals and entities involved, and span over months. Since blockchains allow for transfer of funds anywhere in the world without the use of a traditional bank, it is very expedient for a supply chain that is globalized. In fact, the Australian vehicle manufacturer Tomcar pays its suppliers via the Bitcoin cryptocurrency.

3.6. Food Trust and Supply Integrity

The WEF (2018) suggests that reducing administration barriers in the international supply chain could drive global trade by nearly 15% and global GDP by 5%, providing a huge boost to economies

---

9   https://www.bain.com/insights/customer-experience-tools-blockchain/

10   Wait times for documents, for example, can be reduced far more than wait times for approval of a credit increase.

and job creation. Aside from making operations sharper and provide more data for retrospection, IoT is making supply chains more secure and transparent.

Sensors can be fitted to shipment to immediately relay if there has been any tampering or damage to the cargo. This is highly relevant to the food industry, where companies are equipping shipments with sensors that detect any breaks in the cold chain or spoilage and notify buyers and sellers immediately. Fraud and theft are also being fought with sensors, since the origin and passage of a transaction can be proven with reference to sensor data. IBM's Food Trust Blockchain solution has already introduced distributed ledger technology into the human food supply chain for the social good (see Figure 7.2). This traverses blockchain technology's mainstream adoption, enabling the data generated from sensors to be accessed through a public blockchain, which gives everyone involved in the process more oversight of the upstream and downstream channels. All these details are stored on a public ledger like that of IOTA,[11] and this can be independently verified and shared with ease.

Another critical IoT application for ensuring integrity in the food industry is farm-to-fork (or end-to-end) oversight of animal welfare conditions and the verification via tagging (genetic or otherwise) to ensure that the goods are as genuine as they are labelled. Fraud in food supply may not seem as pressing, but as the controversy around truffles and olive oil in Europe (with two-thirds being shown to be fake) proves, there is enormous profit to be made from the imitation of food sources or brand names. More seriously, the counterfeiting of drugs and expensive medication has killed about one million people each year due to bogus drugs,[12] according to the Interpol. About 50% of pharmaceutical products sold through rogue websites are typically fake, and up to 30% of drug products sold in emerging markets are counterfeit. Being able to authenticate where pharmaceutical drugs come from will not only help consumers but will also help to save lives.

---

11   IOTA is a public distributed ledger that utilizes an invention called the Tangle at its core, which utilizes the DAG (Directed Acyclic Graph). Sending IOTA will not require a transaction fee, and the token is designed for use as a payment network between machines on the Internet of Things.

12   https://www.insightcrime.org/news/brief/counterfeit-drugs-kill-1-million-annually-interpol/

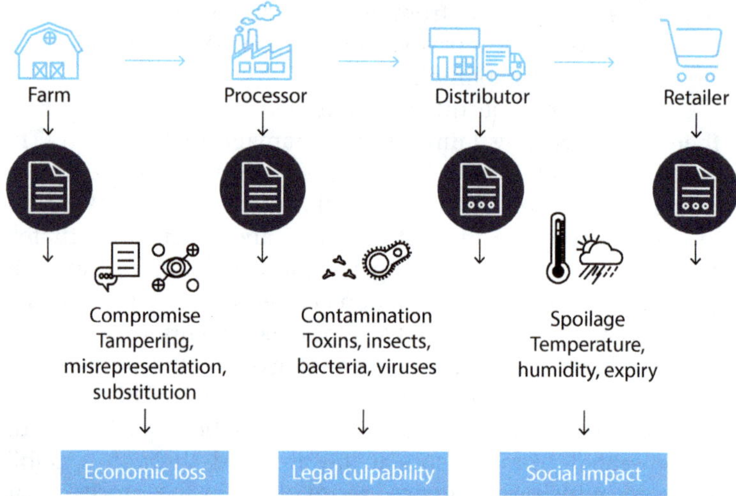

Figure 7.2: Food Trust and Supply Tracking to increase safety and traceability (Source: IBM)

Major suppliers like Unilever, Nestle, Tyson, and Walmart are using the blockchain to keep track of its food supplies sourced from suppliers in China and elsewhere by enabling transparency regardless of loosely-connected sub-suppliers. Figure 7.2 shows food supply tracking that records the parties (source, processor, distributor, and retailer) in the event of compromise, contamination, and spoilage. The blockchain records the origin of each piece of meat, processing plant, storage facility, and its expiry or sell-by-date.

3.7. Interoperability of Information and Systems

The endless succession of communication, feedback, and interface between a variety of cyber-physical systems propels the advancement of a cyber-physical system-of-systems as a whole (van Lier, 2015). This progression is similar to that of natural ecosystems, where organisms engage with their environments and its inhabitants, causing the entire ecosystem to be in a perpetual state of evolution. Due to this evolution of the ecosystem as a whole, the constituent organisms need to have the ability to constantly adapt to new circumstances. A cyber-physical system-of-systems can also be considered as a complex ecosystem made up of people and a wide range of different technological applications that is, as a whole, constantly evolving. According to Greer *et al.* (2019), one example of a cyber-physical system-of-systems is the industrial Internet of Things (IIoT). The development of global networking of sensors, machines, production processes, and factories will inevitably lead to new, digitised, and global industrial system-of-systems. Based on the interconnectedness of machines, production processes, and supply chains, a new and complex sociotechnical industrial whole is developing through the exchange and sharing of data and information. The capability to exchange and share data and information between a diversity of systems and entities based on a relationship of equality and trust is therefore the main condition for the development of this new industrial and sociotechnical whole.

Take the dispensation of healthcare today as an example. In its present state, healthcare depends largely on the patient. They decide when they need to see their doctor, generally only once visible symptoms have appeared or when an accident has occurred. They have to schedule an appointment. Often, they must remember the pertinent details of their medical history, and human beings, of course, they are fallible and forgetful. Instead, with interoperability of information and systems, we can imagine a nation of sensor-equipped patients. Machine learning monitors IoT sensor data built in the patient's home or domicile, and can determine — at an early stage — when something has gone wrong. The patient's virtual assistant can cross-reference their calendar with their doctor's, and schedule an appointment automatically. When the patient arrives, blockchain will ensure that they have a secure and accurate digital medical history for the doctor's reference.

4. Energy Consumption and Efficiency Costs

An exploratory report[13] (Grewal-Carr and Marshall, 2016) from Deloitte approximated that the cost of validating transactions on a blockchain is US$600 million annually, most of which goes into

---

13   https://www2.deloitte.com/content/dam/Deloitte/uk/Documents/Innovation/deloitte-uk-blockchain-full-report.pdf

powering mining operations which consumes a lot of electrical energy. An AI-integrated blockchainized system can possibly help organizations reduce their energy consumption by predicting the priority of transactions. This would allow enterprises to execute transactions faster by working on transactions that they can do first. Being able to learn and adapt to any environment, combined with blockchain, there is no doubt that AI can add efficiencies to the process and the architecture of the blockchain network.

Similarly, the blockchain can be utilized to sell five minutes of unused power during a downtime to another node that needs the additional power. Trading grid flexibility in this way could provide large efficiency benefits for power grid operators. Alex de Vries (2018) of PriceWaterhouseCoopers (PwC) reported that crypto-mining could actually consume 0.5% of the world's energy[14] and if de Vries' calculations of energy costs of a single Bitcoin transaction are accurate, a single Bitcoin transaction would consume about the same electricity as 100 loads of laundry washed and dried, and over 1,000 loads if they are only washed electrically. The development of an integrated trading system that can allow businesses to trade their option to use electricity during certain periods would definitely help in energy consumption. Alternatively, blockchain developers are working on protocols that are more energy-efficient without giving up its potencies.

5. Challenges to Adoption

Although the global blockchain adoption rate is increasing gradually, as reported by IT analysts such as Accenture, McKinsey, and IBM, the adoption rates in developed countries appear to be rather low. According to our own research, about one-fifth of supply chain professionals see a benefit in adopting blockchain; although there is already considerable interest in how the technology can be applied to issues such as traceability, transparency, and meeting regulatory compliance. The application of blockchain to logistics is clearly in its earliest stages, even if its potential is obvious. There are also several reasons for this. Clohessy, Acton, and Rogers (2019) used the Technology-Organization-Environment

---

14   https://www.crowdfundinsider.com/2019/03/145455-report-shows-bitcoin-is-grossly-energy-consumptive-but-is-proof-of-stake-relevant-for-bitcoin/

(TOE) framework (Tornatzky and Fleischer, 1990) to explain them (see Table 7.1).

Firstly, from a technological perspective, corporations were always concerned about new technology because of disruptions to their current processes. Some concerns that emerged as important were the perceived benefits from adoption measured against the level of complexity in development and deployment and its compatibility to the use case and existing systems. The perceived benefits here referred to the perception of

Table 7.1: Main Blockchain Adoption Considerations based on the Technology-Organization-Environment (TOE) framework

Technological Considerations		Organisational Considerations		Environmental Considerations	
Perceived benefits	10	Organisational Readiness	12	Regulatory Environment	11
Complexity	10	Top Management Support	8	Market Dynamics	9
Compatibility	8	Organisational Size	8	Industry Pressure	5
Data Security	6	Business Model Readiness	4	Government Support	5
Maturity	5	Technology Readiness	3	Business use case	3
Relative Advantage	4	Innovativeness	2	Trading Partner Support	3
Disintermediation	4	Participation Incentives	1	Critical User Mass	1
Smart Contract Coding	2	Blockchain Knowledge	1		
Architecture	1				
Permissions (Public vs. Private)	1				

Source: Clohessy, Acton and Rogers (2019)

the benefits (e.g., irreversibility, security, transaction speed, etc.) that will grow by adopting blockchain technology. Listed by virtue of consideration levels, Table 7.1 compiled all concerns through a detailed literature review. Complexity concerns extend to the intrinsic challenges (e.g., validation processes, smart contract structures, blockchain-programming skills, etc.) of developing blockchain applications. Finally, compatibility denotes the ability of blockchain technologies to interface and work with legacy systems (e.g., supply chain integration, system providers, payment integration, etc.) without conflict.

Next, the top three organizational considerations were organizational readiness, top management support, and organizational size (Clohessy, Acton, and Rogers, 2019). Organizational readiness is referred to as the availability of specific structural resources to adopt new digital innovations, categorised under human resources and financial and infrastructure readiness. These include employees with the mandatory experience, knowledge, and skills to adopt new digital innovations, and the allocated financial resources for new digital technological innovations. Top management support refers to the key-executive beliefs about digital transformation initiatives, participation in those initiatives, and the extent to which top management encourages digital innovation. High-level support for a specific digital innovation can instil long-term vision, ensure the commitment and optimal management of resources, create a conducive environment to innovate, and overcome barriers and resistance to change.

Finally, the top two environmental considerations were the regulatory environment and market dynamics (Clohessy, Acton, and Rogers, 2019). In terms of the regulatory environment consideration, with the introduction of any new technology (e.g., cloud computing and data security agreement) that disrupts an industry, authorities will appraise and undertake steps to assess new regulations for consumer protection, financial integrity, and the lack of legislation which is specific to blockchain. Market dynamics refers to the rapidly changing blockchain technological landscape which is forcing organisations to review their existing business processes to assess how they can adopt blockchain as a technology differentiator or not be left behind.

Every organisation is unique and has a different structure, culture, industry sectors, number of employees, and so on. The combination of these factors affects an organisation's approach to any new technology adoption.

6. Conclusion

Like most industries, data has been an essential component of international trade and its facilitation channels. Remote sensing, telematics, IoT devices, and means of transport produce large amounts of data that will be valuable to the logistics and supply chain industry if they can harness this information and turn it into actionable insights.

This insight can be used everywhere from improving warehouse management to finding the quickest transportation routes; it enables agile businesses to take advantage of rapidly-fluctuating prices for raw materials and manufactured goods. It can even bring much-needed accountability and transparency to enormously complicated supply chains, enabling businesses to prove the provenance of everything from authenticating luxury goods to the ingredients of our frozen dinners. Having the right data to support their AI-enabled algorithms enables such corporations to maximize efficiency across their supply chain, boosting profits, fast-tracking deliveries, and eventually reducing time, resources, and monetary costs for themselves and their customers.

So, the human way to look at the integration and interoperability of AI, blockchain, and IoT systems is that AI and machine learning systems *think*, while the sensing ability of IoT devices *feel*, and the blockchain's distributed ledger technology, *remembers*, via its historical and immutable records.

The integration of AI, blockchain, and IoT systems will optimize the elements of the moving experience across the end-to-end process, making links and connections that simply cannot be done today without unifying current fragmented data sets. In the future, wider access to data across an ecosystem and the advances in automated business logic via smart contracts could enable new and greater access for interoperable machines to traverse business ecosystems and deliver more comprehensive solutions to customers.

Bibliography

Arif, S., and S. Sidek. 2015. Application of Halalan Tayyiban in the Standard Reference for Determining Malaysian Halal Food. *Asian Social Science* 11: 17. doi:10.5539/ass.v11n17p116.

Clohessy, T., Acton, T. and Rogers, N. (2019). Blockchain Adoption: Technological, Organizational and Environmental Considerations, in H. Treiblmaier and R. Beck (Editors), *Business Transformation through Blockchain Volume I* (pp. 47–76). Palgrave Macmillan.

de Reuver, M., Sørensen, C. and Basole, R. C. (2017). The Digital Platform: A Research Agenda. *Journal of Information Technology*, pp. 1–12. https://doi.org/10.1057/s41265-016-0033-3.

de Vries A. (2018). Bitcoin's Growing Energy Problem. *Joule*. 2: 801-805. https://doi.org/10.1016/j.joule.2019.02.007

DHL in cooperation with Accenture (2018). *Blockchain In Logistics — Perspectives on the Upcoming Impact of Blockchain Technology and Use Cases for the Logistics Industry.*

Glaser, F. (2017). Pervasive Decentralisation of Digital Infrastructures: A Framework for Blockchain enabled System and Use Case Analysis, in *HICSS 2017 Proceedings*, pp. 1,543–1,552.

Greer, C., Burns, M., Wollman, D. and Griffor, E. (2019). Cyber-Physical Systems and Internet of Things, in *NIST Special Publication 1900-202*. March 2019. https://doi.org/10.6028/NIST.SP.1900-202.

Grewal-Carr, V. and Marshall, S. (2016). *Blockchain: Enigma, Paradox, Opportunity*, Deloitte, January 2016. https://www2.deloitte.com/content/dam/Deloitte/uk/Documents/Innovation/deloitte-uk-blockchain-full-report.pdf

Hawlitschek, F., Teubner, T. and Weinhardt, C. (2016). Trust in the Sharing Economy. *Die Unternehmung – Swiss Journal of Business Research and Practice*, 70(1), pp. 26–44. https://doi.org/10.5771/0042-059X-2016-1-26.

Iansiti, M., and Lakhani, K. R. (2017). The Truth about Blockchain. *Harvard Business Review*. Retrieved from https://hbr.org/2017/01/the-truth-aboutblockchain. Accessed 5 April 2019.

Kosba, A., Miller, A., Shi, E., Wen, Z. and Papamanthou, C. (2016). Hawk: The Blockchain Model of Cryptography and Privacy-preserving Smart Contracts, in M. Locasto and K. Butler (Chairs), *2016 IEEE Symposium on Security and Privacy* (pp. 839–858), The Fairmont, San Jose, California, 23–25 May, IEEE Computer Society, Washington, DC. Retrieved from https://doi.org/10.1109/SP.2016.55. Accessed 4 July 2017.

Manzouri, M., M. N. A. Rahman, N. Saibani, and C. R. C. H. Mohd Zain. (2013). Lean Supply Chain Practices in the Halal Food. *International Journal of Lean Six Sigma* 4 (4): 389–408. doi:10.1108/IJLSS-10-2012-0011.

Mehta, D. and Striapunia, K. (2017). FinTech 2017, market size, business models, blockchain and company profiles (Statista report). Retrieved from https://www.statista.com/study/45600/statista-report-fintech/. Accessed 5 August 2017.

Mohamed, H. and Ali, H. (2019). *Blockchain, Fintech and Islamic Finance — Building the Future of the New Islamic Digital Economy.* De I G Press, Boston/Berlin.

Nofer, M., Gomber, P., Hinz, O. and Schiereck, D. (2017). Blockchain. *Business and Information Systems Engineering,* 59(3), pp. 183–187.

Paech, P. (2017). The Governance of Blockchain Financial Networks. *The Modern Law Review,* 80(6), pp. 1,073–1,110. https://doi.org/10.1111/1468-2230.12303.

Parker, G. and Van Alstyne, M. (2017). Innovation, Openness, and Platform Control. *Management Science,* November, https://doi.org/10.1287/mnsc.2017.2757.

Pilkington, M. (2015). Blockchain technology: Principles and Applications. *Research Handbook on Digital Transformations* (pp. 225–253). Retrieved from https://doi.org/10.4337/9781784717766.00019. Accessed 5 April 2019.

Schneider, J., Blostein, A., Lee, B., Kent, S., Groer, I. and Beardsley, E. (2016). *Profiles in Innovation — BlockChain: Putting Theory into Practice.* Goldman Sachs.

Tieman, M., J. G. A. J. Van Der Vorst, and M. C. Ghazali. (2012). Principles in Halal Supply Chain Management. *Journal of Islamic Marketing* 3 (3): 217–243. doi:10.1108/17590831211259727.

Tornatzky, L.G. and Fleischer, M. (1990). *The Processes of Technological Innovation.* Lexington: Lexington Books.

Underwood, S. (2016). Blockchain beyond Bitcoin. *Communications of the ACM,* 59 (11), pp. 15–17.

van Lier, B. (2015). The Enigma of Context Within Network-centric Environments. Context as Phenomenon Within an Emerging Internet of Cyber-Physical Systems. *Cyber Physical Systems,* I (1), pp. 46–64.

van Lier, B. and Hardjono, T. W. (2011). A Systems Theoretical Approach of Interoperability of Information. *Systemic Practice and Action Research,* 24 (5), pp. 479–497.

World Economic Forum in collaboration with Bain & Company (2018), *Trade Tech – A New Age for Trade and Supply Chain Finance*, http://www3.weforum.org/docs/WEF_White_Paper_Trade_Tech_.pdf.

World Economic Forum, (2018). Trade Tech – A New Age for Trade and Supply Chain Finance. In Collaboration with Bain & Company. January 2018. http://www3.weforum.org/docs/WEF_White_Paper_Trade_Tech_.pdf

SMART MANUFACTURING AND THE FACTORY OF THE FUTURE

Smart factories represent the fusion of a myriad of technologies and business approaches to production in manufacturing. In its fully-optimized form, smart factories can evolve to be adaptable systems that can enable continuous improvements of processes and optimize supply chain planning.

In this chapter, we explore the convergence and fusion of various technologies to describe the Factory of the Future. We detail how manufacturing will be transformed in the digital era through technologies that have defined it such as AI, IoT, and Machine Learning to form the Digital Twin and the emergence of Cyber-Physical Systems (CPS). We analyze the shifts in manufacturing practices, and illustrate several key factors that will shape the future manufacturing environment such as manufacturing operations, Lean Production principles, advanced prototype modelling, IIoT, and the use of integrated manufacturing analytics and the transformation of value chains to value network. We conclude with our thoughts on sustainable innovation and the workforce of the future with increasing scarcity of proficient IR4.0 professionals to support and build the future.

Keywords: *Cyber-Physical Systems, Digital Twins, IIoT.*

Contents

1. Introduction

Manufacturing is essential for long-term economic growth and economic resilience. The link between a thriving manufacturing sector and economic growth is a direct and significant one, particularly regarding employment and industries that themselves are linked. In fact, manufacturing has the largest multiplier effect of any economic sector (WEF, 2016). However, many of its characteristics are changing profoundly. Physical production processes are increasingly at the centre of much wider value chains. Advancements in new generation information technologies like AI, Big Data, cloud computing, high-performance computing, IoT, etc., have wide applications in many sectors of the economy, including the future of manufacturing. The Artificial Intelligence (AI) market is predicted to grow from US$8 billion in 2016 to US$72 billion in 2021. According to the WIPO (2019), 86% of the top 100 companies in research and development (R&D) spending worldwide are manufacturers. Top technology investment areas for manufacturers include: advanced analytics, cloud computing, modelling and simulation, Industrial Internet of Things (IIoT) platforms, and optimization and predictive analytics. The application of IoT is projected to generate \$1.2 to \$3.7 trillion of value globally by 2025, in four primary forms: (1) operational efficiency; (2) predictive and preventative maintenance; (3) supply chain management; and (4) inventories and logistics (Manyika *et al.*, 2015).

Disruptive technologies will drive digitalization in manufacturing as part of an ecosystem-wide transformation. Companies worldwide are engaging in digital transformation that are revolutionizing the future of manufacturing. This digitalization of manufacturing is changing how products are designed, fabricated, used, operated, and serviced post-sale, just as it is transforming the operations, processes, and energy footprint of factories and the management of manufacturing supply chains. Sophisticated modelling and simulation, data acquisition, analysis and reporting, and breakthroughs in imaging and manufacturing come together for organizations to achieve what was once just a dream. Among the most important of these are the marriage of sensors and software into the Internet of Things (IoT). Smart manufacturing is being driven by the advent and maturation of many technologies, including: high-performance computing (HPC)-powered computer aided design (CAD) and engineering (CAE) software; cloud computing; the Internet of Things (IoT); advanced sensor technologies; 3D printing; industrial robotics; data analytics; Machine Learning; and wireless connectivity that better enables machine-to-machine (M2M) communications.

In this chapter, we explore the convergence and fusion of various technologies to describe the Factory of the Future. In order to do so, we uncover facts and trends to provide understanding of the future of manufacturing through its history, industrial revolutions driven by manufacturing, and its evolution. Next, we detail how manufacturing will be transformed in the digital era through technologies that have defined it such as AI, IoT, and Machine Learning to form the Digital Twin and the emergence of Cyber-Physical Systems (CPS). We analyze the shifts in manufacturing practices, and illustrate several key factors that will shape the future manufacturing environment such as manufacturing operations, Lean Production principles, advanced prototype modelling, IIoT and the use of integrated manufacturing analytics, and the transformation of value chains to value network. As systems scale and integrate with other systems, we include important discussions on data security and important risk mitigation procedures. Lastly, we conclude with our thoughts on sustainable innovation and the workforce of the future with increasing scarcity of proficient IR4.0 professionals to support advanced manufacturing systems that will build the future.

2. Understanding the Future of Manufacturing

Manufacturing in 2050 will look very different from what it is today. It may well be unrecognisable from the manufacturing of 30 years ago. Market-leading firms will be capable of rapidly adapting their physical and intellectual infrastructures to exploit changes in technology as manufacturing becomes faster, more responsive to changing global markets, and closer to customers. Successful firms will also harness a wider skills base, with highly qualified leaders and managers whose expertise combines both commercial and technical acumen, typically in science, technology, engineering, or mathematics.

Manufacturing is no longer just about production; it is a much wider set of activities that create value for the nation and benefits for wider society. Manufacturing often involves significant innovation (improving productivity, research and development), and with it creates jobs that are high-income because it is highly skilled. It also contributes to the rebalancing of the economy, with its strong role on exports and import substitutions.

2.1. *History of Manufacturing*

There have been three stages of industrial revolution (Figure 8.1), whereby the First Industrial Revolution used steam power and water to mechanize and increase production. The Second Industrial Revolution used electric power to create the bulk production. The Third Industrial Revolution used advanced electronics and information technology (IT) to make the production autonomous. Now, we are in the Fourth Industrial Revolution, where the digital revolution is typified by the fusion of technologies and cyber-physical systems that are blurring the lines between the physical, biological, and digital spheres.

2.2. *Evolution of Manufacturing*

Digital experience that visualize and control the entire industrial ecosystem, improve productivity and competitiveness, thereby

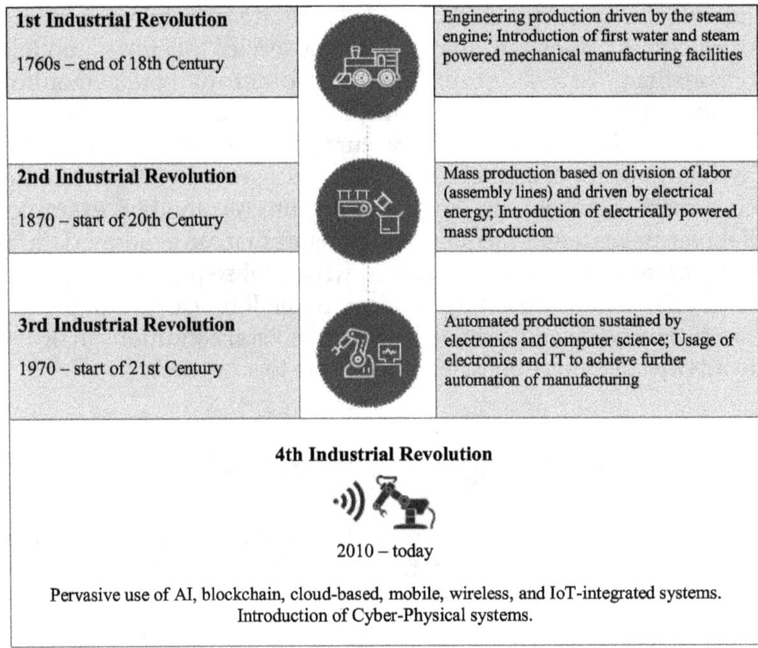

Figure 8.1: The First Three Stages of Industrial Revolution

enabling high-added-value networks in which the real and virtual merge to create, produce, and exchange sustainable experiences and continuously update or improve those experiences through the analysis of real-world user experience feedback.

The quality and skills of the workforce will be a critical factor in capturing competitive advantage. It is essential that governments focus on the supply of skilled workers, including apprenticeship schemes, support for researchers, and the supply of skilled managers. Firms will need to pay much more attention to building multidisciplinary teams to develop increasingly complex products, and also innovative business models.

As far as the business model is concerned, manufacturing-enabled service is becoming the main driving force for defining value. In these cases, manufacturing initiates value creation, and technology enables it. Many manufacturing companies have realized that manufacturing and service are converging because economics has switched from product delivery to continuing interaction with the customer. Advanced and profitable services that are enabled by intelligent sensors and communications are gradually becoming the business model of choice for many manufacturers (Giret *et al.*, 2016). There are increasing numbers of successful blended manufacturing-service business models (Esmaeilian, 2016). For example, in order to better monitor performance and detect problems, Rolls-Royce uses sensors in its jet engines. In fact, this company turned its product into a service by charging its customers for engine usage rather than having customers purchase an engine outright. As another example, Babolat makes tennis racquets with sensors that can generate data to analyze the player's tennis strokes, which subsequently allows the enterprise to offer coaching services. Some John Deere equipment can receive and send data on weather and soil conditions in order to advise customers on when and where to sow seeds.

3. Manufacturing in the Digital Era

The Future of Manufacturing is based on the concept of the smart factory, which interconnects machinery and systems on production sites, but also outside to clients, partners, and other production facilities. It is a digitalization of manufacturing processes directed by new ways of inventing, learning, producing, and trading that are disrupting all sectors of the economy and society. Advancements in new generation technologies like AI, Big Data, cloud computing, IoT, etc., have wide applications in smart manufacturing, coupled with advanced algorithms to process huge amounts of data and analytics in the cyber world will define the future of smart manufacturing, and intelligent companies.

3.1. *AI, IoT, and Machine Learning = Digital Twin*

The advent of the Industry 4.0 revolution realized that if the production systems are made intelligent and smart, they can function more efficiently and reduce costs. There have been many developments to enable this, one of which is the digital twin (Grieves, 2014).

The "digital twin" is a concept that creates a model of a physical asset for predictive maintenance. This model will continually adapt to changes in the environment or operation using real-time sensory data and can forecast the future of the corresponding physical assets (Tuegel *et al.*, 2011). It can monitor and identify potential issues with its real physical counterpart. In addition, it allows for the prediction of the remaining useful life (RUL) of the physical twin by leveraging a combination of physics-based models and data-driven analytics. It consists of three main parts: (1) physical products in real space, (2) virtual products in virtual space, and (3) the connections of data and information that will tie the virtual and real products together. Therefore, collecting and analyzing a large volume of manufacturing data to find the information and connections has become the key to smart manufacturing.

Figure 8.2: A Representation of a Digital Twin Model

Physical object, process, or system can be represented with the help of the digital twin (Figure 8.2). With the combination of data and intelligence that represent the structure, context, and behavior of a physical system, it offers an interface that allows monitoring the past and present operation and makes prediction about the future (Grieves, 2014). Therefore, the digital twin integrate AI, software analytics, and machine learning data to create digital simulation models that update and change as their physical equivalents change. This provides real-time monitoring and updates from multiple sources at the same time. It creates virtual models for physical objects in the digital way to simulate their behavior (Constante, 2018). The virtual models could understand the state of physical entities through sensing data, to estimate and analyze the dynamic changes. The digital twin would achieve the optimization of the whole production process (Tao *et al.*, 2018).

AI will enhance the functionalities of digital twins in which a dynamic software model is formed of a physical thing or system that relies on sensor data to understand its state, respond to changes, improve operations, and add value. Currently, the Industrial Internet of Things (IIoT) use digital twins for implementation in manufacturing industry, like how IoT devices and IoT systems can be managed and optimized throughout their lifecycle using the mechanism of digital twins (Canedo, 2016).

3.2. Emergence of Cyber-Physical Systems

The digital twin concept gives rise to cyber-physical systems (CPS) that makes possible the analytical data-driven control of the resources or physical environments. The physical systems collect sensory information from the real world and send them to the digital twin computational modules through wireless communication technologies (Figure 8.3). The technologies used for the implementation of smart manufacturing span a wide spectrum of domains, which include related techniques such as the Internet of Services (IoS), CPS, Big Data, and advanced

Figure 8.3: The Physical Asset Collects Data for its Twin Computational Modules After Build

robotics (Loucez and Wang, 2014). The rise of IoT/CPS and mobile phones/tablets have made the products more connected and accessible, from which the wealth of data generated allows for accurate targeting and further enabling the proactive management of enterprises through informed, timely, and in-depth decision execution (Leiva, 2015). As such, the interaction of human agents, raw data, and AI algorithms has far-reaching effects on manufacturing efficiency.

4. Shifts in Manufacturing Practices

The factory of the future will be a system of hybrid systems of robots and humans, additive and subtractive manufacturing, composites and metals, digital and analog processes, cyber and physical systems, and nano and macro scales. Robots will not completely replace humans; rather, they will work collaboratively with a balanced distribution of responsibility.

The new era of global manufacturing is driven by shifts in demand and by innovations in materials, processes, technology, and operations. The prospect for manufacturing has turned global, and new customers will come from developing nations who will also be the source of low-cost production. Due to the proliferation of products to meet fragmenting demands, value-added services and innovation becomes significantly more important. With the greater use of intelligent product design and manufacturing to boost resource efficiency, there is a growing scarcity of technical talent to develop and run manufacturing systems. We discuss the key areas and expectations of future manufacturing practices and what the new manufacturing environment will possibly entail to capture business value in the following sections.

4.1. Manufacturing Operations

The shift brought on by the digital transformation has also brought on the shift in customer behaviour. Companies need to manage new customer demands and expectations for highly customized products and shorter delivery times. Addressing these new challenges requires more flexibility and higher efficiency from their manufacturing assets. The overall challenge is to manage new customer demands, highly customized products, shorter delivery times, and optimize costs to improve margins. From the manufacturing point of view, these can be achieved through:

- Better synchronization across all manufacturing activities
- Improve efficiency of manufacturing assets
- Capitalize, share, and develop operator skills

In terms of increase in efficiencies, this is done through:

- Visibility, control, orchestration, and automation of operational activities
- Business process activities and exhaustive data collection for informed decision support and continuous improvement
- Comprehensive performance monitoring

As for quality, advancements can be made on the margins of:

- Comprehensive and real-time quality management across the enterprise
- Quality, traceability, and genealogy across parts, processes, and resources
- Corrective actions to resolve problems and quality issues

To gain competitive advantage, shorter delivery times require faster speed and more agility in production. This can be done via:

- Business process-driven tasks and exception handling for agility and responsiveness
- Real-time digital continuity across engineering and manufacturing
- Visibility and synchronization of operations across departments to reduce risk

The shift in manufacturing operations requires digital continuity from engineering to manufacturing which provides the ability to interface with IIoT devices installed on the production line. The new manufacturing environment synchronizes all departments to manage operations efficiently, and collaborate easily by consolidating all information in a single platform and making it available in the context of each team. It will also deliver the right materials to the right place at the right time, while having records of detailed genealogy on components for traceability.

They have ready access to production-activity information — Line Monitoring Cockpit and team information with list of actions and issues. All this information are made available for more collaborative work and stronger team involvement.

4.2. Lean Production Principles

Industry 4.0 can be integrated in Lean Production and, beyond that, improve Lean Production by increased integration of ICT. This benefit accelerates the shift of Industry 4.0 from science to reality. In practice, new solutions must add value to users and must have an acceptable risk. The integration of Industry 4.0 solutions, which are in general connected with high investments, is especially lucrative in areas where cost-saving and simple methods of Lean Production are not completely fulfilling today's requirements.

Key routines in operational management are mainly coming from the Lean principles, which involve the team to continuously improve overall performance. The goals for successful management of production facilities are faster and better reaction to manufacturing issues, stronger collaboration within and between teams, and fewer non-value-added tasks. To achieve them, production needs to increase efficiency with digital lean by:

- digitalizing Lean and facilitate Lean practices across organizations for continuous improvement
- managing operational performance and Lean KPIs

and digitize sustainable continuous improvement through:

- Best-practice benchmarking and sharing for operational processes
- Cross-functional and cross-organizational collaboration for greater awareness

and improve team intelligence via:

- Collaborative worker interaction and creativity within and across peer groups
- Capitalized know-how of the company for better collective intelligence

Such improvement initiatives can be done via integrated platforms that combine Lean Best Practices and Operational Metrics on a single collaborative virtual experience platform.

Besides isolated applications, the framework should define interfaces how such solutions can complement each other and how to embed them into an existing environment. Similar to service-oriented architectures (SOA), in the domain of Lean Production, CPS can offer required services of a working station to nearby and superior systems. By this, working stations can be flexibly added to production lines and are able to process commands from a superior production control system. Furthermore, CPS can exchange data with sensors, actuators, or PLCs, or can interact via human machine interface with employees at working stations. As a result, manual working stations can be updated with automation technology and vice versa, without changing superior manufacturing execution system.

4.3. *Modelling Prototypes and Builds*

Model-based manufacturing allows manufacturers to model and perform "what if" analysis on manufacturing assets, products, and processes to address current and future challenges. A fusion of technologies blurs the lines between the physical and digital domains, collectively referred to as cyber-physical systems.

Digital twins provide information on the workings of the asset, such as design specifications, engineering models, and the as-built and operational data that are unique to that asset. They effect synchronization between the virtual and real world. The digital thread is the communication framework that connects data from all areas of the asset and provides a combined view of the data for the asset's entire life cycle. Similar to what just in time (JIT) manufacturing was intended to achieve by delivering the "right components to the right place at the right time", the digital thread concept is meant to deliver the right information to the right place at the right time. When employed at the prototyping stage, digital twins can enable manufacturers to develop and validate different scenarios in the work cell before implementing them in the real world.

The overall challenge is to limit risk when investing in new manufacturing assets or existing facility change. This can be done through virtual simulation and validation to validate projected results in advance. From the modelling perspective, the tasks are to reduce cost and time to digitalize existing resources to generate models for simulation, manage large numbers of product variants having a high-frequency of product changes, simulate manufacturing processes, and validate asset capability in context of real organizational conditions.

Such actions can increase speed and efficiency by:

- Validating and testing manufacturing strategies, processes, and throughput to understand enterprise behavior
- Reducing time and cost by simulating the impact of product introductions and changes or factory configuration changes

The responsiveness and agility of manufacturing firms can be improved via:

- Identification and reduction the risk of interdependencies and bottlenecks with what-if scenario analysis
- Achievement of real-time digital continuity between product engineering, manufacturing engineering, and manufacturing operations
- Virtually modelling manufacturing processes based on real production constraints and data

It benefits from the intelligence of model and simulation based on real production data and new scenarios to test and run. Concurrently with virtual reality training on the new line configuration, the aggregation of new data can be consolidated for production line optimization.

4.4. IIoT and Manufacturing Analytics

In manufacturing, IoT devices generate the data from product lifecycle, such as design, manufacturing, MRO, etc., (Li *et al.*, 2015). Manufacturing data are generally from the following aspects:

- Data from the manufacturing systems, e.g., MES, PDM, SCM, ERP, etc., and from other computer-aided systems like CAD/CAM, CAE, etc.

- Data from Internet/users, e.g., from e-commerce sites — Amazon, Shopify, or social media sites — Facebook, Instagram, Twitter, etc.
- Data from manufacturing equipment with respect to real-time performance, material of product data, environmental data, etc.

Processing of the collected data should go through various steps to extract the information. As the data collected via various ways like sensors, application programming interface (API), software development kit (SDK), etc., undergoes cleaning before processing and analyzing. This cleaned data integrates with and is stored for the exchange and sharing for manufacturing data at all levels (Zhu *et al.*, 2016). Further, the real-time data or offline data analysis and mining by advanced data analysis methods and tools like AI and Machine Learning, deep learning, etc., utilize cloud computing (Siddiqa *et al.*, 2016). The valuable information extracted from large number of dynamic and fuzzy data enables manufacturers to deepen their understandings of various stages of product lifecycle. Hence, this helps the manufacturers to make more rational and informed decisions.

4.5. *Value Chain to Value Network*

Contemporary manufacturing has evolved from a system of isolated factories as the centerpieces of production towards international production networks that link firms and countries. With the network of sub-networks, machine with machine, factory with factory, and enterprise with enterprise are able to communicate with one another in real time. Sensors, data sharing, and networking provide unprecedented power to industrial and manufacturing companies. These networks are complex value chains, ranging from being global to local. The value chains determine where value is created and distributed, who captures and controls it, and the conditions under which buyers, suppliers, and intermediaries in the system can generate growth and improve productivity.

Good manufacturing requires good planning. Value Network Optimization will show you how to resolve challenges, optimize supply chain planning, and enhance transparency and efficiency. The challenge is to maintain and exceed production rates, maximize asset utilization, and minimize operation, employee, and maintenance costs. To do so, companies need to improve customer service by:

- Optimizing throughput to meet or exceed customer service level commitments
- Continuously balancing production variables for optimal outcomes based on business objectives
- Improving available-to-promise accuracy based on a true reflection of value network constraints

They also need to reduce costs by:

- Enabling dynamic rescheduling to reduce the impact of costly production disruptions
- Lowering inventory without impacting production
- Improving transportation and delivery costs through optimized routing

Technological, regulatory, and market changes also have an impact on value chains, and trends influence design, innovation, fabrication, and distribution. Reshoring and nearshoring will affect the nature of and extent to which outsourcing and offshoring of activities will occur for value chains to grow. A country's capacity to logistically support networks of firms that are segregated by space or distance will also influence value chains.

5. Data Security

Bringing the Internet to the manufacturing industry offers opportunities but also new challenges. The required information flow across many communication networks raises questions about IT and data security that was not relevant when the machines were not programmable and were not connected to any other infrastructure except the power. Therefore, providing security or maintaining the security in the current manufacturing system in organizations are becoming a challenging task due to the cyberattacks and intrusions in current scenario. The security required for the manufacturing system for the following five levels as depicted in the computer-integrated manufacturing (CIM) model (Tuptuk and Hailes, 2018).

CIM is a highly integrated model that has been used and incorporated into many models and standards in the manufacturing industry.

1. *Enterprise/Corporate Level*: At this level, the decisions related to operational management which define the workflows to produce the end product are made.
2. *Plant Management Level*: This level manages the decisions locally on the plant management network.
3. *Supervisory Level*: This level manages various manufacturing cells, each performing a different manufacturing process.
4. *Cell Control Level*: At this level, processes perform different actions.
5. *Sensor Actuator Level*: Here, the sensors, actuators, controllers integrate to perform the physical process.

Depending on its design, individual digitalized manufacturing model is vulnerable to specific security attacks. Some protocols which are used to support such infrastructure — modbus, distributed network protocol (DNP3), industrial Ethernet, PROFIBUS, building automation and control networking (BACnet), etc., are only used for supervisory and control mechanisms but not security and lack mechanisms to provide authentication, integrity, freshness of the data, non-repudiation, confidentiality, and measures to detect faults and abnormal behavior. The following are the cyber liabilities for most of the manufacturers:

- interruption in business,
- data breach,
- cyber extortion,
- intellectual property, and
- third party damage.

In order to prevent such occurrences, measures need to be put in place to counter security discrepancies:

A. Public Key Infrastructure

The implementation of public key infrastructure (PKI) architectures involves the use of digital device certificates. Implementing PKI into embedded systems secures the communication layer, creating a system that verifies the authenticity, configuration, and integrity of connected devices. This makes PKI ideal for large-scale security deployments that require a high level of security with minimal impact on performance (Tuptuk and Hailes, 2018).

B.   Encryption of the data

Highly confidential data must be encrypted to ensure that only authorized users have access by deploying anti-malware and hardening software on all IT and OT systems. In addition, the use of symmetric encryption algorithms, hybrid encryption schemes, cryptographic hash functions, digital signatures, key agreement, and distribution protocols are widely used to ensure only authorized entities.

C.   Intrusion detection systems

It is always necessary to monitor the dynamic behavior of the security systems and seek to find if there is any abnormal activity. Intrusion detection system (IDS) approaches tackle these issues. IDS are classified by source of data (audit source) — also called network-based or host-based and detection technique (the data needed for analysis) — also called knowledge-based or behavior-based. Receiver operating characteristics (ROC) curve, which depicts the detection probability versus false alarm probability, evaluates the performance of IDS. Studies (Roosta *et al.*, 2008; Shin *et al.*, 2010; Carcano *et al.*, 2011) show that most work in this area has been in behavior-based network intrusion systems, since knowledge-based systems require detailed knowledge of previous exploits to define characteristics of the attack. Hence, IDS research for smart manufacturing and IoT systems is still in progress and face a lot of challenges due to limited testbed availability and insufficient data from real incidents.

D.   Policies and Regulations

There are various special guidelines to enforce security mechanisms in smart manufacturing systems. Some of these guides are Guide to Industrial Control Systems (ICS) for SCADA systems, the National Institute of

Standards and Technology (NIST), Distributed Control Systems (DCS), Department of Homeland Security (DHS), the Centre for the Protection of National Infrastructure (CPNI), and so on.

Planning for security involves understanding the nature of threats, identifying vulnerabilities, quantifying the value to be lost if in case of security breaches, and investing in security appropriately. This gives an autonomous model in which products and machines will become active participants in IoT behaving as autonomous agents throughout the production line.

6. Sustainable Innovation and Workforce of the Future

Industry–academia–government collaboration from benchtop to marketplace is increasingly important in order to bring each stakeholder's best strengths to the partnership and avoid breakdowns along the innovation value chain.

Material innovation will continue to be an important topic for science, technology, and economic policy. Manufacturing and materials are inseparable. Materials provide the "work" for manufacturing, whereas manufacturing adds value to raw materials.

A common theme of all the future trends is the need for a highly talented, skilled, and flexible workforce. Lack of a skilled manufacturing workforce is perhaps the greatest threat to next-generation intelligent manufacturing around the world. This shortage comes in at least two dimensions. First, there are not enough people with the necessary skills to fill manufacturing positions. That is to say, the quantity and quality of the workforce carrying out the manufacturing of the future are insufficient. There is a need to consistently reach out to young people in the education system to encourage them to study STEM (science, technology, engineering, and math) subjects to keep their future options open; focusing on accessing and attracting international talent for example through 'science visas'; and building and maintaining existing workforce capability, for example, by encouraging apprenticeship programs, continual vocational education, and training. On top of managing internal workforce, the best companies will establish and manage an extended talent ecosystem, comprising multiple talent pools and spanning multiple generations. By working to address future skills needs and talent instability, leaders can prepare now to operate effectively in the business environment of tomorrow.

7. Conclusion

Manufacturing is indeed the foundation for building economic prosperity in industrialized nations. Today, technology and innovation drive growth within the sector and spur a constant upgrading of its capabilities. Manufacturing evolves through global economic dynamics, as well as advanced equipment and processing technologies, to produce more diverse and sophisticated products. Thus, it opens the door not only for employment that requires higher skill levels at higher wages, but also for a greater convergence of skills. Understanding the changes in manufacturing will enable economies to establish their own capabilities to innovate and set new development opportunities, including multiplying effects on wages.

A forward-thinking company should have the ability to recognize an unknown scenario, break down the problem into pieces, apply knowledge to solve the pieces of the problem that it can solve, and look for data or knowledge outside its data base for solutions to other pieces, or simply ask for human intervention. Once the "new" or "unknown" problem is solved, the manufacturing company becomes more "intelligent" than it was before, because lessons have been learned by the system. This situational awareness and learning capabilities are perhaps the most defining characteristics of Industry 4.0.

Shaping manufacturing's future requires an awareness of environmental constraints and vulnerabilities, as well as a commitment to address both from planetary and social perspectives. Manufacturing must minimize its environmental impact for society to achieve sustainable development. Moreover, an economy's product and material flows need to be designed to restore or recycle materials used in production, delivery and recycling. Clean technologies that refocus the use of rare and high-energy-consuming resources are becoming an important source of sustainable growth and innovation in manufacturing.

Bibliography

Canedo, A. (2016). Industrial IoT lifecycle via Digital Twins. In: Proceedings of the Eleventh IEEE/ACM/IFIP International Conference on Hardware/Software Codesign and System Synthesis, p. 29, ACM.

Carcano, A., Coletta, A., Guglielmi, M., Masera, M., Fovino, I.N., Trombetta, A. (2011). A multidimensional critical state analysis for detecting intrusions in SCADA systems. *IEEE Transactions on Industrial Informatics*, 7(2), pp. 179–186.

Constante, T.A.D.S.L. (2018). *Contribution for a Simulation Framework for Designing and Evaluating Manufacturing Systems*.

Esmaeilian, B., Behdad, S. and Wang, B. (2016). The Evolution and Future of Manufacturing: A Review. *Journal of Manufacturing Systems*, 39, pp. 79–100.

Foresight (2013). The Future of Manufacturing: A New Era of Opportunity and Challenge for the UK Summary Report. The Government Office for Science, London.

Giret, A., Garcia, E., and Botti, V. (2016). *An Engineering Framework for Service-oriented Intelligent Manufacturing Systems Comput Ind*, 81, pp. 116–127.

Grieves, M. (2014). Digital Twin: Manufacturing Excellence through Virtual Factory Replication. White Paper.

Lee, J., Ardakani, H.D., Yang, S., Bagheri, B. (2015). Industrial Big Data Analytics and Cyber-Physical Systems for Future Maintenance & Service Innovation. *Procedia CIRP* 38, pp. 3–7.

Lee, J., Bagheri, B., Kao, H.A. (2015). A Cyber-Physical Systems Architecture for Industry 4.0-based Manufacturing System. *Manufacturing Letters*. 3: 18–23.

Leiva, C. (2015). On the Journey to a Smart Manufacturing Revolution. Ind. Week.

Li, J., Tao, F., Cheng, Y., Zhao, L. (2015). Big Data in Product Lifecycle Management. *International Journal of Advanced Manufacturing and Technology*. 81(1–4), pp. 667–684.

Louchez, A., Wang, B. (2014). From Smart Manufacturing to Manufacturing Smart. Automation World.

Manyika, J. *et al.*, "The Internet of Things: Mapping the Value Beyond the Hype" (McKinsey Global Institute, June 2015), p. 66.

Qi, Q., Tao, F., Zuo, Y., Zhao, D. (2018). Digital Twin Service Towards Smart Manufacturing. *Procedia CIRP* 72(1), pp. 237–242.

Roosta, T., Nilsson, D.K., Lindqvist, U., Valdes, A. (2008). An intrusion detection system for wireless process control systems. In: 5th IEEE International Conference on Mobile Ad Hoc and Sensor Systems, pp. 866–872. IEEE.

Shin, S., Kwon, T., Jo, G.Y., Park, Y., Rhy, H. (2010). An experimental study of hierarchical intrusion detection for wireless industrial sensor networks. *IEEE Transactions on Industrial Informatics* 6(4), pp. 744–757.

Siddiqa, A., Hashem, I.A.T., Yaqoob, I., Marjani,M., Shamshirband, S., Gani, A., Nasaruddin, F. (2016). A Survey of Big Data Management: Taxonomy and State-of-the-Art. *Journal of Network and Computer Applications.* 71, pp. 151–166.

Tao, F., Cheng, J., Qi, Q., Zhang, M., Zhang, H., Sui, F. (2018). Digital Twin-driven Product Design, Manufacturing and Service with Big Data. *International Journal of Advanced Manufacturing and Technology.* 94 (9–12), pp. 3,563–3,576.

Tuegel, E.J., Ingraffea, A.R., Eason, T.G., Spottswood, S.M. (2011). Reengineering Aircraft Structural Life Prediction Using a Digital Twin. *International Journal of Aerospace Engineering.* 154798: 14.

Tuptuk, N. and Hailes, S. (2018). Security of Smart Manufacturing Systems. *Journal of Manufacturing Systems.* 47, pp. 93–106.

Uhlemann, T.H.J., Lehmann, C., Steinhilper, R. (2017). The Digital Twin: Realizing the Cyber-Physical Production System for Industry 4.0. *Procedia CIRP.* 61: 335–340.

World Economic Forum, (2016). Manufacturing Our Future Cases on the Future of Manufacturing. White Paper, May 2016.

WIPO (2019). The Global Innovation Index 2019. https://www.wipo.int/edocs/pubdocs/en/wipo_pub_gii_2019-chapter1.pdf

Zhang, Y., Zhang, G., Wang, J., Sun, S., Si, S., Yang, T. (2015). Realtime Information Capturing and Integration Framework of the Internet of Manufacturing Things. *International Journal of Computer Integrated Manufacturing.* 28(8), pp. 811–822.

Zhu, C.,Wang, H., Liu, X., Shu, L., Yang, L.T., Leung, V.C. (2016). A Novel Sensory Data Processing Framework to Integrate Sensor Networks with Mobile Cloud. *IEEE Systems Journal.* 10(3), pp. 1,125–1,136.

CENTRAL BANK DIGITAL CURRENCY (CBDC) FORMATS AND THEIR IMPLICATIONS

09

Digital currencies using distributed ledgers can be a digitized version of currency while retaining its four major features: (1) anonymity, (2) peer-to-peer (P2P) exchangeability, (3) universality, and (4) a steady titular value. There is a variety of potential solutions (formats) that can be adopted depending on the attributes and impact of each format on the financial system. This chapter characterizes and examines the benefits, opportunities, costs, and challenges of four key formats, and gives its assessment on the feasibility as well as possibility of practical adoption. Finally, it recommends the adoption of a CBDC (non-universal) for the interbank settlement and wholesale payment systems which has a minimal disruption to the economy, stronger monetary policy transmission and suggests way forward for adoption of an interest-free monetary system.

Keywords: *Sovereign Currency, Public Deposit, Policy Tool, Interbank Settlement*

JEL Codes: E43, E58, E61, G20, O33

Contents

1. Introduction

Traditionally, the Central Banks (CBs) provide banks and other financial institutions with electronic accounts for its functionality in the financial system. The public does not have such access and is only permitted to keep CB money in physical forms (i.e., coins and/or notes). If a CB would issue a universal Central Bank-issued digital currency (CBDC), all the economic actors (regardless if they are individuals, firms, institutions, governments, and central banks) could store assets and make payments using the Central Bank-issued digital currency (Cerqueira *et al.*, 2017). In consequence, this could have important shifts and repercussions for financial stability, monetary policy, and the relation of economic actors to the financial system. There are few papers in the literature (although there are some CBs already conducting research and pilot projects) that address questions on the feasibility of a CBDC implementation and its impact on monetary policy, the financial sector, and the economy (Danezis and Meiklejohn, 2015; Rogoff, 2016; Barrdear and Kumhof, 2016). However, most of these papers are descriptive or are focused on regulatory frameworks and the legal implications, while others are unable to define clear use cases and as a result, confuse the implications of a possible CBDC deployment.

The objective of this chapter is to analyze the possibilities for implementing a CBDC in viable formats that may have the capacity to tackle issues plaguing the current financial system. The possible scenarios and the resulting impact of CBDC on financial markets, monetary policy, on consumers, SMEs, banks, and even central bank independence will be discussed. In each format discussed, the benefits, costs, and incentives faced by stakeholders and end each section with our assessment on the probability of adoption are described. This chapter will also study the implications of the four scenarios described in Cerqueira *et al.* (2017) which have been adapted in our CBDC formats. These formats are assessed separately in Sections 3, 4, 5, and 6 broken down by their projected impact, consequences, and possible adoption assessment in terms of cost-benefit and feasibility.

2. The Possible Scenarios and Formats for the CBDC Regime

Cash is a financial instrument and physical asset that combines four features: (1) it is anonymous (2) it is universal (anyone can take possession); (3) it is exchanged peer to peer (without knowledge of the issuer); and (4) it does not yield any interest by itself. The Central Bank-issued digital currency (CBDC) is a digital alternative to cash that is also peer-to-peer (P2P), but it gives more flexibility in the treatment of the other three features:

1. They can be anonymous (like cash) or identifiable (non-anonymous like current accounts). The first corresponds to the idea of token-based CBDCs, and the second to account-based CBDCs.
2. They can be universal or restricted to a particular set of users. Likewise, distributed ledger (DL)-based tokens can be public (open) or private (closed), for instance, limited to banks or financial institutions.

3. They can be designed to pay or not give returns (in the absence of interest). The delinking of cash from paper–money opens the possibility of including yield as a feature, either in the account based or in the DL-based variant (or crypto-tokens).

These options can be melded in different ways to generate useful formats of the CBDCs for practical applications. Such amalgamation for purposeful solutions may involve these objectives: (1) to enhance the operations of wholesale payment systems; (2) to replace or support cash with a more proficient substitute; (3) to broaden and enrich tools for monetary policy, especially when confronted with the zero lower bound; and (4) to strengthen overall financial stability by decreasing the occurrences of banking and financial crises.

For the purposes of this discussion, the assumption is that the possible CBDC formats are maintained at a 1:1 parity with cash already in the economy. This assumption is held for all formats under discussion, as uneven parity would create a series of aggravations and too many probabilities to ascertain any practical assessment.

Table 9.1: The four formats discussed in this research.

Format	Use Case	Characteristics
1	CBDC as a Sovereign Currency (similar to Cash/Fiat)	Anonymous, universally-accepted, and non-yield bearing
2	CBDC as Public Deposit in Central Bank	Identified (non-anonymous), universally-accepted, and non-yield bearing
3	CBDC as a Monetary Policy Tool	Anonymous, universally-accepted, and yield bearing
4	CBDC for Interbank Settlement	Identified, restricted use, and non-yield bearing

3. CBDC as a Sovereign Currency (similar to Cash/Fiat)

This CBDC format retains all four attributes of cash: (1) anonymity, (2) peer-to-peer (P2P), (3) universality, and (4) non-yield bearing.

Banks would remain as money creators and maintain their inimitability at keeping reserves at the CB. Yves Mersch (2017) of the ECB, defined this CBDC format as "value-based" in collocation to an "account-based" CBDC (analyzed later in Format 2).

Anonymity in CBDCs would have the same issues with security and safety as cash. Like cash, stolen CBDCs would be hard to recover once stolen or lost, although CBDCs would be less likely to be stolen or lost as compared to cash. P2P exchangeability allows its exchange between counterparties without intermediaries. Universality means that anybody can take possession of it, use, and store it. Finally, this CBDC would not bear any yield just like cash.

3.1. *Impact*

By focusing on the three defining roles of money — unit of account, medium of exchange, and store of value — the performance of the CBDC is assessed in the following paragraphs relative to the three most relevant types of money: (1) bank deposits, (2) cash, and (3) other private/foreign currencies.

Its performance as a unit of account would be similar as that of physical cash, as long as they remained pegged to each other.[1] As such, it should serve as a better price reference than private and foreign currencies, both of which would remain vulnerable to exchange rate instability under current standard monetary practices, on top of the risk of capital controls.

As a medium of exchange, this format would compete with and at the same time complement both cash and bank deposits, but it would remain an imperfect and also uncertain substitute for both. Its usage would surely increase as people become more familiar with online transactions, but it would remain a poor substitute for cash for those who are less technologically savvy or who reside in places with poor Internet access. It is worth noting that this format would not curb illicit transactions, as it would retain anonymity.[2] Compared to bank deposits, this format would

---

1   The implementation of this CBDC format would be akin to the issuance of a new "coin" or "note", although this note would be digital hence effortlessly traded online and infinitely divisible.

2   This format could even facilitate illegal activities, as transaction, transportation, and storage costs are lower than those of cash,

facilitate long-distance and/or large-quantity payments, but it would not necessarily offer additional services.[3] That said, it would facilitate the offering of such services by firms other than banks — FinTechs and small players — thus further commoditizing the payment infrastructure and reducing the comparative advantage of deposits (BIS, 2015).

As a store of value, in this format, the CBDC would remain riskier than bank deposits, at least those deposits up to the amount guaranteed by authorities — anonymity implies that it would be untraceable if it were stolen or the password to the wallet forgotten. As argued by Broadbent (2016), if "all CBDC did was to substitute for cash…people would probably still want to keep most of their money in commercial banks" simply because it is familiar and there is a custodian for safe-keeping.

3.2. Consequences

The introduction of this format would impede cash usage and potentially diminish (but not severely) bank deposits. Cash would still dominate in cash-driven economies but in increasingly cashless economies where cash usage has been falling regardless, the CBDCs would swiftly replace cash.

For end users, the total advantages of this format would compensate for its costs. The CBDC in this format is a digital representation of cash without the volatility and price instability of sovereign currencies and lack of liquidity of current non-government crypto-currencies, such as Bitcoin (BTC), Ethereum (ETH), and Ripple (XRP). However, in this case, the CBDC holders would also benefit from the advantages of currencies like Bitcoin, Ethereum, and Ripple — mainly cheaper and faster money transfers whose advantages would turn to productive gains (Barrdear and Kumhof, 2016). It would also promote financial inclusion, namely where banks have had difficulties in establishing branches due to geographical remoteness or where physical cash are ineffective compared to digital versions (IMF, 2019). For example, Nepal

---

   although this may be unlikely considering that it is CB-issued, and there is a possibility of overturning anonymity in exceptional cases.

3 It is highly unlikely that CBs would provide FI-type financial services, despite certain types of services can be inherent to a CBDC through a tech-centric platform as opposed to a bank-centric one.

has recently embarked in the Digital 2020 initiative to accelerate digital financial inclusion and access to finance. In ASEAN, the ASEAN Financial Innovation Network (AFIN) "aims to facilitate broader adoption of fintech innovation and development" in the region. According to a January 2019 from the Bank of International Settlements (BIS, 2019), 70% of central banks (based on 63 central banks that participated in the survey) are currently researching the issuance of a CBDC. The majority of the countries currently investigating to launch of a digital currency, cited 'financial inclusion' as the main reason for exploring CBDCs.

For consumers and small and medium enterprises (SMEs), transactional payments, transfers and remittances would take place much faster and at a lower cost since accessibility becomes easy to perform these transactions (Cerqueira *et al.*, 2017). This feature is particularly useful for developing countries, as remote and rural areas have accessibility challenges. Savings would also be improved since the CBDC as an instrument would allow money to be stored effortlessly.

Also, for monetary authorities the benefits would likely outweigh the costs. Efficiency gains would be higher in emerging markets, especially in countries with high inflation, where maintenance and issuance of physical cash are especially costly. Moreover, the CBDC would also allow CBs to compete and potentially limit the end user incentives for using private or foreign digital currencies with the lack of control that the latter generally entail. Importantly, the CBDC strengthens monetary policy transmission mechanism in that it brings the latter closer in line with the objectives of monetary policy. On the side of costs, monetary authorities would need to finance the implementation and maintenance of a completely new infrastructure that demands first hand equipment and a novel set of skills.

However, for banks, the costs would likely outweigh the benefits. More specifically, this format would make most intermediation for payment transactions redundant, bringing to an end the banks' payment business.[4] Banks would probably continue to offer payment services as part of an encompassing service of financial management.

---

4   Faced with bank fees (no matter how minimal), even people who prefer traditional accounts would consider converting their deposits to frictionless CBDC for more efficient payments. International transfers are already affected.

Banks' credit business would also suffer because of the partial substitution of CBDC for deposits. It is worth noting that the format would not only reduce the volume of deposits, but it would also increase their volatility (due to customers' greater ease of wealth reallocation away from deposits into a broader range of alternatives). As a result of increased volatility, asset and liability management by banks would be more difficult. If consumers decide to keep savings in their wallets and outside the formal financial system, deposits in the banking system would fall, as well as the money multiplier. In addition, the banks would lose critical data that they use to draw up credit scores based on consumer wealth and repayment behaviors.

On top of that, incumbents in the banking sector would face the entrance of new and potentially less-regulated players. New entrants would probably start with services in the payments business, but would eventually broaden their scope to eventually offer credit and full-fledged alternatives to deposits.

With respect to the potential benefits for banks, they would indeed benefit from any aggregate output gains, just like other stakeholders would. Furthermore, banking regulation might ease as the sector would be less concentrated and their activities might turn out to be less prone to systemic disruptions. Potential benefits might ensue from new business opportunities facilitated by the CBDC, such as the management and protection of the keys for CBDC wallets, although it is more likely that this will be adopted by banks themselves.

3.3. Adoption Assessment

The eradication of cash is always an option, or at least a partial eradication as suggested by Rogoff (2016), where only low-denomination bills and coins are maintained. The recognition of such a possibility is particularly pertinent under this format, where the CBDC can be seen as a digital version of physical cash, albeit only in high amounts.

Eradicating cash poses a great challenge, especially in cash-dependent economies. However, it would be easier in developed economies where most transactions already use no cash. Hence, eliminating cash could save bank fees but generate some other costs for end users, although they would enjoy the social benefits from the reduction in informality and illicit activities. Although the

CBDC remains anonymous, there might be a greater reluctance to use CBDC for illicit purposes, for tax evasion, etc., at least if there is a possibility that anonymity can be overturned at any point for AML/CTF investigation purposes.

So, in general, the elimination of cash would be beneficial for banks, if users of cash would convert (some or most) of their money into bank deposits. For authorities, the benefits of eliminating cash (viz. reduced informality and potentially lower maintenance costs) would have to be balanced with the risks related to the exclusive reliance on a digital platform.[5]

For the finance industry, a CBDC means increased efficiency in payment and transfer systems, which translates into greater profits. Also, if the banks safeguard the passwords of the wallets, new businesses could emerge based on this type of service. However, if there is a reduction in deposits and the CB does not adopt compensatory measures, it is most probable that commercial banks will need to find additional capital from the financial markets or by other means. The most immediate consequence could be a drop in the amount of credit granted or an increase in the cost of credit, if there are no CB compensatory measures or stabilization policy. In such a scenario, financial stability and the credit markets could be negatively affected.

4. CBDC as Public Deposit in Central Bank

This format generates a very disruptive configuration of the CBDC because it proposes an identifiable money which is non-anonymous. Practically, "having a CBDC held by the general public is the equivalent of keeping a deposit in the central bank, so that the authority's power to supervise and monitor it would be substantially greater than it is today" (Cerqueira *et al.*, 2017). Being identifiable and non-anonymous, non-compliant activities can be detected. As a deterrent and a regulatory tool in combating illegal activities, it would require the eventual elimination cash and limit the use of alternative assets for this CBDC format to be absolutely effective, which is not easy to do. Two possible scenarios for the adoption of a CBDC with these characteristics have two main differentiating and important elements.

---

5   Potential risks range from a loss of connectivity or a serious cyber-attack on the infrastructure.

In the first scenario, particularly in countries where there is a high volume of illegal activities — such as attempts to launder money and evade taxes — makes the adoption of this CBDC format useful for the government. In the second scenario, the CBDC as a recognized transformation of deposits in the banking system into deposits in the Central Bank can offer greater financial stability to the country.

However, the consequent reduction in bank deposits would shrink credit markets significantly, as falling bank deposits would mean that credit creation becomes severely limited. Every deposit then would be backed by sovereign wealth (i.e., cash, central bank reserves, and government securities), which would be akin to full-reserve banking (FRB). FRB endeavors to "separate the payments system from the financing system as well as monetary policy from credit policy" (Laina, 2015). Preventing private money creation would ensure financial stability as initially proposed in the UK Bank Charter Act of 1844, the US Acts of 1863 and 1864, the Chicago Plan of 1930s forbade "private money creation through fractional-reserve banking by requiring that bank notes (which were the prevailing means of payment) should be fully-backed by government money". This format opens a discussion on allocating government-backed liquidity and the criteria that the CBs could use to build up liquidity in the banking system with framework adjustments for new rules and policy instruments for reserves and/or open market transactions.

4.1. *Impact*

The fact that CBDC is non-anonymous, as are indeed bank deposits, means that it will be less desirable than cash as a medium of exchange, at least for some. However, the demand for the CBDC as a medium of exchange will rise as a consequence of it being a more efficient technology to carry out monetary transactions. All in all, in this format, the CBDC would be less in demand as a medium of exchange than in both formats as a sovereign currency (Format 1) and as a monetary policy tool (Format 3) when it does not bear negative rates.

In contrast, the demand for the CBDC as a store of value would increase in comparison to other scenarios because it is now a safer money than before. In fact, it will likely be a safer money than physical cash not only due to technological issues but also because it is identified, which means that recovering it will be easier in cases of loss, theft, etc. Moreover, it will be a safer money than bank deposits, as the risks of maintaining it at the CBs are clearly lower than maintaining it as a deposit in a bank. However, in spite of this advantage, some would still demand bank deposits due to higher remuneration and services, and banks would prefer higher credit levels in a fractional reserve system for higher profitability.

4.2. Consequences

From the point of view of end users, deposits at the CBs are much safer than bank deposits, among other things, because they do not carry any credit risk. Due to that feature of CBDC deposits, the situation for end users is comparable to keeping deposits in a so-called narrow-bank, i.e., in a financial institution that is compelled by authorities to maintain the public's resources under custody in a liquid and safe form, such as in government bonds, rather than leveraging on them in order to create credit. This would likely lead to a narrow-banking system due to CBs accepting the CBDC deposits and making the CBDC non-anonymous.[6]

It is important to note that even with the CBs functioning broadly as a narrow-bank, banks will likely continue to work according to a fractional-reserve banking model, i.e., transforming part of the public's deposits into credit and keeping only a fraction of them as reserves.[7] In that sense, we can refer to this format as a partial narrow-banking system, as opposed to a full narrow-banking system in which banks are also compelled to operate as narrow-banks rather than as fractional-reserve banks.

From the point of view of the monetary authority, the increase in the demand for CBDC means that the CBs will have

---

6   As bearing credit risk is a common feature of bank deposits and not of the CB's liabilities, the narrow-bank concept applies suitably to a bank, but not necessarily to a CB.

7   For that reason, in a fractional-reserve system banks are exposed to bank runs, while in a typical narrow-bank — and also in a CB — that is not the case. Moreover, it is worth noting that another difference between the two systems is that deposits held in a fractional-reserve style system represent a mechanism through which banks create money, while that is not true in the case of a narrow-bank.

more resources under its management. In other words, the size of the CBs' liabilities will increase, generating an increase in the size of its balance sheet. To match the increase in its liabilities, the CBs will increase the size of its assets through purchase of predominantly safe and liquid assets, such as GDP-linked bonds and public securities, to counterbalance CBDC deposits.

4.3. Adoption Assessment

The CBDC in this format will work as a proper unit of account, like cash and bank deposits, and in contrast with private and foreign currencies (Cerqueira *et al.*, 2017). In this particular format, the CBDC will be in general a better store of value and a worse medium of exchange than in other formats, its adoption will very much depend on how the government and its people value financial stability, safety, and anonymity.

On a cautionary note, the deposits that the CB obtains with a recognized CBDC should not be used to either grant loans to the non-financial private sector or finance governments. First off, it would be problematic as the CB lacks the expertise to do so and a non-independent CB could, for example, have incentives to compete more aggressively with banks, in order to gather more deposits, and lose its focus on its original objectives as a market supervisor and regulator. Although this format may reverberate changes to a more financially-sound and stable system, like all systems, its moral risks remains. In the guise of improving financial stability, moral hazards include unscrupulously generating unreasonable incentives for the government, increasing the risks of fiscal slippage, and creating problems for the CBs with regards to its independence.

5. CBDC as a Monetary Policy Tool

In this format, the CBDC is still similar to cash (i.e., universal and anonymous) in some ways but with the special feature of possibly being interest-bearing (Cerqueira *et al.*, 2017). An interest-bearing currency as a monetary policy instrument gives the Central Banks autonomy to meet their inflation targets, by dropping the nominal value of the digital currency, which would be akin to reducing the interest rates without any lower bound (refer to Barrdear and

Kumhof (2016) or the following Section 7). Similarly, if there is a rise in interest rates, the nominal value of the CBDC would rise, leading to an increase in the monetary base. In such a format, monetary policy would be transmitted directly to the economy without having the banking system as a proxy, thus accelerating the transmission of this policy whilst creating unlimited room for action to meet Central Banks' inflation targets. As a consequence, the effectiveness of monetary policy is enhanced considerably. Under the present configuration of monetary policy transmission mechanism, the banks have a crucial role in the effectiveness of this mechanism. It should be noted that the aim of monetary policy is to induce adjustments in the private sector's portfolio (investment and consumption) in order to achieve stability. However, the banking system and monetary policy have two different objective functions. The former maximizes profits while the latter's objective is to achieve financial stability to help growth. More often than not, the two are in conflict. Current monetary policy relies on the banking system to transmit its actions to the private sector to induce it to adjust its portfolio to achieve monetary policy objective(s). As the objective of monetary policy comes into conflict with that of the banking system, it is more than likely that the banking system will serve its own objectives, thus, reducing the strength of monetary policy transmission and thus rendering monetary policy actions impotent. As mentioned, the CBDC in this format has the capacity to reduce the dissonance from the banking system while concurrently enhancing the power of monetary policy transmission mechanism by directly inducing private sector portfolio adjustments.

5.1. Impact

The technology behind the CBDC allows the CBs to alter the face value of the whole stock of CBDC, a prerogative that would transform the CBDC into an interest-bearing currency.[8] An interest-bearing currency would be a revolutionary change which would create possibilities for monetary policy that are currently unavailable, or at least, one that is very difficult and costly to implement.

---

8   It would also be feasible to embed the CBDC with smart contracts that trigger changes in face value contingent on any pre-stipulated event.

Allowing CBs to reduce the face value of digital currency is tantamount to setting rates as negative as monetary authorities may want, unconstrained by any zero lower bound. In other words, this format allows for unlimited financial repression[9] and the possibility, argued by many, of responding aggressively and effectively against recessionary threats. Conversely, a rise in the face value of CBDC would amount to positive interest rates, implying an automatic expansion of the monetary base.

However, technological feasibility does not necessarily translate into political–social desirability. Allowing the CBs to reduce the face value of circulating currency can be easily interpreted as expropriation. It is true that via inflation, expropriation in real terms has been a constant in modern economies, yet it remains to be seen how society would respond to a nominal confiscation of wealth. In terms of legitimacy, allowing the CBs to raise the face value of circulating currency would amount to a transfer of wealth to those holding the currency, which in the current system is the prerogative of fiscal and not monetary authorities. Thus, the introduction of positive or negative interest rates in such a manner raises legitimacy issues for CBs to transmit fiscal policies, or at least a new discussion on a modified or merged function. Furthermore, the role of currency as a unit of account becomes a questionable numeraire[10] for most prices in the market when CBs have control over its face value.

The impact on the banking sector would be similar to that in the previous format, although banks would benefit from the abolition of cash, which would reduce informality. Similar to the first format, some customers would reallocate deposits into virtual wallets and opt for new non-bank sources of finance, which would be readily available thanks to the CBDC. The impact on deposits would be greater, the higher the CBDC interest rate is, especially if it is not set below the policy interest rate.[11] The

---

9   Financial repression is a term that describes measures by which governments channel funds to themselves as a form of debt reduction.

10   This refers to an item or commodity acting as a measure of value or as a standard for currency exchange.

11   Deposits with rates significantly above the policy rate would be unsustainable for banks and might lead to the banking system's unwarranted reliance on CBs or other types of funding. Deposit rates below CBDC yields would be hard to sell to depositors, unless they perceive benefits in bank deposits that counterbalance a lower remuneration.

volatility of bank deposits is likely to be even higher than in the prior scenario, because demand for deposits would not only be impacted on by movements in the policy rate, but also by those in the CBDC yield rate.

5.2. Consequences

This CBDC format retains anonymity, P2P, and universality. However, in contrast to cash, the CBDC would bear interest in this case. It is worth noting that the interest rate applied to the CBDC could be aligned or not with the monetary policy interest rate. Depending on the objectives of the CBs, it could be set at different levels.[12]

The coexistence of cash and the CBDC under this regime would be tricky and problematic. If interest rates were negative, people would deplete their stocks of CBDC in favor of zero-yield physical cash,[13] or, the CBDC could sustain significantly negative rates only if physical cash were mostly abolished. At the other end of the policy lever, if the CBDC bore positive rates, people would transform cash into the CBDC (i.e., get closer to a cashless society).

As in the first format (CBDC as a Sovereign Currency), this CBDC would exhibit advantages in comparison to bank deposits, especially when viewed as a medium of exchange with no intermediaries. Similarly, bank deposits would likely keep their advantage as a store of value (better safeguards) and continue attracting those looking for specific financial services. As a result, and also in Format 1, demand for bank deposits relative to that for the CBDC would depend on the yield spread between them. Consequently, the impact on the level of deposits would probably be similar to that in Format 1. However, one could argue that any

---

12   On the one hand, a lack of harmonisation among them could undermine the effectiveness of monetary policy actions but, on the other, a lower interest rate on CBDC than the official interest rate could safeguard both financial stability and credit markets as banks would have higher flexibility to remunerate deposits above the CBDC yields.

13   More precisely, for any agent, a turning point would emerge when the loss in yield of CBDC were to surpass the costs of storage and transportation of physical cash.

volatility would be higher as the spread between the CBDC and deposits would be fluctuating at both of its margins.[14]

The CBDC would still compete with other currencies and assets. The perceived stability of the CBDCs versus other currencies/assets would certainly play an important role in the demand for CBDC. With regards to foreign currencies, the situation would not necessarily be different to what exists today, where flexible-exchange currencies coexist while maintaining their own level of domestic interest rates. Yet, uncertainty-instability might escalate with negative rates, making CBs willing to impose capital controls as a last resort.[15]

According to the BIS (2018), the CBDCs are considered an autonomous factor for monetary policy implementation for two reasons. First, from the viewpoint of the day-to-day steering of the central bank's balance sheet to control short-term interest rates, daily fluctuations in the demand for CBDC are an exogenous factor, even though the CBDC would be an endogenous factor within the broader monetary policy framework. Second, even if the CBDC was introduced, the amount of digital central bank money held by monetary counterparties (reserves) would still be crucial for control over short-term interest rates.

5.3. Adoption Assessment

This format might incur even greater drawbacks for society than the previous ones. Although positive rates would be an option, in principle, this format would be adopted to allow the CBs to implement negative interest rates, which would imply direct losses to end users of CBDC, losses that are tantamount to confiscation. Moreover, the threat of losing anonymity due to technological

---

14   As suggested before, the CBDC interest rates could be set at a sufficiently low level such as to guarantee that demand for bank deposits does not fall significantly, driving credit levels down.

15   Uncertainty might rise because the CBs are only held accountable for keeping inflation under control (and their credibility on that front has led to stability in international exchange markets). However, CBs are not held accountable for sustaining rates above any level (and for investors in global exchange markets, very negative rates would bring the same loss in value as would very high inflation). It is not clear *a priori* how that uncertainty would be contained.

or legal issues would always be present, yet end users would face the added difficulty of having no cash in hand. In addition, the near elimination of cash would magnify the costs to the end user brought by any internet disruption or power shortage, for example.

As this format demands the near elimination of cash in order to work, authorities would bear the high cost of guaranteeing universal access to the CBDC, reducing barriers on both the technology and the educational fronts. Therefore, before allowing CBDCs to bear interest rates, it would be important in the first place to carefully discuss what the CBs' roles[16] and mandates are, and then to establish a framework to correctly incentivize major stakeholders.

Finally, regarding payment services, while the domestic business would practically come to an end, as in Format 1, the cross-border payment business could be significantly impaired by the eventual adoption of capital controls.

6. CBDC for Interbank Settlement

The current settlement of payments is costly because it needs strict monitoring to avoid any double spending or sudden default. As a result, payment systems currently used by CBs are tiered: only Tier 1 banks can open a settlement account in the CB (which needs to remain continuously funded) for immediate settlement purposes. "Banks in other tiers have to open accounts in Tier 1 banks and go through them to settle their transfers in the CB. Thus, top-tier banks intermediate other banks' transfers while also managing their own customers' accounts" (Cerqueira *et al.*, 2017) (see Figure 9.1).

---

16   Although changing the face value of a currency seem similar to changing its yield, there is an important dissimilarity when effecting such a change as a policy lever. In normal CB operations, interest rates are typically adjusted in open market operations by changing their total balance. In this format, reducing the face value of the CBDC implies the reduction of the CBs' liabilities without a corresponding fall in its assets and conversely, increasing the surplus (or reducing the deficit) of the consolidated fiscal account. "The implementation of such an instrument would thus be a major change of policy rules, where deficits are the sole prerogative of governments, not of CBs." (Cerqueira *et al.*, 2017).

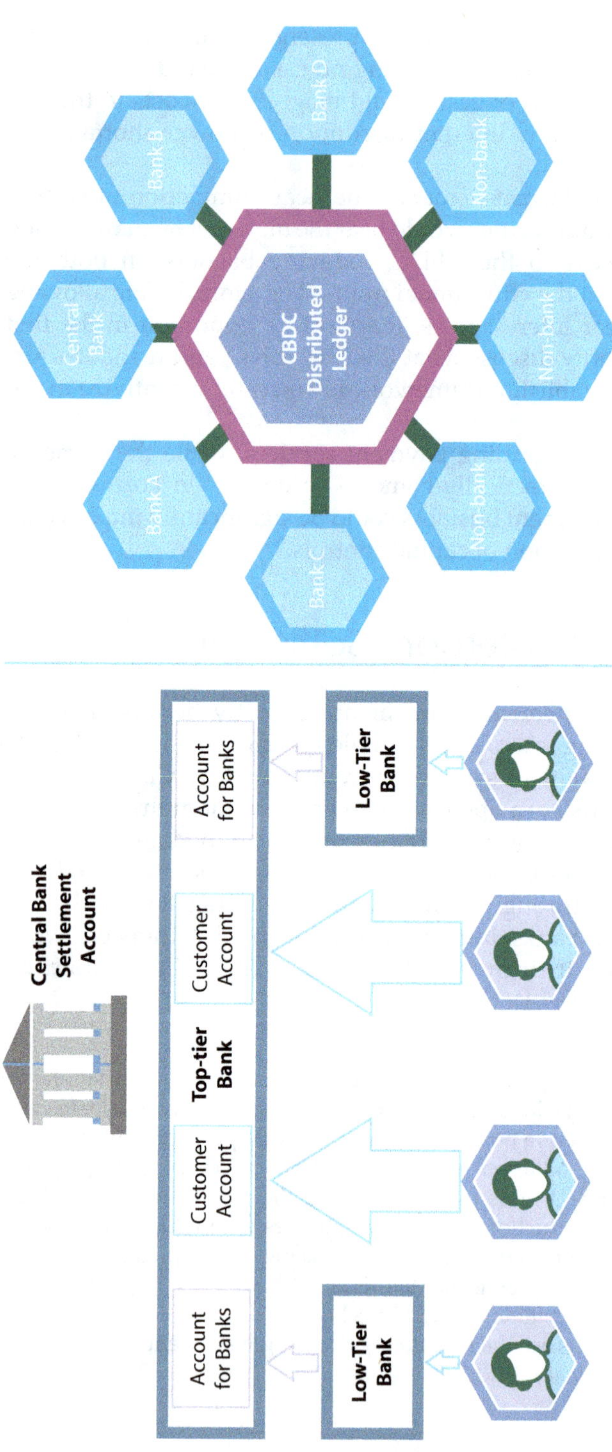

Figure 9.1: Tiered Payment Model versus Distributed Payment Model

In this format, the interbank payment system infrastructure is replaced by one based on DLT, so that the accounts of the participants in the CB are replaced by CBDC wallets and the CB becomes just another node of the network, although with certain privileges. The CB can still access information on all the transactions as a supervisor, decides who can join the system and is the issuer of the cryptocurrency. The main advantages of this scenario lie, on the one hand, in the increased efficiency of the interbank payment system (i.e., cost reduction and speed increase) (BIS, 2018). On the other hand, in the greater resilience of a system of this type to cyberattacks since there is no vulnerable central point. The less efficient and insecure the system is, the greater the net benefits of adopting a CBDC (BIS, 2019), discounting the cost of implementing the new infrastructure and, therefore, the more probable its adoption.

6.1. *Impact*

This format achieves what modern payments systems set out to do — P2P and more rapid payments, and involving FinTech companies (or other NBFIs) which have the expertise but are not necessarily focused in banking services. This would separate the financial business of credit and payments, where payments now can become commoditized through innovation for better services and use. Overall, all parties, including consumers, will benefit from faster, better, and cheaper services from the efficiencies gained.

The creation of a shared payments ledger system would allow for real-time and traceable transactional information about capital flows, which is progressing towards dynamic monitoring and better management of systemic risk. Furthermore, the CBs will have to compete with other digital currencies/ledgers[17] in order to keep full control (supervision) of the settlement system. In fostering competition, it will expand accessibility without incurring traditional payment infrastructure costs. The marginal cost of adding a new participant would be considerably lower — adding a new node to the network is technologically and operationally simpler and cheaper. As a result, more players would have direct access to the wholesale payments business, increasing

---

17   In this research, other digital currencies are defined as those not issued by the CB, like Libra, Bitcoin, etc.

competition. All these benefits would come at a high initial cost of implementation[18] and subsequent infrastructure maintenance costs (although the maintenance costs could be lower than the current system).

However, Tier 1 banks would lose their privileged role as ultimate settlers in CB accounts, and would lose part of the payment business in favor of Tier 2 banks, and all of them in favor of non-banks. Additionally, direct access to the wholesale payments settlement system would allow non-banks to provide end-to-end payment services and, as a consequence, increase their market share. Such new entrants might negatively impact the revenues of banks. However, the benefits in terms of efficiency, infrastructure costs savings, resilience, transparency, and innovation could well outweigh such loss of revenue.

This format would further push banks to focus on the credit business, where they would maintain a competitive advantage — mostly due to both their expertise in risk management and the resources needed to enter into the business. Anyway, given the important role that non-banks will have in the new competitive landscape, potential partnerships between banks and non-banks could naturally arise, with the aim of complementing knowledge, skills and processes to build a win-win value proposition in payments and credit services.

From an operational point of view, this scenario would force banks to excel in management of their CBDC wallets because prefunding of wallets is mandatory in a DL-based system, which would mean that banks cannot operate in overdraft. CB settlement accounts in RTGS today are quite similar, as they are periodically pre-funded with accurate calculated funds enough to cover the payment needs. However, in this scenario, banks need to balance the amount of CB money both in its traditional form and in CBDC at all times.

6.2. Consequences

For central banks, the utilization of a DL-based infrastructure allows for the full availability (365 days a year, 24 hours a day, seven days a week) of the system, which can operate without

---

18   Implementation costs include the development of new skills needed in the CBs in order to be able to make full use of data stored in the ledger.

interruption, unlike the current RTGS systems, such as TARGET2 in Europe, which have predetermined operating schedules. In addition, a decentralized system is much more resilient to potential cyber-attacks because there is more than a single point of attack in order for it to fail.

For banks, the main benefits would be concurrent with the ones of the CB — full availability and resilience under cyber threats. Additional benefits would be speed and cost efficiency in the whole settlement process, including infrastructure costs. Also, higher competition would reduce transaction fees to more accurately reflect the marginal cost of verification. The effect on the aggregate financial industry would be a reduction in the transactional costs associated with payments.

On the payment front, competition would shift from the transaction itself to the offering of additional services. The transactional part of payments would be easily covered by any kind of player since they could have direct access to the CB settlement system. Therefore, the value creation in the payment business would have to be based on a seamless and intuitive user experience and a broad range of value-added services, mainly built upon the payment insights and knowledge extracted from transactional data. Although end-customers do not have access to the CBDC in this scenario, they would benefit from cheaper, safer, and faster money transfers.

One area where there is a huge potential for efficiency gains is in cross-border payment systems (IMF, 2017). Cryptocurrencies offer an opportunity for dramatic cost reductions, which may translate into faster and less expensive transactions, for instance, in remittances. However, it is unclear whether the CBDCs may compete with cryptocurrencies in this, being based on national payment systems. Central banks may, however, have incentives to develop interconnected payments systems for cross–border transactions if threatened by the competition of cryptocurrencies.

6.3. Adoption Assessment

This CBDC format is highly probable not only because of its benefits but also because it could serve as an intermediate step to start testing the more disruptive scenarios of Formats 1, 2, and 3. CBs such as the Bank of England are currently working on modernizing their RTGS systems, and a DL-based infrastructure is being given serious consideration.

7. Countercyclical Measures and Fiscal Policy Interactions with CBDC

In another study, Barrdear and Kumhof (2016) of the Bank of England investigated the properties of a specific format of CBDC (Format 3) which can be held by the non-bank private sector (unlike reserves) — that it is bears yield (unlike cash), and that it rivals the internally created private bank-issued money. Their quantity or price rules react to inflation, in the same way it responds to the policy rate.[19] Hence, the quantity and price rules for the CBDCs have a very similar potential for countercyclical policy responses to standard shocks (discretionary monetary stimulus or money supply shock). The choice between quantity and price rules must therefore mostly be based on the fact that price rules, as mentioned above, perform better under money demand shocks. Barrdear and Kumhof (2016) also found that "the relative performance of countercyclical quantity and price rules depends critically on the elasticity of substitution between CBDC and bank deposits, with a lower elasticity implying that smaller quantity responses and larger interest rate responses to inflation are required to achieve the same degree of countercyclicality".

In order for the CBDC price rule and countercyclical quantity rule to be sufficiently effective, Barrdear and Kumhof held the assumptions that the steady state quantity of CBDC amounts to 30% of GDP (significant enough to make sizeable withdrawals of CBDC possible without hitting a 'quantity zero lower bound'), that the CBDC is used frequently enough by its prospective users, and that the steady state efficiency gains of CBDC issuance are sizeable over the expected scale measured.

Within this model, Barrdear and Kumhof found that a system of the CBDC offers a number of clear macroeconomic advantages, including large steady state output gains of almost 3% for an injection of CBDC equal to 30% of GDP, and considerable gains in the efficacy of systematic or discretionary countercyclical monetary policy.[20] Their analysis suggests that the only restrictions

---

19 They visualized that the CBDC would be an economically relevant monetary aggregate as long as the quantity outstanding is sufficiently large and its substitutability with other monetary transactions media is sufficiently low.

20 This is particularly if a sizeable share of shocks is to private credit creation or to the demand for monetary transaction balances, and if

required to obtain these gains are that an adequately large supply of CBDC is circulated in steady state, and that the central bank only utilizes the CBDC when it trades against government debt instruments.

8. Analysis and Recommendations

To overcome the confusion and improper assessments of digital currencies, specifically CBDCs, each practical option (format) has to be categorized and independently evaluated. This chapter attempts to clearly define each format according to its use case, while thoroughly appraising their consequences and impact to the monetary and financial system. Working on a format that improves efficiency for payments (Format 4) can show advancements that may buy-in more changes moving forward. For financial stability, Format 2 has the greatest potential, and is rooted in ideas which are fundamentally sound and not necessarily new. However, the impact on credit creation is a reality that needs to be dealt with by all stakeholders. It will slow growth and restrain profitability for those who are solely profit-driven on credit, which will lead them to explore real risk-sharing investments and question critical decision-making to balance profit-seeking with financial stability and economic responsibility.

Format 3 is the only format that does not appear to be viable, in the author's opinion. An interest-bearing currency format would be a radical shift that could create possibilities for monetary policy that are currently unavailable without being constrained by any "zero lower bound", but would incur losses in value for these CBDC holders, equivalent to confiscation, domestically and internationally. Practically, it will be problematic and unpopular as its trade-offs would be unattractive.

In Format 1, the partial replacement of cash in low denominations may be feasible to facilitate the majority of transactions. Eliminating cash could save bank fees and other transaction costs for end users. Unlawful transactions through large denominations may be reduced, although the CBs may be able to trace illicit transactions via the blockchainized system even if large denominations were also implemented.

---

the substitutability between CBDC and bank deposits in transaction technologies is low.

However, the interest rate as the pricing mechanism and policy lever here then requires a little more in-depth discussion. It is intended to explain the Islamic financial perspective which effects a ban on interest, including interest rate as a pricing mechanism. The concern for justice and equity involves non-discriminatory exchange and fairness in financial transactions, including getting the market prices right through proper pricing mechanisms so as to not suffer the consequences of mispricing.

'Getting the prices right' means letting market forces function naturally to produce market prices that reflect all opportunity costs that correspond to them. John Maynard Keynes (1936) had already indicated that "the interest rate policy had deviated the true opportunity cost of financial resources", and James Tobin (1969) pointed out that "there was no such thing as a 'market rate of interest' in an environment in which policy drove the 'market rate of interest'". Monetary policy had the ability, Tobin argued, to force a deviation between market valuation of capital and its replacement cost. His "fundamental-valuation efficiency" concept, interpreted as "allocative efficiency", would ascertain the opportunity cost of financial resources that guides and necessitates their worthiest uses.

According to the "get the prices right" doctrine, in a market where prices were not allowed to reflect their opportunity cost, repression ruled — which was the McKinnon-Shaw argument for liberalization of the financial sector of developing countries (Mirakhor, 2017). Financial repression, the deviation of "administered interest rate" from the "market interest rate", led to market distortions, which has resulted in poor savings, inadequate investments and stunted economic growth. In the subsequent decades of financial liberalization to chase economic prosperity, Mirakhor laments that "a basic question never asked was how and in what sense did the 'market rate of interest' reflect the true opportunity cost of financial resources".

One of the central problems of major economies is the uncoordinated and mismatched balance sheets of the real, financial, household, and government sectors. Ideally, it is presumed that the market would work freely to coordinate the balance sheets and allow for equilibrium to surface. Unfortunately, the current state of economics suffers from a runaway financial sector, which is decoupled from the real sector. In our current state, we have an economy that apportions only a very small fraction of market trades to capital formation in the real sector,[21]

---

21 About 0.8% of US$33 trillion, according to John C. Bogle's *Clash of Cultures*, 2012.

resulting in a real sector with corporations overflowing with cash, but not investing. Micro-, small- and medium-sized enterprises (MSMEs) become starved for financial resources and are unable to grow and survive, while government sectors amass huge debts to fund their programs, unable to coordinate its balance sheets. The market's inability has spawned a "paper economy" without much connection to the real sector, when in fact, the economy needs a real sector rate of return to replace the mis-pricings of opportunity cost of financial resources.

Where the interest rate mechanism is no longer available to misallocate financial resources, monetary policy becomes even more effective in inducing private sector portfolio adjustment as it relies on the rate of return to investment in the real sector of the economy (as the true opportunity cost of financial resources) to guide its policy actions. Such systemic change is required for a systemic problem that has gone on for far too long, and it came come in the form of the alternative Islamic financial system.

For Islamic Finance, the CBDC in public deposit format (Format 2) is closest to what the intellectuals of the industry have been proposing. A full-reserve system where every deposit is backed by sovereign wealth (i.e., cash, central bank reserves, government securities, and assets) would ensure financial stability which the current fractional-reserve banking system has been grappling with as it is inherently flawed. Preventing private money creation for the sake of financial stability is not a new idea, as it was initially proposed in the UK Bank Charter Act of 1844, the US Acts of 1863 and 1864, and the Chicago Plan of 1930s, as mentioned in Section 4. There are constant trade-offs in economics, but we cannot trade the stability of our financial future for unrestrained profits through the aggressive expansion of credit.

9. Conclusion

For the CBDCs to be practical, they have to provide pragmatic implementable solutions that will solve existing problems that cannot be solved by current tools or instruments. The impending structural changes in the monetary system requires CBs to carefully consider which formats work for their needs and then implement them in prudent, deliberated ways in order to mitigate risks and work out unintended and unforeseen consequences. Current policies and frameworks will remain ineffective to existing problems so long as fundamental flaws which are systemic are not rectified. They cannot be resolved by "patch" solutions which only treat the symptoms (not the root) where increasingly outdated and flawed mechanisms have masked their compounding detrimental effects. DL-based solutions like the CBDC in its various formats offer alternatives in tackling some of these important issues as we work towards a freer marketplace, a more stable financial and considerably more prosperous economic system.

Acknowledgment

The author would like to thank Professor Abbas Mirakhor for his invaluable inputs and suggestions.

Bibliography

Agarwal, R. and Kimball, M. (2015). Breaking Through the Zero Lower Bound, IMF Working Paper, WP/15/224.

Bank for International Settlements (2019). Proceeding with Caution — A Survey on Central Bank Digital Currency, Monetary and Economic Department, January 2019.

Bank for International Settlements (2018). Central Bank Digital Currencies, Committee on Payments and Market Infrastructures, March 2018.

Bank for International Settlements (2015). Digital Currencies, Committee on Payments and Market Infrastructures, November 2015.

Barrdear, J. and Kumhof, M. (2016). The Macroeconomics of Central Bank Issued Digital Currencies. Staff Working Paper No. 605, Bank of England.

Bogle, John C. (2012). *Clash of Cultures: Investment vs. Speculation.* John Wiley & Sons, Hoboken, New Jersey.

Broadbent, B. (2016). "Central banks and digital currencies". Speech given at the London School of Economics on 2 March 2016.

Cerqueira, G. O., Enestor Dos Santos, Santiago Fernández de Lis, Alejandro Neut and Javier Sebastián, (2017). Central Bank Digital Currencies: Assessing Implementation Possibilities and Impacts. BBVA Research, March 2017.

Danezis, G. and Meiklejohn, S. (2015). *Centrally Banked Cryptocurrencies.* University College London.

Dyson, B. and G. Hodgson (2016). "Digital Cash: Why Central Banks Should Start Issuing Electronic Money", Positive Money.

Fung, B. and H. Halaburda (2016). Central Bank Digital Currencies: A Framework for Assessing Why and How. Bank of Canada Staff Discussion Paper No. 2016-22.

IMF (2019). Fintech: The Experience So Far. IMF-WBG Policy Paper, June 2019.

IMF (2017). Fintech and Financial Services: Initial Considerations, IMF Staff Discussion Note, SDN 17/05.

Keynes, John Maynard (1936). The General Theory of Employment, Interest and Money. London: Macmillan (reprinted 2007).

Koning, J.P. (2016). Fedcoin: A Central Bank-issued Cryptocurrency. November 15, 2016.

Kotlikoff, L. (2010). *Jimmy Stewart Is Dead: Ending the World's Ongoing Financial Plague with Limited Purpose Banking*. John Wiley & Sons, Hoboken, NJ.

Laina, P. (2015). *Proposals for Full-Reserve Banking: A Historical Survey from David Ricardo to Martin Wolf*. University of Helsinki.

Mersch, Y. (2017). Digital Base Money: an assessment from the ECB's perspective. Speech at the Farewell ceremony for Pentti Hakkarainen, Deputy Governor of Suomen Pankki – Finlands Bank. Helsinki, 16 January 2017.

Mirakhor, A. (2017). "Islamic Finance and Financial Repression". *Global Halal Investing Journal*, URL: https://journal. wahedinvest.com/islamic-finance-and-financial-repression/. Accessed 5 July 2019.

Pfister, C. (2017). "Monetary Policy and Digital Currencies: Much Ado About Nothing?" Bank of France, Working Papers, No. 642.

Raskin, M. and Yermack, D. (2016). "Digital Currencies, Decentralized Ledgers, and the Future of Central Banking", NBER Working Paper No. 22238, May 2016.

Rogoff, K. (2016). *The Curse of Cash*, Princeton University Press.

Stevens, A. (2017). Digital currencies: Threats and Opportunities for Monetary Policy, National Bank of Belgium, Economic Review, June.

Sveriges Riksbank (2017). The Riksbank's e-krona Project – Report 1, September.

Tobin, James (1969). A General Equilibrium Approach to Monetary Theory, Journal of Money, Credit and Banking, 1, February, pp. 15–29.

MODERNIZING FARA'ID, WAQF, AND ZAKAT

Responsible governance is a crucial issue in strengthening the performance of Islamic Social Finance institutions, viz. waqf, zakat, and those pertaining to inheritance (fara'id). Although past research has found that good governance in these institutions has been well implemented in some aspects, they, however, have not been implemented comprehensively.

This research aims at elaborating good governance from the perspective of Islam and proposing technology to fill gaps in governance due to various factors, by effectively tracking and tracing assets such that it ends up to the deserving beneficiaries with minimal leakages.

In this chapter, we provide ways as to how technologies like the blockchain and AI can operationalize the transparency and accountability that is required of important social institutions that govern the dispensation of fara'id law, and the management and distribution of waqf and zakat. These areas go beyond efficiency benefits in processes or projected cost-savings, but demand the highest level of ethical implementation of governance.

Keywords: *Accountable Management, Distributed Digital Ledgers, Smart Contracts.*

Contents

1. Introduction

Accountability and responsible governance are crucial factors in the context of strengthening the performance of zakat institutions. As a public organization, the performance of zakat institutions, especially in management and service, are the benchmark for the growth of public trust. The principles of accountability, duty, justice, and transparency are the foundation of shaping the framework in achieving good governance in all public institutions — Islamic or otherwise. For Muslims, the sources of the Shariah (Qur'an and Sunnah) and the established Islamic jurisprudence (fiqh) provide the framework for Islamic corporate governance to achieve the maqasid (objectives) of Shariah (Divine Law).

Latest developments in Fintech promises more efficiency and reduced costs, causing significant shifts in the financial landscape with the introduction of sophisticated and disruptive technologies like AI and the blockchain. However, in public institutions, the utilization of such technologies is focused on transparency and enforcing accountability rather than cost and efficiency benefits alone. The ability to audit and monitor the movement and transfer of assets to the intended beneficiaries is crucial in dispensing the duty of the authorities, and subsequently establishing trust and improving social capital between citizens and the governing authorities. Providing the public with the appropriate information and the performance of waqf and zakat assets are mechanisms where the entrusted authorities can enhance and gain support from the public to continue paying zakat to their collection centers and endowing waqf channels. Failure to do so will result in diminishing pools of waqf assets and reduction in zakat collections, which are critical sources of funds for socioeconomic development of Muslim communities (ummah).

In this chapter, we discuss ways as to how technologies like the blockchain and AI can operationalize the transparency and accountability that is required of important social institutions that govern the dispensation of fara'id law, and the management and distribution of waqf and zakat in order to eradicate poverty, circulate wealth, and enhance micro-, small-, and large-scale infrastructure for social and economic development, and thus share prosperity for a just social system that enables a more secure and sustainable economy.

1.1. *Shariah Basis for Fara'id, Waqf, and Zakat*

Whether Muslims realize it or not, the waqf and zakat institutions are some of the most powerful public/social institutions in the world. Unlike formal financial institutions that have resulted in excluded groups that are unbanked or deemed unbankable due to their financial status and lack of assets or resources, these Islamic institutions are meant to serve the disadvantaged and disenfranchised as prescribed by the Almighty Creator.

1.1.1. Fara'id

Islamic Inheritance jurisprudence is a field of Islamic jurisprudence that deals with inheritance, a topic that is prominently dealt with in the Qur'an. This branch of Islamic law is technically known as 'ilm al-farā'id, and it determines the manner and order of distribution of the assets of a deceased Muslim is known as Fara'id. The principles of Fara'id are to be found in the Holy Quran, the traditions and sayings of the Prophet ﷺ and the majority opinion of Islamic scholars.

Farā'id is regarded as one of the most important branches of Islamic law and the subject of the most detailed provisions revealed in the Quran. The Prophet himself is reported to have said: "Learn the law of intestate inheritance (Fara'id) and teach it to people, for I am someone who will be taken from you, and this knowledge will be taken from you and calamities will ensue, until two men will one day disagree about the obligatory appointment and will not find anyone to judge between them" (Nasif, undated). The Prophet also warned his community that Fara'id would be the first area of knowledge to be removed from the Muslim community and therefore, it is not surprising that Fara'id has received a great deal of attention from the Muslim jurists and scholars up to the present day.

1.1.2. Waqf

Awqaf (i.e., the plural form of waqf) institutions may comprise several types and can be aimed at different beneficiaries. They can be either religious or philanthropic. Religious awqaf include mosques, shrines, graveyards, Islamic educational institutions like madrasahs, and so on. Philanthropic awqaf include the waqf of a property or asset for a specific philanthropic purpose, like medical aid, general education, inns, and so on. Similarly, the beneficiaries of a waqf may be family members (waqf ahli/dhurri), or the general public (Ahmed, 2004).

The creation of waqf is a way for waqf founders to attain righteousness:

> "By no means shall ye attain righteousness unless ye give (benevolently) out of that which ye love; and whatever ye give, Allah surely knows it."
>
> (Quran 3: 92)

The creation of waqf is one of the ways to generate continuous rewards for the founder even after his death:

> "When a man dies his acts come to an end, except three things, recurring charity, or knowledge (by which people benefit), or pious offspring, who pray for him."
>
> (Reported by Abu Hurairah, Sahih Muslim)

The perpetuity of waqf implies that waqf property needs to be preserved and the benefits can be gained without consuming it (Kahf, 2003). When a waqif (i.e., a person who waqf his/her assets) surrenders his/her properties as waqf, the properties are no longer his, as the ownership of any waqf property belongs to

Allah s.w.t. Therefore, an administrator or trustee (mutawalli) has to be appointed to manage the properties in order to ensure perpetuity and that the benefits will be continually disseminated to the beneficiaries.

Historically, Prophet ﷺ built the Quba and Nabawi Mosques in Madinah as a waqf for the benefit of Muslims to do their prayers. Prophet ﷺ taught his companions to create awqaf whenever they realized any pressing need in their society. He dedicated his land in Khaybar for the building of a guesthouse for newly-converted Muslims as their numbers grew. The creation of waqf spread to include not only the building of mosques, houses, guesthouses, lands, and wells, but almost all goods and social services during the Ummayad and Abbasid eras. As years past, the role of waqf was extended to other socioeconomic welfare of the society, such as building and maintaining universities, schools, hospitals, graveyards, orphanages, and others (Mahamood, 2000). The perpetuity of waqf renders it the characteristic of a sustainable development instrument, which is potent for poverty alleviation as well as inclusive finance.

Generally, there are three types of waqf:

1. Waqf khayri (public waqf): Endowment made by the founder to support the general good and welfare of the poor and the needy in society. Usually, the founders create such awqaf in the form of buildings, such as mosques, schools, hospitals, orphanage houses, guesthouses, or in the form of basic infrastructure, books, land for cemeteries, and wells.
2. Waqf dhurri (family waqf): Endowment made by the founder for his children, grandchildren, relatives, or for other persons he specifies. When the beneficiary dies, the waqf asset will be transferred to public welfare purposes.
3. Waqf al-mushtarak (mixed waqf): Endowment created by a founder to support both the public and his family.

The waqf administration structure is typically an independent administration (mutawalli) to ensure proper governance — a state-appointed authority (or Chief Judge) is usually entrusted to supervise all waqf assets to protect from misuse. Founders typically manage their own waqf assets, or this responsibility is given to their respective beneficiaries or appointed persons.

Waqf institutions can be viewed as three sections — (1) waqf procurement section, (2) waqf utilization section, and

(3) income distribution section. Hence, waqf institutions should procure highly competent personnel not only in management but also in Islamic finance and investment management. In addition, the waqf institutions should be administered by experienced professionals with deep investment knowledge and skills to keep the assets highly productive and income generating.

1.1.3. Zakat

Zakat is no doubt one of the most significant institutions of Islam. In early Islamic history, zakat proved to be an extremely effective tool for poverty alleviation and inclusive finance. During the rule of Umar ibn al-Khattab between 13 Hijri to 22 Hijri (634–644 CE) and the reign of Umar ibn Abd al-Aziz (r. 99–101 Hijri/ 717–720 CE), the distribution of zakat was so successful that, at one stage, no one was qualified to receive zakat, due to the people's improved financial conditions.

Despite tremendous success of poverty alleviation through zakat disbursement in early Islamic history, its immense potentials still remain untapped in the contemporary Muslim world. The current performance of zakat management in the Muslim world is quite poor, with a few exceptions. In many Muslim majority countries, there is no official authority responsible for the management of zakat (Nagaoka, 2014). An Islamic Development Bank (IDB) report estimates that the current annual zakat collection is only around USD10 billion per annum. In reality, zakat could potentially generate at least US$200 billion, implying that only 5% of total potential zakat is actually being collected throughout the Muslim world. This is only 0.15% of the OIC member countries' GDP, given the fact that the GDP of the OIC member countries is US$6 trillion (IDB-UNDESA, 2014). These figures indicate that there is a need for a massive reform and revitalisation of the institution of zakat, which is undoubtedly an important tool for the development of inclusive finance and poverty eradication.

2. Utilizing Technology for Fara'id, Waqf, and Zakat

Blockchain coupled with the artificial intelligence cluster of technologies (AI as well as machine learning, natural language processing, machine vision, etc.) are especially applicable to the contractual formulation and documentation portion of Islamic social services. This is because AI has been proven to be most useful when it is fed large volumes of data (e.g., legal research archives, e-Discovery electronic stored information, "ESI") (Mohamed and Ali, 2019). They are also useful in automating time-consuming mundane formulaic tasks like screening research and filling out legal templates. As such, AI can save the consumer on massive legal fees from expensive man-hours that traditional lawyers charge.

The digitization of legal data constitutes another megatrend transforming workflows and business models. The volume of data used in legal advice has increased exponentially — a pattern seen in many other industries as well. A variety of legal technologies has emerged, enabling the digitization and automation of these and other legal-work activities (Veith *et al.*, 2016).

2.1. *Digitalized Fara'id Systems*

In regard to the distribution of the inheritance among the heirs, the Shäfi'i, Mäliki, and Hanbali schools consider that it should be proceed in the following order (i) firstly to the ashab al-Furud or Quranic sharers, (ii) to the 'asabah al-Nasabiyyah, or agnate by blood relationship, (iii) to the al Mu'tiq (patron), (iv) to the bait ul-mal (state treasury).

Once the laws of the land and practices recommended by fiqh scholars have been adhered to, the disbursement of the inheritance according to the wishes as stated in the wasiyyah (will) of the deceased or in its absence, according to the Islamic intestate laws.

From the technology perspective, a platform can be built to facilitate the assembly of such contractual agreements. Digital technologies can enable the management and automation of legal contract creation and automatically produce customized templates based on limited input for customization. The said platform can review documents for key and non-standard clauses, and can also organize and classify volumes of contracts according to each category for better contract management (Figure 10.1).

From the social perspective, it reduces a lot of counter claims when an asset has been dealt with clearly through a wasiyyah, and becomes an effective form of dispute resolution when ownership rights transfers are unambiguously determined.

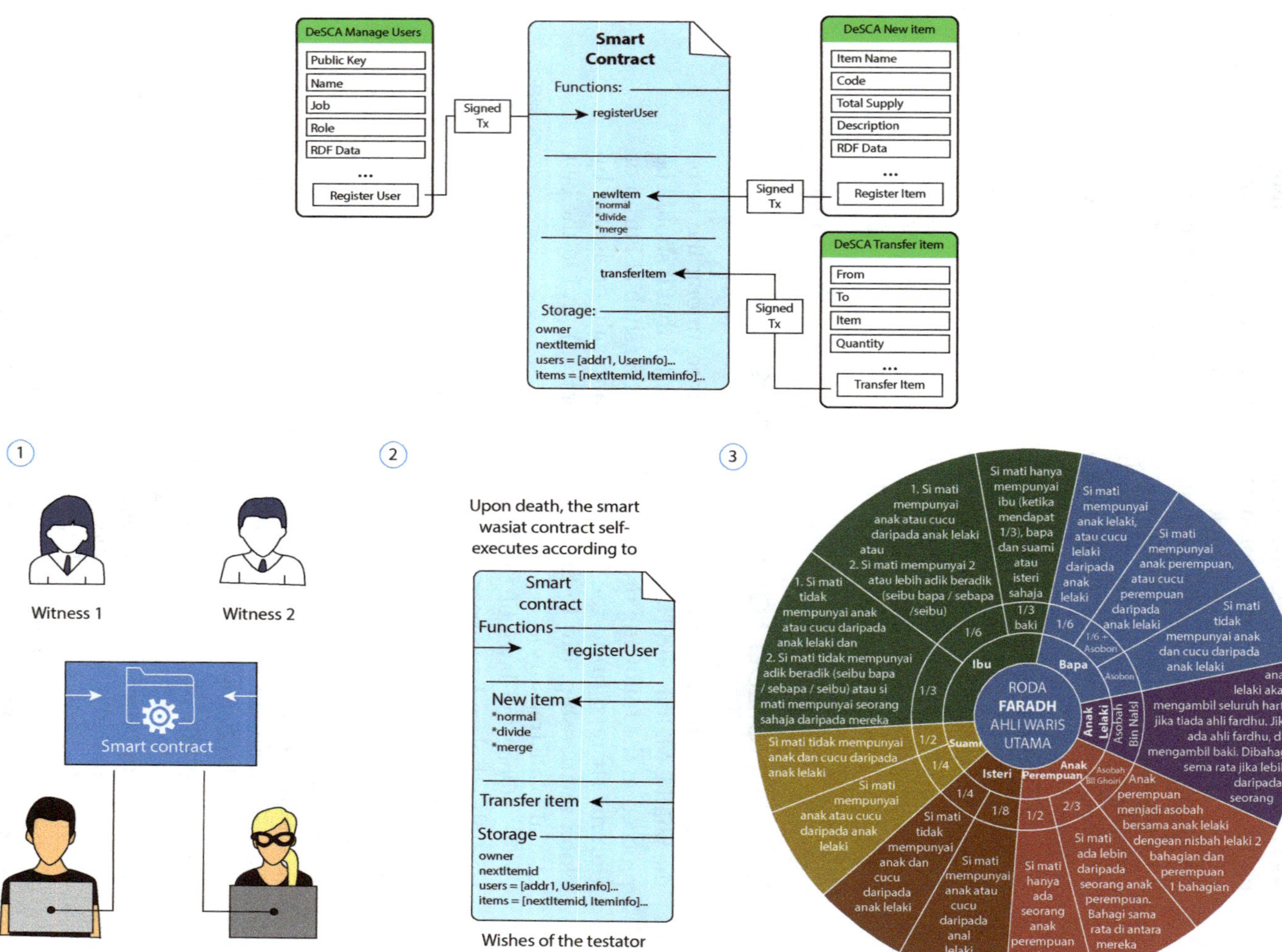

DeSCA Manage Users
Public Key
Name
Job
Role
RDF Data
...
Register User
Signed Tx
Smart Contract
Functions:
registerUser
newItem
*normal
*divide
*merge
transferItem
Storage:
owner
nextItemid
users = [addr1, Userinfo]...
items = [nextItemid, Iteminfo]...
DeSCA New item
Item Name
Code
Total Supply
Description
RDF Data
...
Register Item
Signed Tx
DeSCA Transfer item
From
To
Item
Quantity
...
Transfer Item
Signed Tx
1
Witness 1
Witness 2
Smart contract
2
Upon death, the smart wasiat contract self-executes according to
Smart contract
Functions
registerUser
New item
*normal
*divide
*merge
Transfer item
Storage
owner
nextItemid
users = [addr1, Userinfo]...
items = [nextItemid, Iteminfo]...
Wishes of the testator as stated in the wasiat
3
RODA FARADH AHLI WARIS UTAMA
Ibu
Bapa
Anak Lelaki
Asobah Bin Nalsl
Suami
Isteri
Anak Perempuan
Asobah Bil Ghoiri
1/3
1/6
1/6
1/6 + Asobon
Asobon
1/2
1/4
1/4
1/8
1/2
2/3
baki
1. Si mati tidak mempunyai anak atau cucu daripada anak lelaki dan
2. Si mati tidak mempunyai adik beradik (seibu bapa / sebapa / seibu) atau si mati mempunyai seorang sahaja daripada mereka
1. Si mati mempunyai anak atau cucu daripada anak lelaki atau
2. Si mati mempunyai 2 atau lebih adik beradik (seibu bapa / sebapa /seibu)
Si mati hanya mempunyai ibu (ketika mendapat 1/3), bapa dan suami atau isteri sahaja
Si mati mempunyai anak lelaki, atau cucu lelaki daripada anak lelaki
Si mati mempunyai anak perempuan, atau cucu perempuan daripada anak lelaki
Si mati tidak mempunyai anak dan cucu daripada anak lelaki
anak lelaki akan mengambil seluruh harta jika tiada ahli fardhu. Jika ada ahli fardhu, dia mengambil baki. Dibahagi sema rata jika lebih daripada seorang
Anak perempuan menjadi asobah bersama anak lelaki dengean nisbah lelaki 2 bahagian dan perempuan 1 bahagian
Si mati ada lebih daripada seorang anak perempuan. Bahagi sama rata di antara mereka
Si mati hanya ada seorang anak perempuan sahaja
Si mati mempunyai anak atau cucu daripada anal lelaki
Si mati tidak mempunyai anak dan cucu daripada anak lelaki
Si mati mempunyai anak atau cucu daripada anak lelaki
Si mati tidak mempunyai anak dan cucu daripada anak lelaki

Figure 10.1

2.2. Digitalized Waqf Systems

In regard to the distribution of the inheritance among the heirs, the Shäfi'i, Mäliki, and Hanbali schools consider that it should be proceed in the following order (i) firstly to the ashab al-Furud or Quranic sharers, (ii) to the 'asabah al-Nasabiyyah, or agnate by blood relationship, (iii) to the al Mu'tiq (patron), (iv) to the bait ul-mal (state treasury).

Once the laws of the land and practices recommended by fiqh scholars have been adhered to, the disbursement of the inheritance according to the wishes as stated in the wasiyyah (will) of the deceased or in its absence, according to the Islamic intestate laws.

From the technology perspective, a platform can be built to facilitate the assembly of such contractual agreements (estates, wills, and trusts). Digital technologies can enable the management and automation of legal contract creation and automatically produce customized templates based on limited input for customization (Figure 2). The said platform can review documents for key and non-standard clauses, and can also organize and classify volumes of contracts according to each category for better contract management.

From the social perspective, it reduces a lot of counter claims when an asset has been dealt with clearly through a waqf nuzriah (oath) or wasiyyah (will), and becomes an effective form of dispute resolution when ownership rights transfers are unambiguously determined.

For waqf, such accountability and proper administration, particularly in its longevity, is required. In order to be valid and legitimate, a waqf is subject to three key restrictions:

i. Irrevocability: Once the waqf deed is pronounced in verbal terms or signed in written form, it cannot be revoked.
ii. Inalienability: Once the deed is performed; the corpus of waqf (principal of the fund) can never be alienated as gift, inheritance, or sale etc.
iii. Perpetuity: It is mandatory upon the trustee to ensure the safeguard of corpus of cash against any loss or reduction, so the benefits of the same may continue forever.

In Figure 10.2, permissioned access can be given to state authorities to verify the previous ownership of the waqf assets, or

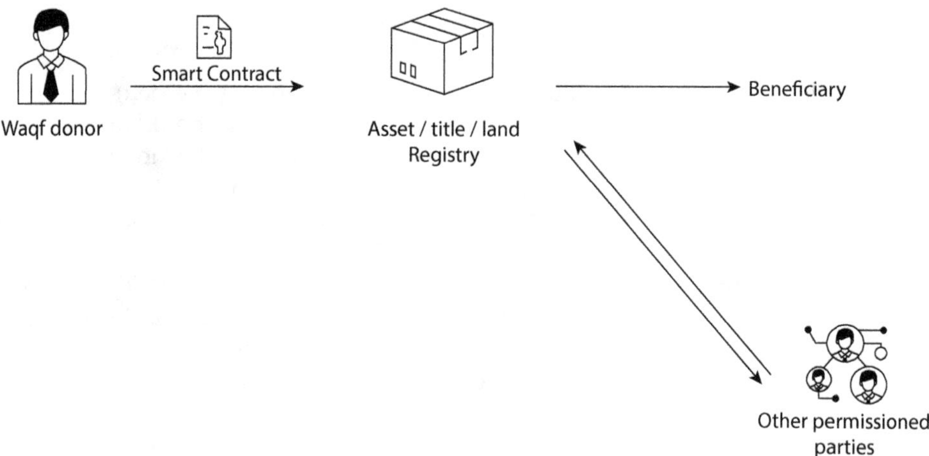

Figure 10.2: Digitalized Waqf System

the stipulated wishes of the waqf founder, if required for whatever purposes that may arise.

2.3. *Digitalized Zakat Systems*

It is often recognized that zakat disbursements are opaque to zakat-payers, with it becoming increasingly difficult to identify where the zakat money ends up.

By integrating blockchain architecture to AI systems, complex processes can be mechanized by a framework of automation, trusted data sets and support system integration (Figure 10.3). Multi-party stakeholders can work from a unified platform that covers the majority of logistical processes and can enable faster assessment and financial transfers.

This allows for those involved in this transaction — including state-level regulators or Shariah authorities — to retrace every zakat contribution to its place of origin/destination for whatever reason (see Figure 10.3). The decentralized ledger makes it impossible for anyone to manipulate this data, giving the authorities (State and Shariah) an effective tracking and accountability system where fraud or other breaches of compliance can be detected.

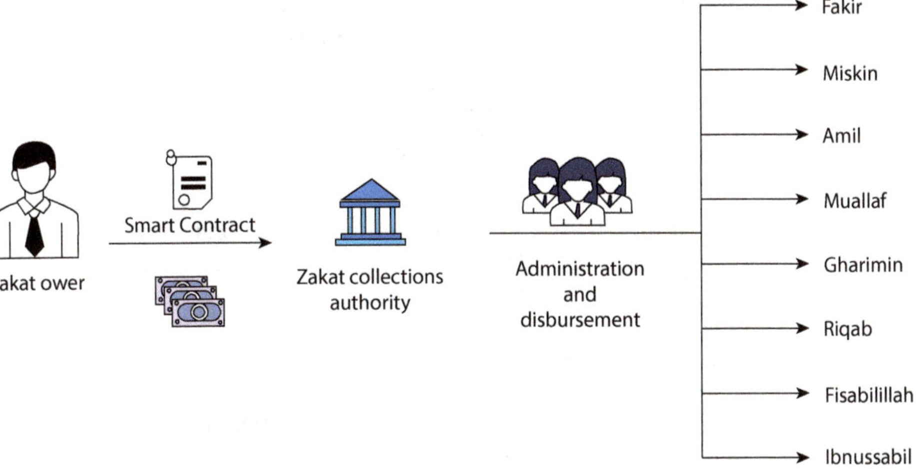

Figure 10.3: Digitalized Zakat System

AI and blockchain applications in zakat collection and disbursement:

i. *Fraud Detection and Risk Mitigation*

Due to its ability to provide a public ledger across multiple unknown parties, blockchain has the potential to eliminate errors and detect fraudulent activity. A decentralized digital repository can independently verify the authenticity of zakat contributors, disbursement policies, and financial transfers by providing a complete historical record.

ii. *Better Processing and Management*

The collection of zakat from a mobile phone app or physical collection at mosques or authorized collection centers reduces risks and increase contributor satisfaction, with blockchain systems facilitating transparency and coordination among all parties working on a unified platform.

iii. *New Disbursement and Payment Models*

Increased automation to capture risk data in contracts also offers new opportunities to build market knowledge, streamline payments, and manage agency risks better. At the very least, zakat administrators can use blockchain to cut zakat management costs by reducing the costs required to collect and subsequently disburse the funds to the beneficiary groups.

iv. *Transparency and Traceability*

The ability to track and monitor transactions of zakat contributions physically in the real world with greater transparency builds trust between the State and its citizens, between collector and contributor. This will improve future collections. It also facilitates data collection for reporting and the publication of annual reports for zakat collection and the disbursement to beneficiaries by percentage for that year.

3. Benefits of Digitalized Processes for Islamic Social Systems

These new systems will make traditional processes of Islamic social systems better and more efficient in their process flows to existing cumbersome processes which are fraught with agency issues and leakages. In this manner, a blockchainized transaction is publicly accessible and ensures that the data is protected against tampering and revision, and it is virtually impossible for individuals to modify or replace parts of the blockchain secretly. Any form of concealment, fraud, or attempt at misrepresentation violates the principles of justice and fairness in Shariah. A full copy of the blockchain contains every transaction ever executed, making information on the value belonging to every active address (account) accessible at any point in history.

The ability to track and monitor transactions waqf assets and zakat collections physically in the real world with greater transparency builds trust between the State (authorities) and its citizens, the people they serve. This will improve future collections, and their reputation as a credible mediator and regulator.

Automated collections, tracking, and processing replaces the laborious auditing and monitoring of fraud and monetary leakages between collection and disbursement, going back-and-forth between claimants, assessing rightful ownership in cases of disputes, and counter-claims.

The simplicity and speed of execution will increase overall efficiency and usability for authorities put in-charge of such religious duties. It also leads to a superior user experience for the users and customers that require such important services.

Since the system is efficient with less repeating steps, or less need to repeat similar steps done by different parties, more time can be put to provide better customer value and enhanced support.

4. Bringing Traditional Islamic Social Institutions into the Future of Global Aid

Given the complexity and likely continuation of current conflicts, by 2030, an estimated 80% of the world's extreme poor will live in areas defined as fragile — the majority of which will be Muslim-majority countries, or states with significant Muslim populations.[1]

Islamic social finance was developed in adherence to the Shariah principles of socioeconomic justice, equality, and collective prosperity. Through the mobilization of tools such as zakat, waqf, sadaqah, and infaq, it can help deliver much-needed financing for the humanitarian challenges caused by climate change.

Zakat (wealth tax and a means of wealth distribution) is a key Islamic institution of harmonizing the relationship between the individual and public interest (maslahah) and minimizing the disparity between the needy and the wealthy. Each year, Muslims are required to donate 2.5% of one year's total cumulative wealth to the poor in the form of zakat. The Islamic Development Bank estimates the global value of zakat to be between US$232 billion and US$560 billion annually.

Waqf is an endowment to a religious, educational, or charitable cause, most frequently used to build schools, hospitals or religious institutions. Given its communitarian nature, waqf is often used to fund social projects and services, and has a high potential for sustainable development due to its perpetuity requirement of the principal.

Infaq and sadaqah are voluntary charities given on a voluntary basis at any time. It is equivalent to the contribution

---

1   https://www.weforum.org/agenda/2019/05/islamic-social-finance-humanitarian-aid-charity-climate-change/

to any charity or donation box. As such, it is irregular in nature and often difficult to tabulate, because there are no fixed rates like the zakat, and depends largely on the generosity of kind souls. Hence, Islamic social finance tools such as infaq, sadaqah, waqf, and zakat have enormous potential to be leveraged and scaled when viewed as a collective whole towards a solution to global humanitarian aid.

For example, the International Federation of the Red Cross and Red Crescent Societies (IFRC) in 2018 used zakat collected in the Malaysian state of Perlis to fund a drought-assistance programme in the Kenyan county of Kitui, pioneering a sustainable humanitarian zakat initiative. The program provided access to clean water and livelihood opportunities to the county residents by using zakat funds to repair boreholes used to extract water and dig new ones. In addition, green gram seeds (a regional staple) were purchased using zakat funds and distributed to local families for farming purposes. On average, each family received two kilograms of seeds, which had the capacity of yielding 180 kilograms of harvest. In the total of US$1.2 million in zakat funding that was channelled to Kitui county, a total return of approximately US$20 million generated from green gram crop sales alone, and on top of that, access to much-needed clean water was also made available to 175,000 families.

5. Conclusion

Zakat and awqaf institutions aim to contribute to the development of society in all possible forms. Historically, significant educational institutions, healthcare services, mosques, and other places of worship, rest houses (traveller inns), huge arable lands producing fruits and agricultural products for beneficiaries, and many other poverty alleviation projects and inclusive finance tools were successfully established and administered from the proceeds of awqaf and zakat collections.

In an era of disruption to long-standing financial institutions, digital technologies can reinforce increased use and broader adoption of mobile apps and intelligent systems for traditional Islamic institutions of fara'id, waqf, and zakat. The many digital innovations that have helped reshape the financial landscape can help to remove friction, human errors, fraud and other agency risks from all of the essential steps of fara'id, waqf, and zakat institutions. The Islamic industry must make calculated investments to take advantage of efficiencies and opportunities that digital technologies can deliver in the long term.

Bibliography

Ahmed, H. (2004). Role of Zakah and Awqaf in Poverty Alleviation, Jeddah: IRTI, IDB, 2004, pp. 72–73

Al-Mubarak, T. (2016). The Maqasid of Zakah And Awqaf And Their Roles in Inclusive Finance. Islam and Civilizational Renewal (ICR), 7(2).

Amalia, E., Rodoni, A., and Tahliani, H. (2018), "Good Governance in Strengthening the Performance of Zakat Institutions in Indonesia" in International Conference on Islamic Finance, Economics and Business, KnE Social Sciences, pp. 223–241. DOI 10.18502/kss.v3i8.2511

Bhatti, M., & Bhatti, M. I. (2010). Toward Understanding Islamic Corporate Governance Issues in Islamic Finance. *Asian Politics & Policy*, 2(1), pp. 25–38.

Coulson, N. J. (1971). Succession in the Muslim Family Law, Cambridge University Press, Cambridge.

IDB and UN-DESA, Summary of "The Role of Islamic Finance in Sustainable Development Financing and the Opportunities in Creating New Partnerships in the Implementation of the Post-2015 Development Agenda," Jeddah: IDB Head Quarters, 2 June 2014; and IDB, "*Waqf* & Zakat: Solidarity-Based Financing for Sustainable Development" presentation available online at 'UN Sustainable Development Knowledge Platform': https://sustainabledevelopment.un.org/content/documents/10289Mahiridrissipresentation.pdf, 6 June 2014.

Ihsan, H., & Ayedh, A. (2015). A Proposed Framework of Islamic Governance for Awqaf. *Journal of Islamic Economics, Banking and Finance*, 11(2).

Kahf, M. (2003). The Role of *Waqf* In Improving the Ummah Welfare. Paper presented at the International Seminar on "*Waqf* as a Private Legal Body," organized by Islamic University of North Sumatra, Medan, Indonesia.

Mahamood, S. M. (2000). The Administration of *Waqf*, Pious Endowment in Islam: A Critical Study of the Role of the State Islamic Religious Councils as The Sole Trustees of a Wqaf Assets and The Implementation of Istibdal In Malaysia With Special Reference to the Federal Territory of Kuala Lumpur. PhD thesis, Birmingham University.

Mohamed, H., & Ali, H. (2019). *Blockchain, Fintech and Islamic Finance — Building the Future of the New Islamic Digital Economy.* De I G Press, Boston/Berlin.

Nagaoka, S. (2014). Resuscitation of the Antique Economic System or Novel Sustainable System? Revitalization of the Traditional Islamic Economic Institutions (*Waqf* and Zakat) in the Post-Modern Era, *Kyoto Bulletin of Islamic Area Studies,* 7 (March 2014), p. 3.

Nasif, M. A. (not dated). *al-Taj al-. Jämi' li al-Usul fi Ahädith al-Rasid, Istanbul, al-Maktabah al-Islamiyyah,* n. d, Vol. 2, p. 250.

Powers, D. S. (1986). *Studies in Qur'an and Hadith: The Formation of the Islamic Law of Inheritance,* Berkeley, University of California Press.

Ramli, N. M., & Muhamed, N. A. (2013). *Good Governance Framework for Corporate Waqf: Towards Accountability Enhancement.*

Samra, E. (2016). *Corporate Governance in Islamic Financial Institutions.*

Sulaiman, M., & Zakari, M. A. (2015). Efficiency and Effectiveness of *Waqf* Institutions in Malaysia: Toward Financial Sustainability. *Bloomsbury Qatar Foundation Journals,* 1, pp. 43–53.

Veith, C., Bandlow, M., Harnisch, M., Wenzler, H., Hartung, M., and Hartung, D. (2016). *How Legal Technology Will Change the Business of Law.* Boston Consulting Group and Bucerius Law School.

Wahab, N. A., & Rahim Abdul Rahman, A. (2011). A Framework to Analyse the Efficiency and Governance of *Zakat* Institutions. *Journal of Islamic Accounting and Business Research,* 2(1), pp. 43–62.

ENHANCING LEGAL AND REGULATORY FRAMEWORK FOR DIGITAL TRANSFORMATION

11

Digital innovation has incorporated advanced technologies in transforming the way we access and use existing financial products and services. The Islamic Economy is becoming increasingly disrupted by revolutionary enterprises using technologies such as cloud computing, extensive use of artificial intelligence (AI) and data analytics, integration of interoperable Internet of Things (IoT) devices, and the blockchained decentralization.

Nevertheless, to sustain such innovation, the Islamic Economy has to fully develop digital ecosystems that nurture and develop both the demand and supply sides of the ecosystem. At the same time, regulatory and legal systems need to be strengthened in order for the ecosystem be protected from cyber risks and threats to allow for the market actors to flourish.

This chapter assesses the key features of the Islamic Digital Economy and its network to foster fair competition, innovation, and the entrepreneurship mindset. On the supply-side, recommendations to continually develop and attract talent, expertise, and capital to ensure sufficient funding for groundbreaking ideas and novel scalable business models will be made. The regulatory issues that comes with technological adoption along with financial stability implications and consumer protection, with suggestions that regulators themselves adopt advanced technologies (SupTech) to embark on the new era of market supervision and monitoring will also be discussed.

Keywords: *alternative capital, cybersecurity, deal flows, suptech*

Contents

1. Introduction

Undoubtedly, Fintech growth is relentless but unleashing the future of Fintech requires a re-engineering of how financial institutions operate and are regulated. E-commerce businesses like Amazon, Apple, Facebook, and Google prove that smart data management can create a customer understanding like no other. Across retail, wholesale, and capital markets, banks are ardently aware that the digital-first model based on high-performance data analysis will create a massive advantage. An effective and conducive regulatory system is key to the success of jurisdictions in order to remain competitive in the global market with the use of FinTech. In this chapter, the evolution, challenges, and recommendations for the Islamic Finance regulators in the management and regulation of new technology will be discussed.

2. Digital Transformation in the New Economy

Digital transformation is imperative for the Islamic Economy to remain competitive and achieve sustainability in the market. The continued existence of economic institutions is connected with the implementation of innovation, and in embracing digital transformation, to radically improve efficiency and performance within the organization. Digital transformation and new technology adoption have changed the way of doing businesses and these new ways have resulted in reshaping the existing models of businesses and the creation of new innovative ones.

Unlike the digitization of developed country wholesale and institutional markets, in general digital economic services in most developing countries has developed independently of the efforts of financial regulators, and have been usually led by mobile telecommunications companies.[1] In many jurisdictions, market regulators only started to address potential risks to consumers and economic stability once mobile payments had already become mainstream in the domestic economic system.

---

1   Daniel Runde, "M-Pesa And the Rise of The Global Mobile Money Market", *FORBES* (12 August 2015), http://www.forbes.com/sites/danielrunde/2015/08/12/m-pesa-and-the-rise-of-the-global-mobile-money-market/.

The digital transformation shift has also changed the expectations and wants of the customers. Today, customers want banking (and other economic services) from anywhere they are and at any time, regardless if they are in the office, at home in the evenings, or while waiting for their next appointment to come. This digital behavior of customers has set a new bar for the services industries, and the industry is trying to cope with the needs of these digital mindsets by using omni channels and advanced technologies. Having better insights into how customers behave in their preferred buying channels also allows businesses to identify the right moment to intervene and develop a comprehensive strategy that works holistically across channels such as search, video, social, and display (Mohamed and Ali, 2019).

The modes in which Fintech has become relevant to every customer without the need for an array of disparate customized solutions are with chatbots and robo-advisory solutions. Built into messaging apps, chatbots come as close to the customer as possible by being a personal assistant in any enterprise. They provide a pertinent answer and allow the clients to complete a purchase immediately with the help that is provided.

3. Regulatory Issues Concerning Disruptive Technology

Technology is accelerating at a scale that presents quickly apparent economic benefits to the economic system and society at large, but it may also have potential risks from unintended consequences. Some of these concerns, though not exhaustive, are as follows.

3.1. Regulation and Supervision

By and large, regulators are aware that digital transformation has the potential to deliver immense economic benefits, by lowering the cost of operations and enhancing competition, and societal benefits, by boosting financial inclusion and delivering more convenient financial services. However, risk and failure are an integral part of innovation in FinTech solutions. Therefore, it is critical for regulators to ensure safeguards are in place to manage the risks (such as institution-specific micro-financial risks and system-wide macro-financial risks). Providing parameters and regulatory clarity through a framework (for digital business models) is essential for digital's mass adoption in order to ensure the financial stability of the system. Regulatory sandboxes are only one of the approaches to manage FinTech and may not fit circumstances in different situations and jurisdictions. Market supervisors will have to ensure that financial institutions or firms have robust governance frameworks and such surveillance could be complemented by data-driven supervision.

Other risks include those associated with the usage of such digital currency, which the public may not be aware of. Initial Coin Offerings (ICOs) were new ways of raising capital through decentralized means, which has the potential to side-step rigorous regulation requirements for funds-raising established by authorities. In addition, there is serious trepidation on the risk of money laundering and financing of terrorism, termed as anti-money laundering/counter-terrorism financing AML/CFT, which requires financial institutions including banks to have adequate measures to counter the risk of AML/CFT.

Another significant risk management concern is the operational risk that reflects cyber-security, fraud and theft, data privacy, and legal issues. Similar to the Basel Committee on Banking Supervision (BCBS), the Islamic finance standard-setting body known as Islamic Financial Services Board (IFSB) prescribes a capital regime for operational risk which does not really address risk-related operational issues. While regulatory instruments such as BCBS/IFSB capital requirements can create incentives to address certain operational risks, such as business continuity, capital is not sufficient to restore operations if a financial institution suffers a cyber-attack. Cyber-security and Critical Information Technology Infrastructure (CITI)'s resilience has to be given considerable attention by market supervisors of all sectors, especially the banking/financial sector.

Specific to Islamic Finance, the innovative solutions for Islamic Financial Services should be consistent with Shariah rules and principles, and it takes adequate knowledge in the relevant economic, financial and technical (AI, Blockchain, IoT, Machine Learning) areas. This is huge concern in the role of the Shariah Supervisory Board (SSB) in the overseeing the product innovation at the institutional level, which impacts Shariah compliance issues for enhanced supervision. The assessment of Shariah-compliance too should include the procedural processes from creation to the result of any crypto-assets and its mechanisms. In this respect, the General Council for Islamic Banks and Financial Institutions (CIBAFI) has recently suggested (in its comments submitted to the BCBS's consultative document) that Islamic banks will need to consider how they can safeguard the end-to-end transactions according to the Shariah, including the rights and ownership at each stage. While other bodies, such as the IFSB, have also highlighted the challenges that FinTech innovations cause, a thorough guidance covering all the modalities of the FinTech issues for Islamic finance is unrealistic, and such expectations need to be reframed. The appropriate regulations will have to be created (or adjusted) as the technology itself evolves. The assumption that regulations, once crafted, will then remain in place unchanged for significant periods of time has been overturned in today's environment. As new business models and services such as sharing services (e.g., Airbnb and Grab) and ICOs emerge, government agencies are challenged with creating or modifying regulations, enforcing them, and communicating them to the stakeholders, while working within legacy frameworks and striving to foster innovation.

3.2. *Financial Stability and Consumer Protection*

Market supervisors will need to ensure that financial institutions including banks have robust plans in place for scenarios that could threaten their own stability or the larger macroeconomic stability. For instance, in robo-advisory services, which rely on algorithms and portfolio management to analyze investors' data and automatically recommend investment portfolios, need to be within approved products, or companies offering such services need to be compelled to disclose more information when required. Similarly, third-party service providers or vendors to financial institutions are becoming more common and critical, especially in the areas of cloud computing and data services. Such third-party technology providers may need to be regulated in order to manage related operational risks, which may impact financial stability indirectly.

Under financial stability, consumer protection including personal data protection is one of the areas that are highly focused on. The danger of cyber-attacks and hacking, as well as the need to protect sensitive consumer and corporate financial data, is very real. Unquestionably, a number of recent incidents involved fraud and theft, and there have been breaches of personally identifiable information, which raises many issues including data privacy, ownership and administration, and legal liability. In order to avoid any undesirable situations, much work needs to be done on boosting cyber-security and alleviating cyber risks. The author will make recommendations and discuss that in greater depth in the following sections on RegTech and SupTech.

3.3. *Domestic and Cross-Border Arrangements*

Both domestic and cross-border transactions are important for supervisors. Domestically for FinTech developments, there has to be a coordination among the supervisory agencies regulating financial institutions. A common approach and strategy need to be in place to address FinTech issues at the national and also the international levels. Hence, regional cooperation will be integral in regulating FinTech that scale beyond borders. Furthermore, innovations in cross-border lending, trading, and payment transactions, including via smart contracts, raise questions about the cross-jurisdictional disputes, and enforceability issues.

3.4. *Expertise and Capacity Building*

Talent and the right expertise are one of the areas that requires attention and needs to be addressed moving forward. Though traditionally for supervisors, this has not been a key concern, there are serious challenges for building staff capacity in new areas of the required technical expertise. As traditional roles within some areas of the Islamic bank become automated, forward-thinking planning for capacity building and innovation-related expertise has to be part of the overall strategy in order to provide proper market supervision.

Financial Market and Conduct supervisors should feature greater emphasis on ensuring that they have the adequate resources and skillsets to deal with the evolving nature of FinTech. Additionally, authorities should ensure regulators and financial institutions work collaboratively early on towards the development of next-generation IT infrastructure and cloud-based systems to build in transparency and accountability.

4. RegTech and SupTech — Digital Reporting and Compliance

Around the world, regulators are facing the challenges of the rapid emergence of new FinTech technologies and non-traditional market entrants, all at extraordinary speed. Authorities are faced with the task to develop regulatory approaches that do not hamper development and innovation while still limiting risks to consumers and financial stability.

RegTech and SupTech are largely seen as a category that focuses on technologies that may facilitate the delivery of regulatory requirements more efficiently and effectively than existing capabilities.[2] However, Arner *et al.* (2016) view RegTech and SupTech as more than just efficiency tools but rather a pivotal change leading to a paradigm shift in regulation. To them, RegTech and SupTech holistically represent the next logical evolution of financial services regulation and should develop into a foundational base underpinning the entire financial services sector.

The application of technology to monitoring and compliance offers massive cost savings to established financial companies and potentially massive opportunities to emerging FinTech start-ups, IT, and advisory firms (Shedden and Malna, 2016). From a regulator's perspective, SupTech will enable the prospect of continuous monitoring that would improve efficiency by both liberating excess regulatory capital, decreasing the time it takes to investigate a firm, fostering competition, and upholding their directives for financial stability (both macro and micro) and market integrity (Gutierrez, 2014). From the financial institution's perspective, RegTech will allow them to comply to the constantly evolving regulatory requirements and effectively manage regulatory change within their organizations.

---

2   Feedback Statement, Financial Conduct Authority, Call for Input on Supporting the Development and Adopters of RegTech, (July 2016). RegTech refers to applications of innovative technologies that support compliance with regulatory and reporting requirements by regulated financial institutions. SupTech, on the other hand, refers to technologies used by supervisory agencies themselves.

4.1. Cybersecurity

While regulators regulate prescribed market behaviors, there is a need for an independent agency that enforces and acts when there is a security breach in the Critical Information Technology Infrastructure (CITI) within corporations and government information systems. Hence, a National Cybersecurity Agency (NCsA) is recommended to establish a legal framework for the oversight and maintenance of national cybersecurity in the country. The agency will also be responsible to develop and enforce cyber-secure framework to be used in conjunction with any existing Systems Development Lifecycle (SDLC) methodologies adopted by organizations, as well as complementing government policies, standards, guidelines, and directives.

While most organizations acknowledge that security is an important consideration in developing computer systems, costs, and business performance often take precedence over security. Even though awareness has been elevated on security issues, most organizations focus on applying security only at the commissioning stage of the system development and try to force-fit security into the final design, resulting in ineffective application of security.

An effective way to protect computer systems against cyber threats is to integrate security into every step of the SDLC, from initiation, to development, to deployment, and the eventual disposal of the system. Control Gates or decision points are specific milestones where the security implementations are evaluated. They specify to the corporation that security considerations are addressed, adequate security controls are built in, and identified risks are clearly understood before the system development advances to the next lifecycle phase. The Agile approach can be adopted to continuously update and improve on standards.

Security planning is to be conducted as part of integrating security in SDLC, and should include:

- Identifying and confirming key security roles in the system development project
- Outlining key security milestones and activities for the system development
- Connecting the use of secure design, IT architecture and coding standards

- Warranting all key stakeholders have a shared understanding of the goals, implications, considerations and requirements of performing security

These values integration is crucial in responding to potential security threats as it highlights to key stakeholder the important areas of systems development progress, and that critical decisions made will have security implications.

In addition, a Bill or an Act can be enacted to:

4.1.1. Empower NCsA to prevent and respond to cybersecurity threats and incidents

The Act can empower an authority (e.g., a national cybersecurity agency like NCsA) to investigate cybersecurity threats and incidents to determine their impact and prevent further harm or cybersecurity incidents from arising. The powers that may be exercised are adjusted to the severity of the cybersecurity threat or event and the appropriate measures required for response. The CITI sectors are Banking and Finance, Emergency Services, Health (hospitals, etc.), Transport (air, land and sea), Information Communications (media, etc.), Power and Water.

4.1.2. Create a framework for sharing cybersecurity information

The Act can also facilitate information sharing, which is critical as timely information helps the government and owners of computer systems identify vulnerabilities and prevent cyber incidents more effectively. The Act can also provide a framework for NCsA to request information, and for the protection and sharing of private, restricted or sensitive information.

4.1.3. Launch a licensing framework for cybersecurity service providers

NCsA can act to license different types of service providers, namely cyber-threat penetration testing, cyber-defense and managed security operations monitoring. These services are prioritized because providers of such services have access to sensitive information and hence have a significant impact on the overall security landscape. The licensing framework allows for a balance between security needs and the development of a vibrant cybersecurity ecosystem.

4.2. Institution-specific Micro-financial Risks

An effective way to protect computer systems against cyber threats is to integrate security into every step of the SDLC, from initiation, to development, to deployment, and eventual disposal of the system, which is called the Security-by-Design (SBD) approach.

Security-by-Design is an approach to software and hardware development that seeks to minimize systems vulnerabilities and reduce the attack surface through designing and building security in every phase of the SDLC. This includes incorporating security specifications in the design, continuous security evaluation at each phase and adherence to best practices. The values of integrating security into SDLC include:

- Early identification and mitigation of security vulnerabilities and misconfigurations of systems.
- Identification of shared security services and tools to reduce cost, while improving security posture through proven methods and techniques.
- Facilitation of informed key stakeholder decisions through comprehensive risk management in a timely manner.
- Documentation of important security decisions throughout the lifecycle of the system, ensuring that security was fully considered during all phases.
- Improved systems operability that would otherwise be hampered by isolated security of systems.

Specific to cybersecurity, the SBD addresses the cyber protection considerations throughout a system's lifecycle. This includes security design specifically for the identification, protection, detection, response, and recovery capabilities to strengthen the cyber resiliency of the system.

4.3. *System-wide Macroprudential Policy for Financial Stability*

Macro-financial issues related to systemic importance are embedded in the FSB SIFI[3] framework, which recommends that financial institutions identified as systemically important should have more intense supervisory oversight, higher loss absorbency, as well as recovery and resolution plans. The majority of regulatory changes and clarifications have been made in the areas of payments, capital raising, and to a lesser extent investment management, as many of these economic functions naturally fit within existing regulatory regimes. Only a few regulatory changes to include FinTech innovations in insurance and market support were mentioned (FSB, 2017).

International cooperation will be crucial given the commonalities and global dimension of many FinTech activities. There is potential for international bodies, like the IFSB, FSB, the GPFI and SSBs — such as the BCBS, IAIS, IOSCO and CPMI — to provide avenues for authorities to get together to share experiences on FinTech implications for financial markets. Increased cooperation will be particularly important to mitigate the risk of fragmentation or divergence in regulatory frameworks, which could impede the development and diffusion of beneficial innovations in financial services, and limit the effectiveness to promote financial stability.

As innovations in financial services are developing fast, authorities may further wish to consider the following issues:

4.3.1. Cross-border legal considerations and regulatory arrangements

Cross-border cooperation and coordination among authorities are important to a well-functioning financial system. Financial innovations in cross-border lending, trading, and payments, via

---

3   Systemically important financial institutions (SIFIs) are financial institutions whose distress or disorderly failure, because of their size, complexity, and systemic interconnectedness, would cause significant disruption to the wider financial system and economic activity.

behavioral systems, begs the question about the cross-jurisdictional compatibility of national legal frameworks. The legal validity and enforceability of smart contracts and other applications of DLT are in some cases uncertain, and should be discussed in greater detail. In addition, in some cases, certain technological structures around DLT and smart contracts may not necessarily be designed to comply with the laws of all potential jurisdictions, thus affecting their scale on a cross-border applications.

4.3.2. Governance and disclosure frameworks supporting big data analytics

Applications of Big Data are becoming more prevalent as a basis for financial services across the full range of economic functions, including lending, investment and insurance. Big Data analytics gives rise to several ways for the financial services industry to achieve business advantages by mining and analyzing data. They include enhanced detection to identify exposure in real time across a range of sophisticated financial instruments like derivatives. Predictive analysis of both internal and external data results in good, proactive management of a wide range of problems across industries with the ability to conduct extensive analytics rapidly and enhance risk identification and assessment. Similar to the use of algorithms in other domains, such as securities trading, the complexity and opacity of some Big Data analytics models makes it difficult for authorities to assess the robustness of the models or new unforeseen risks in market behavior, and to determine whether market participants are fully in control over their systems.

4.3.3. Study alternative configurations of digital currencies

The repercussions of hybrid configurations of cryptocurrencies for national financial systems, and the global monetary framework should be investigated. Digital currencies and alternative payment arrangements based on new technology are developing at different speeds across jurisdictions, along with a decline in the use of cash for transactions in some jurisdictions (FSB, 2017). On top of monitoring developments, relevant authorities should examine the potential implications of cryptocurrencies for monetary policy, financial stability, and the global monetary system.

4.4. *Shariah Compliance*

The main risk that Islamic financial institutions (IFIs) face which is unique to them is the Shariah compliance risk. In addition to managing the risks faced by conventional banks, such as credit, market, operational risks, an Islamic financial institution also has to ensure that it complies to Shariah rulings as this carries significant reputational risk to the institution. Fintech products (including cryptocurrencies and tokens) and services need to be treated differently according to the fiqh understanding of the Shariah as well as the regulatory authorities because of its nature and usage. Due to this, its treatment by the regulators as well as Islamic jurists will be in accordance to its nature and utilization — the way they are used as well as the way they were intended to be used — and this should be done first by effectively categorizing such products before fiqh rulings can be applied to them.

The assessment of Shariah-compliance too should include the procedural processes from creation to the result of any digital crypto-assets and its mechanisms. For compliance and legitimacy, before launching a project of any digital crypto-assets it should be scrutinized as per fiqh guidelines (from Shariah committees), and in the absence of those guidelines, clarification should be sought from Shariah experts who have the relevant economic, financial, and technical (blockchain and token experience) capability. Shariah advisory scholars now need to be adept with the underlying technology, which drives digital Shariah solutions to adequately assess Shariah compliance. These Shariah scholars also need to be versed in conventional and Islamic economics and finance to make sound decisions and would require future scholars to be multidisciplinary.

5. The SupTech Trajectory

Policymakers and watchdogs will confront rapidly transforming financial systems in coming years. Building the necessary infrastructure to support their regulation will necessitate the increasing use and reliance on SupTech. This will have to take place in close cooperation with all industry participants. The development of SupTech so far has primarily been driven by the financial services industry wishing to decrease costs, especially in light of the fact that regulatory fines and settlements have increased 45-fold (Kaminsky and Robu, 2016). The next stage is likely to be driven by regulators seeking to increase their supervisory capacity by automating compliance and regulatory surveillance through SupTech.

5.1. Cooperation and Mutual Learning

Interoperability, coordination, and collaboration are the essential elements of any developed and successful ecosystem around the globe. This involves different governments, public, and private sectors indigenously and outside the region. Public and private sectors can establish safe, secure, reliable, and affordable open and shared platforms for digital payments, banking services, and other financial alternatives by converging their offers via omni-channels (offering the customers integrated consistent financial platforms), including regulatory supervision. The regulator can initiate market meetings, discussions, and consultations, and also begin regulatory sandbox experiments. The main contribution of a sandbox from a regulator's perspective may not be in the controlled experimental safe space, but instead, in communicating regulator flexibility towards innovative enterprises, and the regulator's desire to understand new technologies. For many regulators, their doors need to stay open to facilitate knowledge transfer in an era of rapid technological change.

5.2. Updating the Regulatory Toolkit

So far regulators have applied various tools from their regulatory toolkit:

- Traditional approaches of regulating or decision not to regulate;
- Thoughtful testing through forbearance, special charters, or restricted licenses;
- Controlled, transparent experimentation through regulatory sandboxes or piloting.

An increasing number of regulators are beginning to experiment with novel approaches, seeking to unlock innovative potential by seeking to generate innovation while minimizing risks, preserving consumer protection, and market stability. This iterative process has gradually increased regulators' sophistication in their understanding of FinTech innovations and business models.

5.3. *Improving Regulations and Responding to Market Evolution*

FinTech's growth has drawn the need for RegTech and SupTech, the need to use technology, particularly in managing large datasets and audit trails, in the context of regulation, monitoring, reporting, and compliance. Colleges, business schools, and universities should also enhance the training of next-generation talent through updating their current curriculum by adding courses that focus on FinTech, Design Thinking, Coding and Product Development, Micro-Financial Risk Management, and Macro-Prudential Supervision of the impacts and unintended consequences of FinTech, and of course, Cybersecurity.

6. Conclusion

The main entities within the innovation ecosystem are the regulators, Islamic Fintech companies, IFIs, venture capitalists, government agencies, strategy, and technology consultants, media, and academia (Mohamed and Ali, 2019). These entities make up the demand and supply sides of the digital ecosystem. Every crucial component gives support to each other and strengthens each other for the attainment of common and collective objectives. Each stakeholder plays its role and uses its resource and capability to provide solutions. Regulators may provide innovation-friendly policies and an environment that gives incentives to Islamic Fintech platforms to test and refine their innovative ideas, and IFIs may provide financial services or access to their internal sources and financial expertise. Incubators and regulatory sandboxes allow for the trial of prototypes in a controlled environment, while the media and academia may provide insights into trends and conduct proof-of-concept research to determine viable solutions for the gap in the industry. Stakeholders must ensure their organizations can pivot with market shifts, even dropping or switching partnerships if the market turns. The ability to adapt to new conditions will be a driving factor in maintaining a prosperous and dynamic digital ecosystem, as technology and its use cases change and market needs evolve.

Bibliography

Arner, Douglas W. and Barberis, Janos Nathan and Buckley, Ross P. (2016), "FinTech, RegTech and the Reconceptualization of Financial Regulation," Northwestern Journal of International Law & Business, Forthcoming; University of Hong Kong Faculty of Law Research Paper No. 2016/035. Available at SSRN: https://ssrn.com/abstract=2847806

Avgouleas, Emilios (2015) "Regulating Financial Innovation," in N. Moloney, E. Ferran & J. Payne, eds., *The Oxford Handbook of Financial Regulation*, Oxford, UK: Oxford University Press, pp. 659–689.

Barr, Michael S., Jackson, Howell E., & Tahyar, Margaret E. (2016). *Financial Regulation: Law and Policy*, New York: Foundation Press.

Brummer, Chris, & Gorfine, Daniel (2014). *FinTech: Building a 21st Century Regulator's Toolkit*, Santa Monica: Milken Institute.

Butler, Tom & O'Brien, Leona (2019). "Understanding RegTech for Digital Regulatory Compliance", in T. Lynn *et al.* (eds.), *Disrupting Finance, Palgrave Studies in Digital Business & Enabling Technologies*, https://doi. org/10.1007/978-3-030-02330-0_6.

Financial Stability Board (2017). *Financial Stability Implications from FinTech: Supervisory and Regulatory Issues that Merit Authorities' Attention.* 27 June 2017.

Gutierrez, Daniel (2014). Big Data for Finance — Security and Regulatory Compliance Considerations, Inside Big Data (20 October 2014), http://insidebigdata. com/2014/10/20/big-data-finance-security-regulatory-compliance-considerations/

Kaminski, Piotr and Robu, Kate (2016). A Best-Practice Model for Bank Compliance, McKinsey, Exhibit 1 (January 2016), http://www.mckinsey.com/business-functions/risk/ our-insights/a-best-practice-model-for-bank-compliance.

Mohamed, Hazik & Ali, Hassnian (2019). *Blockchain, Fintech and Islamic Finance — Building the Future of the New Islamic Digital Economy*. De I G Press, Boston/Berlin.

Runde, D. "M-Pesa And the Rise of The Global Mobile Money Market", *FORBES* (12 August 2015), http://www.forbes. com/sites/danielrunde/2015/08/12/m-pesa-and-the-rise-of-the-globalmobile-money-market/

Shedden, Adrian & Malna, Gareth (2016). "Supporting the Development and Adoption of RegTech: No Better Time for a Call for Input", Burges Salmon (January 2016), https:// www.burges-salmon.com/-/media/files/publications/ open-access/supporting_the_development_and_ adoption_of_regtech_no_better_time_for_a_call_for_ input.pdf

MANAGING REGULATORY CHANGE FOR FINANCIAL INSTITUTIONS

12

The persistent financial crises in the last few decades have transformed the global regulatory framework radically, in a concerted effort to enhance the resilience of financial institutions, recapture investor confidence, and improve the overall financial system.

Many financial institutions are struggling with ever-changing regulatory requirements and increased burden of complex rules. Often, such global and local due diligence rules can be conflicting, and non-compliance or the inability to meet the deadlines subject institutions to hefty penalties and multi-dollar fines for lapses in anti-money laundering, know your customer (KYC) and over-the-counter (OTC) trading regulations.

In this chapter, we map out the ongoing regulatory milestones globally and use the snapshot between Q3 2019 to Q2 2021 to illustrate the key regulatory priorities by region, and propose how banks can effectively manage regulatory change within their organizations through an AI-driven regulatory management model. We discuss the evolution, challenges, and recommendations for financial institutions (including Shariah compliance) in the change management for regulations using a structured approach that addresses regional priorities.

Keywords: *Anti-Money Laundering, Customer Due Diligence, Data Privacy and Protection, OTC Reform, RegTech*

Contents

1. Introduction

An effective and conducive regulatory system is key to the success of jurisdictions in order to remain competitive in the global market with the use of FinTech. Persistent financial crises in the last few decades have transformed the global regulatory framework radically, in a concerted effort to enhance the resilience of financial institutions, recapture investor confidence, and improve the overall financial system.

International cooperation will be crucial in view of the harmonies and shared dimension of many global financial activities. "There is potential for international bodies, like the IFSB, FSB, the GPFI and SSBs — such as the BCBS, IAIS, IOSCO and CPMI — to provide avenues for authorities to get together to share experiences on FinTech implications for financial markets" (Mohamed and Ali, 2019). "Increased cooperation will be particularly important to mitigate the risk of fragmentation or divergence in regulatory frameworks, which could impede the development and diffusion of beneficial innovations in financial services and limit the effectiveness to promote financial stability".

There appears to be "no regulatory let-up in sight, setting the stage for another busy year in terms of regulatory priorities, with a continued focus on data privacy, OTC (over-the-counter) derivatives reform and cybersecurity" (Dunphy and Glynn, 2018). Dunphy and Glynn observe that "while regulators in the U.S. are largely focused on regulatory reform, many of their European counterparts are still working through implementation of the Fourth EU Money Laundering Directive and preparing for the impact of Brexit". Meanwhile, in the Asia Pacific, regulators adopting the "wait-and-see" approach are now catching up in anti-money laundering, financial crime, and data privacy regulations.

In this chapter, we map out ongoing regulatory milestones globally over the Q3 2019 to Q2 2021 to illustrate the crucial regulatory priorities by region, and proposed how banks can effectively manage regulatory change within their organizations through an AI-driven regulatory management model. We also discuss the evolution, challenges, and recommendations for financial institutions (including Shariah compliance) in the change management for regulations using a structured approach that addresses regional priorities.

2. Regulatory Reforms and the Evolving Financial Landscape

The pace of regulatory reform did not wane in the last few years. A "number of key deadlines came into effect from January 2018 onwards, including the introduction of MiFID II",[1] when the

---

1   https://www.fca.org.uk/markets/mifid-ii/legal-entity-identifier-lei-update

legal entity identifier (LEI)[2] became "mandatory for transaction reporting, and the implementation of the General Data Protection Regulation (GDPR), which modernized and harmonized data protection legislation across Europe". In the US, "FinCEN's Final Rule (CDD) introduced significant new customer due diligence requirements for financial institutions".[3]

It is critical for regulators to ensure safeguards are in place to manage the risks (such as institution-specific micro-financial risks and system-wide macro-financial risks). Providing parameters and regulatory clarity through a framework (for digital business models) is essential for digital's mass adoption in order to ensure the financial stability of the system. Market supervisors will have to ensure that financial institutions or firms have robust governance frameworks and such surveillance could be complemented by data-driven supervision.

Another significant risk management concern is the operational risk that reflects cybersecurity, fraud and theft, data privacy, and legal issues. Similar to the Basel Committee on Banking Supervision (BCBS), the Islamic finance standard-setting body known as Islamic Financial Services Board (IFSB) prescribes a capital regime for operational risk which does not really address risk-related operational issues. "While regulatory instruments such as BCBS/IFSB capital requirements can create incentives to address certain operational risks, such as business continuity, capital is not sufficient to restore operations if a financial institution suffers a cyber-attack" (FSB, 2017). In addition, "there is serious trepidation on the risk of money laundering and financing of terrorism, termed as AML/CFT, which requires financial institutions including banks to have adequate measures to counter the risk of AML/CFT".

Specific to Islamic Finance, the innovative solutions for Islamic Financial Services should be consistent with Shariah rules and principles, and it takes adequate knowledge in the relevant economic, financial and technical (AI, blockchain, IoT, and machine learning) areas. This is critical concern in the role of the Shariah Supervisory Board (SSB) in the overseeing the product innovation at the institutional level, which impacts Shariah

---

2   https://www.emissions-euets.com/internal-electricity-market-glossary/839-lei

3   https://www.fincen.gov/resources/statutes-and-regulations/cdd-final-rule

compliance issues for enhanced supervision. The appropriate regulations will have to be created (or adjusted) as the technology itself evolves. The assumption that regulations, once crafted, will then remain in place, unchanged, for significant periods of time, has been overturned in today's environment.

Market supervisors will need to ensure is that financial institutions including banks have in place robust plans for scenarios that could threaten their own stability or the larger macroeconomic stability. For instance, robo-advisory services, which rely on algorithms and portfolio management to analyze investors' data and automatically recommend investment portfolios, need to be within approved products or companies offering such services need to be compelled to disclose more information when required. Similarly, third-party service providers or vendors to financial institutions are becoming more common and critical, especially in the areas of cloud computing and data services. Such third-party technology providers may need to be regulated in order to manage related operational risks, which may impact financial stability indirectly.

For financial stability, the danger of cyber-attacks and hacking, as well as the need to protect sensitive consumer and corporate financial data, is very real. Unquestionably, a number of recent incidents involved fraud and theft, and there have been breaches of personally identifiable information, which raises many issues including data privacy, ownership and administration, and legal liability.[4] In order to avoid any undesirable situations, much work needs to be done on boosting cybersecurity and alleviating cyber risks.

For domestic and cross-border transactions, there has to be a coordination among the supervisory agencies regulating financial institutions. A common approach and strategy need to be in place to address AML and counter-terrorism financing (CTF) issues at the national and also the international levels. Hence, regional cooperation will be integral in regulating digital applications that scale beyond borders. Furthermore, innovations in cross-border lending, trading, and payment transactions, including via smart contracts, raise questions about the cross-jurisdictional disputes and enforceability issues.

---

4   Data Protection Law: An Overview https://fas.org/sgp/crs/misc/R45631.pdf

3. RegTech — Digital Reporting, Audit and Compliance

Around the world, regulators are facing the challenges of the rapid emergence of new FinTech technologies and non-traditional market entrants, all at extraordinary speed. Authorities are faced with the task to develop regulatory approaches that do not hamper development and innovation while still limiting risks to consumers and financial stability.

RegTech is largely seen as a category that focuses on technologies that may facilitate the delivery of regulatory requirements more efficiently and effectively than existing capabilities.[5] However, Arner *et al.* (2016) view "RegTech as more than just an efficiency tool but rather a pivotal change leading to a paradigm shift in regulation". To them, "RegTech holistically represents the next logical evolution of financial services regulation" and should develop into a foundational base underpinning the entire financial services sector.

The application of technology to monitoring and compliance offers massive cost savings to established financial companies and potentially massive opportunities to emerging FinTech start-ups, IT, and advisory firms (Shedden and Malna, 2016). From a regulator's perspective, RegTech will enable the prospect of continuous monitoring that would improve efficiency by both liberating excess regulatory capital, decreasing the time it takes to investigate a firm, fostering competition, and upholding their directives for financial stability (both macro and micro) and market integrity (Gutierrez, 2014).

3.1. Regulatory Priorities by Region

As we look ahead in the regulatory landscape, the key upcoming regulatory milestones identified over the next two years are — anti-money laundering and customer due diligence, OTC reform, and data privacy and protection, with slightly different priorities for different regions. Globally, both data privacy and data protection

---

5   Feedback Statement, Financial Conduct Authority, Call for Input on Supporting the Development and Adopters of RegTech, (July 2016).

are significant regulatory priorities.[6] The lead up to GDPR has created a ripple effect of new and revised data protection and data privacy regulations worldwide in order to ensure the continuation of data flows between jurisdictions.

In the US, "regulatory reform, conflicts of interests and cybersecurity feature prominently on the list of regulatory priorities".[7] The regulatory impacts of Brexit on US investors and securities markets are also key concerns. The Securities and Exchange Commission (SEC) are particularly anxious that companies are not adequately disclosing the potential impact of Brexit. To combat this, they have instructed manpower to "focus on the exact disclosures that companies are making about Brexit".[8] Cybersecurity is another key supervisory priority, specifically in terms of data breach prevention and cyber-related misconduct in the markets.

"Prudential requirements are under analysis, especially with the Current Expected Credit Loss regime came into effect in January 2020".[9] The US is also under increased pressure from the EU to appoint a Data Privacy Ombudsman, as per Privacy Shield requirements.[10]

The European Union focused on REFIT (regulatory fitness) for 2019, i.e., reviewing their current book of legislation, particularly with regard to reporting measures. "Continued development of the Capital Markets Union and securitization supervision have been called out by the European Securities and Markets Authority (ESMA) as key regulatory priorities".[11] Governance and culture are also coming to the forefront, with increased emphasis on accountability, which translates into

---

6   https://www.pdpc.gov.sg/-/media/Files/PDPC/DPO-Connect/March-20/Seven-Global-Personal-Data-Protection-Priorities-for-2020.html

7   https://blogs.thomsonreuters.com/answerson/top-10-concerns-for-u-s-compliance-officers-in-2019/

8   https://tax.thomsonreuters.com/blog/the-sec-is-watching-part-2-brexit-disclosures/

9   https://www.occ.treas.gov/news-issuances/bulletins/2020/bulletin-2020-27.html

10   https://www.euractiv.com/section/data-protection/news/us-to-appoint-permanent-privacy-shield-ombudsperson-following-eu-pressure/

11   https://www.esma.europa.eu/sites/default/files/library/esma80-199-332_confidential_supervision_ar_2019_wp_2020.pdf

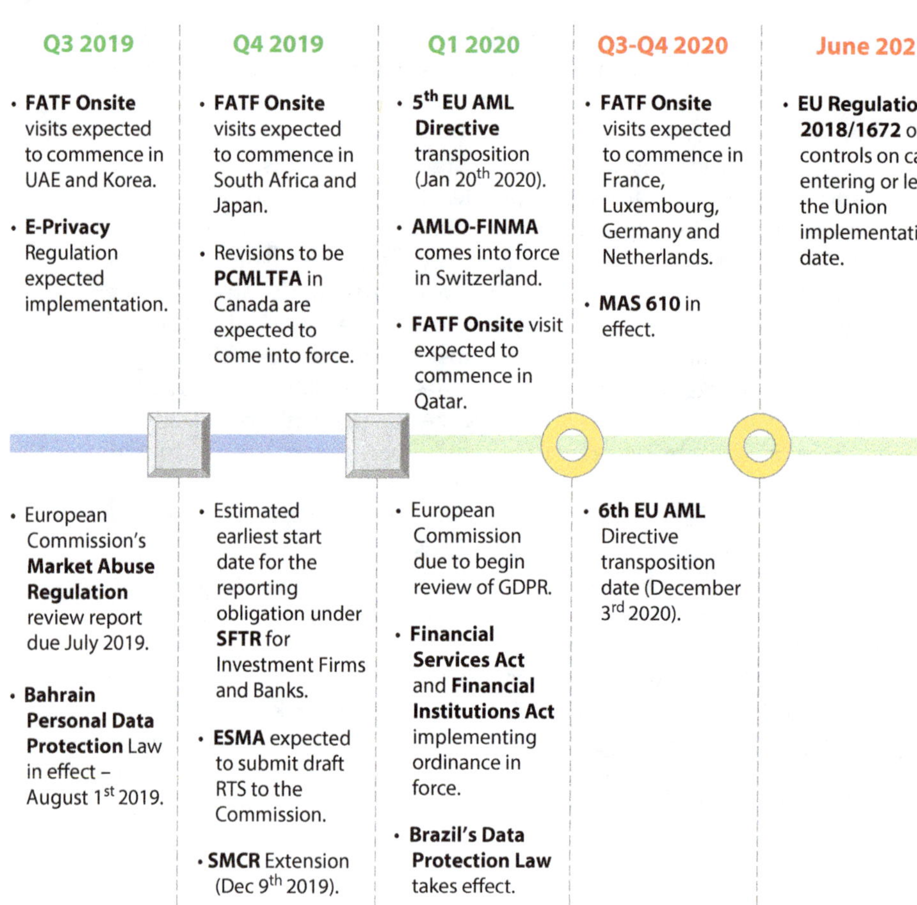

Figure 12.1: Snapshot of Global Regulatory Outlook for Q3 2019–Q2 2021 to Illustrate Regional Priorities (compiled from various sources)

holding senior managers responsible for breaches and failures of the firm and staff. This also applies to retail and wholesale misconduct risks.

Indeed, the theory of culture has moved from the classroom to the boardroom in recent years. The European Banking Authority (EBA) published draft "guidelines on internal governance in the 2017".[12] The area of outsourcing has also

---

12　https://eba.europa.eu/regulation-and-policy/internal-governance/guidelines-on-internal-governance-revised-

been highlighted by several European regulators, specifically outsourcing IT security and IT risk. "Draft guidelines have been formulated by the EBA around establishing a framework for the due diligence process of institutions with the objective of ensuring that functions are only outsourced to reliable service providers so that the ongoing provision of services and compliance with regulatory requirements is ensured" (Dunphy and Glynn, 2018).

Cybersecurity is high on the agenda of the APAC regulatory priorities list. A number of regulators have already issued "specific cyber-risk management and information security guidance, including on the importance of effective cybersecurity risk management"[13] (i.e., Hong Kong SAR) and on "early detection of cyber intrusions"[14] (i.e., Singapore).

3.1.1. Anti-Money Laundering, Cryptos & Ultimate Beneficial Owner (UBO)

In the US, "compliance with the Bank Secrecy Act (BSA) remains a key area, with an increased focus on stress testing and risk testing programs to ensure they are able to stand up to risk".[15] Cryptocurrencies also continue to be a key talking point, but it is "unlikely there will be any formalized rules around this yet".[16] In its place, the urgency in 2019 has been to monitor the crypto space.

In the Asia Pacific, "AML and beneficial ownership regulatory reform progressed with the Anti-Money Laundering Bill taking effect in Hong Kong, along with the removal of a two-tiered approach to ultimate beneficial ownership to align with FATF (Financial Action Task Force) standards".[17] Historically, a dual threshold was required where 25% was applied as standard, with the threshold reducing to 10% where there is an increased

---

13 https://www.hkma.gov.hk/media/eng/doc/key-information/guidelines-and-circular/2015/20150915e1.pdf

14 https://www.mas.gov.sg/regulation/circulars/srd-tr-012015-circular-on-early-detection-of-cyber-intrusion

15 https://www.fincen.gov/news/news-releases/federal-bank-regulatory-agencies-and-fincen-improve-transparency-risk-focused

16 https://www.loc.gov/law/help/cryptocurrency/world-survey.php

17 https://www.fatf-gafi.org/media/fatf/documents/reports/mer4/MER-Hong-Kong-2019.pdf

risk. Several financial institutions have elected to retain the dual threshold approach or apply 10% across all entities.

Macro-financial issues related to systemic importance are embedded in the FSB SIFI[18] framework, which recommends that "financial institutions identified as systemically important should have more intense supervisory oversight, higher loss absorbency as well as recovery and resolution plans" (FSB, 2017). The majority of regulatory changes and clarifications have been made in the areas of payments, capital raising, and to a lesser extent, investment management as many of these economic functions naturally fit within existing regulatory regimes. Only a few regulatory changes to include FinTech innovations in insurance and market support were mentioned (FSB, 2017).

3.1.2. Customer Due Diligence (CDD)

Over the past year, there has been a lot of change and movement in AML legislation within Europe. Even in terms of the Fourth EU Money Laundering Directive, which is long past its implementation date, there are a number of countries that have yet to formally transpose this rule into law, a few of which have been referred to the European Court of Justice. Member States are required to transpose the Directive by January 20, 2020 (Dunphy and Glynn, 2018). Following closely, the "Sixth AML Directive was adopted in October 2018 and must also be transposed by Member States by December 3rd, 2020".[19]

Moving to the US, the "FinCEN Final Rule (CDD) came into effect for all new accounts opened on or after May 11th, 2018, implementing a dual-prong approach to beneficial ownership".[20] Under the rule and unless an exemption applies, beneficial owners are split into two distinct types: (1) those who own 25%

---

18 Systemically important financial institutions (SIFIs) are financial institutions whose distress or disorderly failure, because of their size, complexity and systemic interconnectedness, would cause significant disruption to the wider financial system and economic activity.

19 https://ec.europa.eu/commission/presscorner/detail/en/qanda_20_821

20 https://www.fincen.gov/sites/default/files/2018-04/FinCEN_Guidance_CDD_FAQ_FINAL_508_2.pdf

or more of the equity interests of the legal entity customer and (2) a control person, described as the individual with significant responsibility to control, manage, or direct the legal entity. Until 2018, ultimate beneficial ownership thresholds had primarily been applied on a best practice approach in the US. Covered financial institutions must not only know who their customers are and from where their sources of funds originate, they also need to develop an accurate risk profile based on a culmination of all available client data and documentation. To achieve this, an appropriate level of due diligence checks must be applied to all beneficiaries.

3.1.3. Cybersecurity

Cybersecurity is another high-priority program in the list of APAC regulatory agenda. As mentioned earlier, several regulators have already issued specific cyber-risk management and information security guidance in Hong Kong and Singapore. In Australia, the "Australian Prudential Regulation Authority (APRA) sought to implement enforceable standards around information security"[21] (CPS 234), which commenced July 1, 2019. The standards on third-party outsourcing are being reviewed, including if 'outsourcing' remains relevant, given that banking supply chains have evolved and are much more complicated.

3.1.4. Data Privacy and Data Protection

The final draft of the ePrivacy Regulation still remains to be published.[22] The "Regulation is intended to increase the effectiveness and level of protection for privacy and personal data in electronic communications. The final version of the Regulation on a framework for the free flow of non-personal information, known as the fifth freedom of the European Union, was published in November 2018 and has been directly

---

21 https://www.apra.gov.au/sites/default/files/cps_234_july_2019_
for_public_release.pdf

22 https://www.lexology.com/library/detail.aspx?g=5e41c7c1-
691b-4179-87f1-553d8d638c7a

applicable from May 2019".[23] The Regulation will prohibit non-personal data localization. Member States continue to implement national legislation to account for permitted derogations. "Given the increased scrutiny on data breaches of late, it would not be too long before national authorities begin imposing enforcement measures — although this has already started in some Member States" (Dunphy and Glynn, 2018). The "European Data Protection Board, formerly known as the Article 29 Working Party,[24] is still in the process of publishing guidance on several matters, most recently on GDPR's extraterritorial impact". Member States are still waiting on a final text of the e-Privacy Regulation to prepare for the implementation of the Free Flow of Non-Personal Data Regulation.

Countries in APAC have "begun reviewing — and, in some cases, introducing — legislation relating to data protection in the wake of the implementation of GDPR".[25] In the Asia Pacific, "Thailand, India, Indonesia and Vietnam have all published draft data protection bills as several jurisdictions begin to seek adequacy status".[26] In direct conflict with the EU's new data localization prohibition, India and Vietnam are following closely in neighboring China's footsteps, implementing strict data protection regimes with data localization provisions. "New Zealand has also begun reviewing current data protection provisions ahead of a likely review of its EU whitelist status".[27] Conduct and culture are another key regulatory focus in the region, driven by the Royal Commission in Australia (New Zealand recently undertook a review of banking culture), to align with the process of reform in banking culture and the way it conducts financial service throughout the industry worldwide.

---

23   Ibid.
24   https://ec.europa.eu/information_society/newsroom/image/document/2016-51/wp243_en_40855.pdf?wb48617274=CD63BD9A
25   https://www.regulationasia.com/managing-regulatory-change-as-a-business-as-usual-activity/
26   https://www.dataprotectionreport.com/2020/01/reflecting-on-apac-data-protection-and-cyber-security-highlights-for-2019-and-what-lies-ahead/
27   https://mlexmarketinsight.com/insights-center/editors-picks/area-of-expertise/data-privacy-and-security/new-zealands-privacy-law-revamp-to-come-under-scrutiny-in-eu

3.1.5. OTC Reform

The year 2019 marked 10 years since the G20 commitment to reform OTC derivative markets in response to the financial crisis. Some of the measures taken is the introduction of initial margin requirements globally in phases. "September 2018 was the most recent deadline (becoming applicable for Phase 3 entities), bringing a larger number of counterparties into scope for those requirements. Most recently, Singapore Central Clearing came into effect in October for Singapore and US class currency accounts, while Canadian Central Clearing was phased in from August 2018" (Dunphy and Glynn, 2018).

OTC reform had some key impacts on EU regulation in 2019. Notably, the "Securities Financing Transaction Regulation (SFTR) — the reporting obligation for investment firms and financial institutions — was expected to come into effect in Q3 2020 (following the European Commission's extension of the scrutiny period of the RTS by three months)".[28] There are also "additional changes under global investor protection in Switzerland, highlighted in the Regulatory Outlook Calendar under January 2020, with the introduction of the Financial Services Act (FinSA) and the Financial Institutions Act (FinIA)".[29]

3.2. *Shariah Audit, Compliance and Monitoring*

The main risk that "Islamic financial institutions (IFIs) face which is unique to them is the Shariah compliance risk. In addition to managing the risks faced by conventional banks, such as credit, market, operational risks, an Islamic financial institution also has to ensure that it complies to Shariah rulings as this carries significant reputational risk to the institution" (Mohamed and Ali, 2019). FinTech products (including cryptocurrencies and tokens) and services need to be treated accordingly to its use cases and

---

28   https://www.esma.europa.eu/policy-activities/post-trading/sftr-reporting

29   https://www2.deloitte.com/content/dam/Deloitte/ch/Documents/financial-services/deloitte-ch-fs-financial-markets-regulatory-outlook-switzerland-2020.pdf

the fiqh understanding of the Shariah, as well as the regulations in place.

The assessment of Shariah-compliance too should include the procedural processes from creation to the result of any new financial products, or digital assets and its mechanisms. For compliance and legitimacy, the regulations for them can be coded as per fiqh guidelines (from Shariah committees), and automated as an algorithm-driven AI module. Such rulings or fatwas that have been previously determined as sound, can be accumulated in a database for future cross-referencing and limit additional resources and fees required for Shariah compliance assessments. Through the use of new regulatory audit mechanisms and validation technology (i.e., RegTech), the compilation of various schools of thought (mazhabs, etc.) can be organized productively and Shariah compliance can be reconciled in a structured and efficient manner.

4. Managing Regulatory Change

Policymakers and regulatory authorities have monumental task in confronting rapidly transforming financial systems in the coming years. "Regulatory change management has the potential to impact divisions beyond the compliance function, including data management, operations, client-facing teams, client experience and time to revenue" (Dunphy and Glynn, 2018). Regulatory change has to be managed and precisely calculated, as wide-ranging changes can ultimately use up the allotted discretionary budget and resources. The continuing regulatory changes embroil uncertainty in operating environments, and anticipated regulatory change has already impacted today's business decisions and existing business operations.

Operationally, financial institutions face day-to-day challenges with the constant addition and modification of hundreds and thousands of regulations with multi-jurisdictional requirements. They are also increasingly pressured to achieve categorical compliance with limited budgets and substantial resource limitations. Such constraints impact both the financial and operational performance of financial institutions, as they are subjected to the continual adjustment of resources to meet compliance deadlines. Financial institutions have traditionally responded by throwing more bodies to remediate and collect

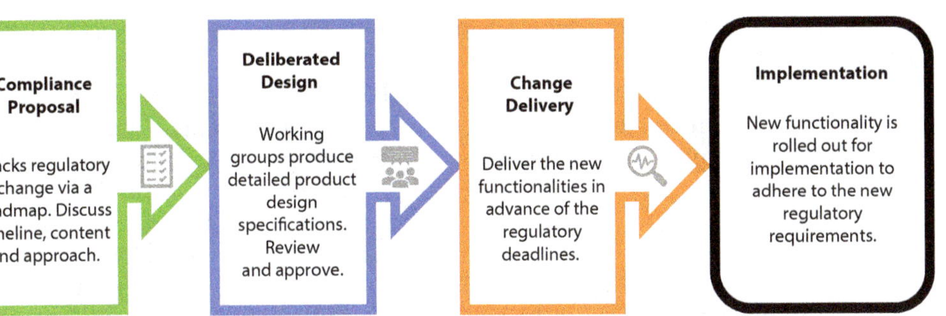

Figure 12.2: Regulatory Change Process Flow
Source: Author's own.

information, driving up the overall cost of compliance at the expense of customer experience.

To overcome this anticipated revolving door of regulatory changes, banks will necessitate the increasing use and reliance on technology in order to build the necessary infrastructure to support the changing regulations. The "development of RegTech so far has primarily been driven by the financial services industry wishing to decrease costs, especially in light of the fact that regulatory fines and settlements have increased 45-fold" (Kaminsky and Robu, 2016). The next stage of regulatory supervision is likely to increase their capacity by automating compliance and regulatory surveillance through AI and machine learning. Likewise, financial institutions will need the help of AI technology and systematic strategies within a regulatory framework to adapt to these changes.

4.1. *Keeping Track of Regulatory Changes*

The reality that financial institutions are bombarded by regulatory news, updates, and commentaries creates a lot of garbled noise, most of which distracts rather than focuses an organization into regulatory action. Debates resulting from asymmetric perspectives from a host of sources only makes the situation worse as financial institutions try to decode and extract useful information from the boisterous clamor of the industry. Instead, a trusted supply of structured information that enhances accurate regulatory interpretation is needed to properly assess its impact to the organization. In such a manner, the organization will then be able to transmute this analysis into risk-assessed and evidence-based actions.

In the current climate, regulatory compliance requires the internal harmonization between departments within the organization, processes and technology. Internally, the organization must find ways to align their objectives to market supervision goals. Furthermore, it is not only the regulatory environment that is hampering compliance and regulatory change management abilities. Much of it now also rely on interdisciplinary competencies which require understanding of technology and compliance through auditing and monitoring. Every financial institution is managing regulatory change processes internally and as a result, doing so independent of the rest of the industry. Having incomplete expertise will handicap the organization from being able to adequately implement the changes required. Establishing channels to leverage on the collective expertise would speed up processes and up-level expertise competencies.

4.2. Establishing Clear Objectives and Goals

The first step in assessing the primary goals of regulatory change management solutions is to understand that there are two principal objectives:

1. the first aim is concentrated on ensuring regulatory compliance. This assures the right processes are in place, and the recommended data and documentation requirements are achieved;
2. the second objective is to cascade the compliance across the organization — for instance, within onboarding tools, there may be specific tax information around FATCA (Foreign Account Tax Compliance Act) and CRS (Common Reporting Standard) that can be captured to synchronize a change with the overall compliance requirements.

When both these objectives are clearly aligned throughout the organization, compliance will be safeguarded during the client onboarding process whilst facilitating post-onboarding compliance in terms of the tax reporting obligations placed upon the financial institution. Synchronizing process changes and integrating them with existing processes and the organization's goals clarifies the direction within internal teams towards external regulatory objectives and how they complement each other.

4.3. *Developing a Regulatory Adaptation AI-driven Model*

MiFID II and EMIR regulations, among others, often consist of several thousand pages of documentation. As such, having an automated regulatory framework (possibly through an AI-driven model) will allow financial organizations to make sense of this, and with less mistakes. Utilizing such a model will help them to identify areas where they are obligated to enforce, and areas where they need to facilitate other parties to manage. The need for RegTech to manage large data-sets and audit trails, in the context of regulation, monitoring, reporting, and compliance, will enhance many capabilities that the tasks calls for. This will involve design thinking, coding, and product development to deal with micro-financial risk management and macro-prudential supervision. The finalized model has to also account for the impact and unintended consequences of technology, while being attuned to the increased need for cybersecurity. The goal is to develop a technically-cohesive and cyber-resilient model for assessing regulation and implementing its requirements.

When managing regulatory change, the effective approach goes beyond just reading the regulatory documentation, but putting it into a structure that allows buy-in and orderliness that can be applied. Regulatory change is not trivial because financial institutions are challenged by limited IT budgets and have to develop solutions, often within tight deadlines, that do not create other issues within their organization.

Each regulation is typically distinctive and will usually involve very specific requirements. The proposed Regulatory Framework above can be modelled into an AI-driven system to manage regulatory compliance in a consistent and structured manner. The key component algorithms of the AI model should incorporate:

1. *Scoping Rules and Assessing Data Requirements* — Scoping help to determine the rules dictated by the regulation, according to when they apply and their particular characteristics. It also determines if they are applied through business processes or the regulatory rules engine.

Figure 12.3: Regulatory Modelling Components
Source: Author's own.

Once the regulation is in range, additional data requirements need to be assessed. The two main facets of this are:

- Re-use of data that is already available, or source data from third-party services if needed,
- Managing multiple data-sets across all relationships

2. *Document Requirements* — Depending on the regulations, automatic or conditional documentation may need to be acquired from the counterparty. The regulatory data-set will determine if the data captured applies by default or conditionally required.

3. *Rule-Based Logic and Authentication* — Rules-based algorithms are used to compute values associated to compliance levels and push authentication alerts and monitors according to regulation.

4. *Ongoing Controls* — Processes that concern ongoing controls involve the triggering of requirements for updates or reassessments based on changing circumstances of certain clients.

5. Conclusion

Regulators may provide innovation-friendly policies and an environment that "gives incentives to digital platforms to test and refine their innovative ideas, and financial institutions may provide financial services or access to their internal sources and financial expertise" (Mohamed and Ali, 2019). Stakeholders must ensure their organizations can adopt to market shifts, even making difficult operational changes if the market turns. The capability to adapt to new regulations and managing those changes internally will foster a prosperous and dynamic financial ecosystem, towards better business conduct and service culture.

With the upcoming regulatory requirements and expectations, ensuring compliance will be challenging for global firms in the coming years, and the continuing review has become the new normal in an uncertain and demanding regulatory environment. Although the "pace of regulatory reform has slowed in Europe and the US, geo-political factors, such as Brexit, combined with new regulatory priorities and ongoing supervision will increase the regulatory burden on global organizations" (Dunphy and Glynn, 2018). In the Asia Pacific, its regulators continue to trudge forward with the accomplishment of proposed reforms according to internationally agreed standards. Improving the financial industry's culture and business conduct will be a vital supervisory priority for the subsequent years ahead across jurisdictions, emphasizing on individual accountability within institutions and organizations. Reform for OTC trading and data protection will endure to be prevailing premises, as will cybersecurity, where essential service institutions will face increased pressure to build cyber-resilient eco-systems for economic security and resilience.

Bibliography

Arner, Douglas W. and Barberis, Janos Nathan and Buckley, Ross P. (2016), "FinTech, RegTech and the Reconceptualization of Financial Regulation," *Northwestern Journal of International Law & Business*, Forthcoming; University of Hong Kong Faculty of Law Research Paper No. 2016/035. Available at SSRN: https://ssrn.com/abstract=2847806

Avgouleas, Emilios (2015) "Regulating Financial Innovation," in N. Moloney, E. Ferran & J. Payne, eds., *The Oxford Handbook of Financial Regulation*, Oxford, UK: Oxford University Press, pp. 659–689.

Barr, Michael S., Jackson, Howell E., & Tahyar, Margaret E. (2016). *Financial Regulation: Law and Policy*, New York: Foundation Press.

Brummer, Chris, & Gorfine, Daniel (2014). *FinTech: Building a 21st Century Regulator's Toolkit*, Santa Monica: Milken Institute.

Butler, Tom & O'Brien, Leona (2019). "Understanding RegTech for Digital Regulatory Compliance", in T. Lynn *et al.* (eds.), *Disrupting Finance, Palgrave Studies in Digital Business & Enabling Technologies*, https://doi.org/10.1007/978-3-030-02330-0_6.

Dunphy, Joe and Glynn, Laura (2018). Global Regulatory Outlook 2019–2021, Dublin: Fenergo.

Financial Stability Board (2017). Financial Stability Implications from FinTech: Supervisory and Regulatory Issues that Merit Authorities' Attention. 27 June 2017.

Gutierrez, Daniel (2014). Big Data for Finance — Security and Regulatory Compliance Considerations, Inside Big Data (Oct 20), http://insidebigdata.com/2014/10/20/big-data-finance-security-regulatory-compliance-considerations/

Kaminski, Piotr and Robu, Kate (2016). A Best-Practice Model for Bank Compliance, McKinsey, Exhibit 1 (Jan 2016), http://www.mckinsey.com/business-functions/risk/our-insights/a-best-practice-model-for-bank-compliance.

Mohamed, Hazik. (2020). "The Future of FinTech in ASEAN". In Anshari, M., Almunawar, M. N., & Masri, M. (Eds.), *Financial Technology and Disruptive Innovation in ASEAN* (pp. 63–79). IGI Global.

Mohamed, Hazik and Ali, Hassnian (2019). *Blockchain, Fintech and Islamic Finance — Building the Future of the New Islamic Digital Economy*. De l G Press, Boston/Berlin.

Raden Aji Haqqi, A. (2020). "Strengthening Islamic Finance in South-East Asia Through Innovation of Islamic FinTech in Brunei Darussalam". In Ordoñez de Pablos, P., Almunawar, M. N., & Abduh, M. (Eds.), *Economics, Business, and Islamic Finance in ASEAN Economics Community* (pp. 202–226). IGI Global.

Shedden, Adrian & Malna, Gareth (2016). "Supporting the Development and Adoption of RegTech: No Better Time for a Call for Input", Burges Salmon (Jan 2016), https://www.burges-salmon.com/-/media/files/publications/open-access/supporting_the_development_and_adoption_of_regtech_no_better_time_for_a_call_for_input.pdf

INDEX

A

accountability, 13, 15, 23, 37, 57,
61, 110, 114, 139, 193, 194, 195,
201, 202, 216, 233, 245
AI+blockchain technology, 11–12,
38, 85–86, 124–125
algorithmic bias, 9
Anti Money Laundering (AML),
31, 35, 80, 83, 173, 229, 230,
231, 235, 236
authentication, 4, 75, 158, 244
server, 110

B

behavior, 10, 69, 84, 127, 149, 155,
158, 159, 212, 221
behavioral biases, 76
business models, 52, 75, 85, 95,
101, 123, 147, 148, 199, 209,
213, 214, 224, 230

C

capital controls, 169, 180, 181
Central Bank Digital Currency
(CBDC), 17, 165–190, 178
centralized blockchain, 30
centralized databases, 26
centralized systems, 11, 82
consumer protection, 17, 138, 209,
214–215, 224
cooperation, 93, 220, 223, 228, 229,
231
countercyclical measures, 186–187
counterparties, 15, 32, 35, 62, 130,
132, 169, 180
of trade transactions, 27
counter-terrorism financing (CTF),
35, 83, 173, 231
creditworthiness, 45, 49, 60
cross-border cooperation and
coordination, 220–221
cross-border flow of goods and
services, 15
cross-border investments, 51, 52
cross-border payments, 94, 181,
185
cross-border transactions, 95, 101,
215, 231
cryptocurrencies, 95, 130, 170, 185,
221–222, 235, 239
cryptocurrency, 33, 132, 183
customer due diligence (CDD), 31,
236–237
customer insights, 3
cyberattacks, 28, 30, 37, 60, 157,
183, 214, 231
cyber liabilities, 158
cyber-physical systems (CPS), 16,
134, 143, 145, 150–151, 154

S

T

U

V

W

CPSIA information can be obtained
at www.ICGtesting.com
Printed in the USA
BVHW091941061220
594983BV00001B/2